Both Career and Love

A Woman's Memoir 1959-1973

Anne Rankin Mahoney

outskirts
press

Outskirts Press, Inc.
http://www.outskirtspress.com

ISBN: 978-1-9772-2941-0

Outskirts Press and the "OP" logo are trademarks belonging to Outskirts Press, Inc.

PRINTED IN THE UNITED STATES OF AMERICA

For my children Katherine and Michael,
my grandchildren Maya, Sofia, and Audrey
and to Barry,
without whose love this book
could not have been written.

Disclaimer: Many names and identifying characteristics of individuals have been changed to protect their privacy.

Also by Anne Rankin Mahoney

Couples, Gender, and Power:
Creating Change in Intimate Relationships.
Carmen Knudson-Martin and Anne Rankin Mahoney, Eds.
New York: Springer Publishing Company. 2009

Juvenile Justice in Context.
Anne Rankin Mahoney
Boston: Northeastern University Press. 1987

Ruts: Gender Roles and Realities.
Editors: Anne Rankin Mahoney, Marilyn Colter,
Dorothea Deley, and Kara Colter
Red Feather Lakes, CO: Red Mesa Publishing. 1996

Travel
Exploring Florida
Anne Rankin
NY: Hippocrene Books, Inc. 1992

Table of Contents

Acknowledgements

THANKS TO MY granddaughters for urging me to write about what they call the 'olden days,' to my daughter Katie for heightening my interest in the project by presenting me with several books about writing memoirs, and to my son Mike, whose enthusiasm about the book helped me overcome occasional writer's block. I thank Shari Cauldron for her excellent memoir workshops at Lighthouse Writers, Denver's phenomenal writing center. Her advice to start our stories 'where the energy is' gave me the direction I had been seeking. I knew immediately where that formative energy of my young adulthood was—New York City. I felt it when I visited Manhattan while I was in graduate school at Northwestern University near Chicago, and it fueled my life there from my arrival in Manhattan in 1961 through the time I left in 1973.

This book is much better in every way because of the honest and acute critique of many drafts over several years by members of my long-term writers' group, Lynn Hall, Lois Hjelmstad, and Esther Starrels. Their encouragement was unfaltering. I also want to thank numerous classmates in my Lighthouse classes who taught me good writing by example and their thoughtful comments on my and other participants' work.

I especially thank my husband Barry for his ongoing and loving support of this and all my projects. The memoir has more accuracy, fewer errors, and greater coherence because of his close readings of several drafts. He is not only a New Yorker by birth and a good editor and proofreader, he asks hard questions that push me to think further and research more.

Author's Note

I FINISHED THE final version of this memoir as peaceful protestors from a cross-section of America were demonstrating against the abuse of power and demanding equality for all people. Individuals of color, native Americans, and other minorities have been waiting too long for the end of bias and police violence against them and for the rights and freedoms that they have been promised for generations. Like many of us who are white and sympathetic with the demonstrators' causes, I have had to look inward in new ways and with greater honesty than ever before. As part of this self-reflection I viewed the book I had just completed from a new perspective. It is about my efforts as a woman in the 1960s to overcome male privilege and enter a 'man's occupation.' What I saw, along with my struggle as a woman encountering male privilege, were examples of my own white privilege. I did not have to face the reality of potential violence and humiliation that accompanies racism. I also had some 'breaks' along the way—like a recommendation from a teacher, help paying for school, and work with a tutor—that I might not have had if I had not been white and middle class. As we live our lives and pursue our dreams we are *all* entitled to a wide range of opportunities, safety, and a few positive breaks along the way.

—Anne Rankin Mahoney

Part One
No Image of Myself Anywhere

CHAPTER 1

The Best Fit for You, But...

"IT LOOKS LIKE college teaching would be the best *fit* for you," my career counselor announced with a note of caution in her voice.

I leaned forward excitedly. That sounded right. I loved school.

"There are a couple of concerns, though," she continued carefully. "You would need a Ph.D...."

"No problem," I interrupted, "I'm planning to start graduate school next fall..."

"And," she broke in, "college teaching is primarily a *man's* occupation."

"That's okay," I said, "I like men."

It was 1958, early in my senior year at Kent State University in Ohio. The crystal ball of scientific testing had given me the perfect answer to my career question. Professors did all the things I liked to do--explain things, read, talk, write, think. The fact that college teaching was considered a man's job seemed irrelevant. In my rural town in western Pennsylvania I'd grown up with the idea that America was the land of equality, and individuals could do anything they wanted if they worked hard. As a student of sociology, I should have known better, anticipated that breaking into a profession dominated by men might be difficult. But discrimination is rarely mentioned when it isn't being challenged. I thought all I had to do was work hard to get my credentials. I liked sociology, and it had always been easy for me. This seemed like an attainable goal. I didn't grasp then that the percentage of women in my chosen occupation was in the low single digits and might not even hit ten percent by the end of the next decade.

My larger concern at that time was how I could combine career and family. In 1958 a woman was expected to raise a family. If she couldn't find a man, she might decide to have a career. I wanted both career and family together, at the same time! My friends just smiled knowingly and explained I would change my mind when I fell in love. My mother worried that no man would be interested in me if I got too much education. I didn't want to accept either of those perspectives. I was left in a quandary. If I pursued my work too diligently I might never find love. If I fell in love I might feel compelled to let go of my professional ambitions. How could I be whole? Achieve and balance both love and work in my life?

So far, falling in love had not been an isssue. I hadn't met anyone I could really get excited about, but I was terrified that if I fell in love before I'd made some progress toward my career as a college teacher I might give up my goals. My plan was to start graduate school in September, get a master's degree in a year, and then work for a couple years before going back for the doctorate. My immediate concern, however, was finding a graduate program. This was not easy in the late 1950s, before computers and the internet, especially since I wanted to strike out into new territory beyond Ohio and Western Pennsylvania.

"Go talk to the chairman of the sociology department," my professors suggested. "He'll have ideas."

His only suggestion was his own alma mater, the University of North Carolina, from which he had graduated more than thirty years earlier. It was my only lead, so I applied, even though I'd never been there and knew nothing about it. No one helped me with the application or suggested the possibility of applying for student aid. I didn't even realize until the beginning of June, after I'd graduated from Kent State and was about to start a summer job in Chicago, that I needed to take the Graduate Record Exams (GRE). I'd never even heard of them before. The tests were offered only periodically in different sites around the U.S. Luckily they were scheduled in Chicago in early July and I learned just in time to make the signup deadline. The exam brochure for the three tests, verbal, mathematics, and sociology, said I didn't need to study so, except for looking briefly through my old *Introduction to Sociology* textbook, I didn't.

Chicago was exhilarating, as special as Carl Sandburg, one of my favorite poets, had described it in his writing. After growing up in a small town, I had come to realize that I loved cities. The previous year I had worked at a settlement house in Cleveland, but Chicago was even more vibrant and exciting. As the summer wore on, I became romantically involved with one of my work colleagues, and toward the end of the summer he asked me if I would consider staying in Chicago. I said yes. Without a second thought I wrote to North Carolina to withdraw my application and cancel my housing arrangements. Going there had never felt real anyway. The school was mostly someone else's idea.

I was still set on going to graduate school in September however, and immediately began learning about Chicago-area sociology departments. In August, after studying its catalogue, I decided on Northwestern University in nearby Evanston and sent in an application and my newly minted GRE scores. I had no idea what were considered 'good' scores, but they looked okay, even mathematics, which at that time was ranked separately for men and women to boost a woman's percentile ranking. The practice gave some indication of the academic world's view of both women's career interests and their innate mathematical abilities.

My experience with higher education was so limited that it never dawned on me that I probably had little chance of getting into Northwestern, especially at the last minute. To this day I remain stunned by my audacity, ignorance ... and the letter of acceptance from Northwestern that arrived just after I got home from my summer job. It didn't matter by then that my brief romance had ended.

My parents had always encouraged me to make my own decisions and adjusted, at least outwardly, to my sudden change of plans. We had already agreed that they would drive me to graduate school and would give me money to cover my graduate school tuition for a year, with the expectation that I would find a job to cover my housing and food. My dad put aside the AAA travel maps he had gotten to drive to North Carolina, ordered a new set for Evanston, Illinois, and off we went. Because I had had no time to arrange for a place to live, our first stop at Northwestern was the Women's Housing office where the graduate school catalogue said I could pick up a list of off-campus rooms for rent to women students.

"I should be back in a couple minutes," I assured my parents as I climbed out of the car in front of the administration building.

When I asked the secretary in the Women's Housing Office for the list of rooms for rent, she immediately slapped a lengthy application in front of me. Surprised, but compliant, I dutifully filled it out and sat back down when she said the Director of Women's Housing was busy at the moment but would meet with me soon. Someone had told me that Northwestern was an upscale private school, but this level of scrutiny just to get a list of off-campus rooms for rent seemed excessive.

After what seemed like a long time, especially with my parents waiting outside in the car on a hot September day, I was ushered into the Director's office. She was a spare looking woman in her early sixties, immaculately dressed, her gray hair in a tight permanent. Everything about her was precise, narrow. She greeted me cordially and gave me a quick look that registered everything about me. As I sat waiting, she perused two documents on her desk. One looked like the application I'd just filled out. What was the other? My application to Northwestern? Why would she need that?

"You didn't mention on your housing application that you graduated *cum laude*"

"I didn't think it was relevant for getting a room."

"I see you have two years as an undergraduate dorm counselor. How did you like that?" The Director peered at me intently.

"I enjoyed it."

"I've just lost one of my returning resident dormitory counselors. She decided to quit school and get married. One of those things, I think..." She looked up at me with raised eyebrows and a slight shake of the head. "How would you like to work as a resident dorm counselor and earn full room and board?"

The offer was more tempting than I cared to admit, even to myself. I had really wanted to be on my own in graduate school, live independently, and get a job in the real world. However, although I tried to appear nonchalant to my parents about earning enough money for housing and food, I had little work experience and was acutely worried about finding a job.

I moved into the women's dormitory that afternoon, one of three resident counselors. My immediate boss was housemother Mrs. King, who seemed to have no credentials for the job except good social standing. My first conversation with her shortly after I arrived was unsettling.

"What are you studying, education?' she asked, smiling her social smile.

"No, sociology."

Her smile faded briefly before she put it back on again. "Oh politics, organizing, things like that."

"Not really. We study organizations and social systems."

Her eyes narrowed and she lowered her voice. "I suppose there are still a lot of radical sympathizers in your field?"

I blinked, had never been asked a question like that before and, as far as I knew, had never met or heard about a radical sociology sympathizer on Kent's conservative campus. But it was 1959, just five years after the end of McCarthyism, the era in which Communists were bogeymen and disloyalty was imagined and ferreted out among even the most loyal of Americans. I'd been too young to experience it myself but knew that careers had been destroyed on the slimmest of evidence. A shiver of recognition ran down my spine. It was people like Mrs. King, with a suspicion honed by life-long vigilance in enforcing propriety and political conservatism, who had supported McCarthyism. The word 'sociology' was too much like 'socialism' for her taste.

We counselors all underwent coy questioning from Mrs. King about our personal lives in our first few days in the dormitory. I learned from the other two counselors that she had quizzed each of them separately about my behavior.

"Mrs. King thinks you are fraternizing too much with the freshman girls on your corridor."

"Isn't that what we're supposed to do? Get acquainted with them?" I asked, puzzled.

They shrugged their shoulders.

"Mrs. King seems to think she can nose around in our business," complained one of the other counselors. "That was not my understanding. I'm going to the Housing Director to find out for sure."

Word came back quickly that Mrs. King's job did not and should not include the monitoring of the personal behavior of the resident counselors. Even with that assurance, we all remained guarded around her.

I was beginning to wonder if I had made a mistake in accepting the resident counselor position.

CHAPTER 2

Red Flag—Almost No Women Here

STARTING GRADUATE SCHOOL was like competing in the Olympics after doing well in my first college swim meet. At Kent State I had participated actively in classes and hung out with the graduate students, who didn't seem very different from me. I won the Outstanding Woman in Sociology award when I graduated and had managed to place in the 97th percentile on the Sociology section of the GRE.

Still swathed in my undergraduate enthusiasm and bouncy co-ed persona, I popped cheerfully into my first class, social psychology taught by Dr. Welton. With the exception of one woman my age, my twelve classmates were all older than I and male. Dr. Welton had brilliant white hair and a strong, handsome face that made him look like an academic god. His voice was decisive. He spoke with absolute certainty, though not with great clarity. Within minutes of sitting down I realized I didn't understand what he was talking about, except to appreciate that it didn't seem to have much to do with the assigned books that I had glanced at briefly.

"I'm making a seating chart and will call on you by name throughout the semester," he explained as he began to throw out obscure questions.

The students he chose all had something erudite to say. I tried to avoid eye contact and make myself as small as possible. I met Dr. Welton again two days later in the required statistics class. He filled chalkboards on three walls with complicated formulas. I'd gotten an

A in statistics at Kent State, but could find little connection between what I'd learned there and what the professor was presenting. Before the end of my first week at Northwestern I doubted every aspect of my ability to succeed.

Two parts of me had always jostled for my allegiance. One was the cautious, conforming girl, a member of the silent generation who had experienced the deprivation of the Great Depression and the fear and rationing of World War II. In 1951, just as I was entering high school, *Time Magazine* gave us our name in a generally uncomplimentary column written by its editors entitled "People: The Younger Generation." "The most startling fact about the younger generation is its silence" *Time* declared. Not too long afterwards, William Manchester, a well-known historian, described us in greater detail. We were "withdrawn, cautious, unimaginative, indifferent, and unadventurous." This conservative era, the silent generation of which I was a member, promoted caution, restraint, and pulling back. I excelled at all three of those activities.

On the other hand, my family legacy of independent thought pushed me to think beyond the conservatism of my generation and the small-town environment in which I'd started. During and after World War II, when we played soldiers and nurses during school recess, I was usually the only girl who wanted to be a soldier. As a child I read every book I could find on women seeking entrance into previously male-dominated professions. Yet, true to my generation's propensity for caution and timidity, when I learned to color as a child, I was always careful to color *within* the lines. In fact, I was so worried about staying within them that I left a neat narrow strip of white just inside.

All my life I had vacillated between these two contrasting behaviors and worldviews. In that first week at Northwestern all my silent generation propensities toward caution rose to the forefront. I shut down, developed a sense of inadequacy and a need to protect myself with silence.

This reaction was accentuated when I sought advice from an older graduate student about completing my master's degree in a year, as I had planned to do.

"Forget it," he said. "It's theoretically possible according to the school catalogue and chair of the department, but nobody does it. It usually takes at least two years. Northwestern is focused on the Ph.D. For most students the M.A. is incidental. They get it along the way or bypass it altogether."

What had I gotten myself into?

That first fall in Chicago was especially warm. I took walks whenever I could, shedding my shoes as soon as I was out of sight of the dorm. Ambling barefoot toward Lake Michigan, just a few blocks away, I luxuriated in the sensual pleasure of the smooth sidewalk beneath my bare feet, cool in the shade of old maples, and warm in sun. It was a delicious pleasure, a small deviance that helped me feel part of the beat generation, whose poetry I read, and hang on to the free-spirited girl inside, now threatened by the grown-up worlds of graduate school and dorm counseling.

In college I had focused on English, as well as sociology, and the decision about which field to pursue in graduate school had been agonizing. I finally opted for sociology but, as an undergraduate, I continued to take classes in English literature. Graduate school allowed no such option. Impenetrable academic prose and statistical equations weighed me down. I yearned for the music of poetry and the narrative of stories but there was no time to read anything but sociology. I hit on a solution to this dilemma early in fall semester when we faced our first research assignment. I could indulge my need for literature by doing research on writers and writing.

My first paper was awkwardly entitled, "The Effect of his Minority Status Upon the Negro Author's Poetry." Although I tried to write something more erudite, my main finding was about what wasn't there. In 1959 the illustrious Northwestern University library listed almost nothing on Negro writers. (The terms Black and African Americans were not yet used.) I finally discovered a few references to Negroes in historical materials about the Harlem Renaissance of the 1920s, but the writers and books mentioned, if they were available at all, were buried deep in the stacks of the library.

I prowled dimly lit aisles, pulled out crumbling, thin volumes, breathed in their old-book smell, then curled up in dusty cubicles to read American poets I had never met in my English classes, riveted by their beat, imagery, and articulated pain. How could my education not have included brilliant Zora Neale Hurston, a published, trained anthropologist who wrote plays, poems, and novels? Or Paul Laurence Dunbar, Langston Hughes, or Claude McKay?

I was excited by my discovery of minority writers who had produced a rich body of work, but distressed that they were invisible to white America and that I had not studied them in college. It was the beginning of my uncovering a naivete and ignorance that I hadn't known I had, in an era in which many of us were also beginning to face up to inequalities in America that we had previously chosen not to see. In 1954 the U.S. Supreme Court had ruled in Brown v. Board of Education that school segregation was unconstitutional. In 1956, after Rosa Parks refused to give up her bus seat in Montgomery, Alabama and a city bus boycott of over a year, the Supreme Court ruled that segregated seating was unconstitutional. Two years later in 1957, we watched the "Little Rock Nine" integrate Central High School in Little Rock, Arkansas. We were about to see the Woolworth sit-ins in Greensboro, North Carolina.

In my small research paper, I had also become aware and distressed by a kind of discrimination for which, at that time, most of us barely had words. I did not have the understanding then, nor the language, to ask the kinds of questions that many of us would ask a few years later in regard to both the Civil Rights and Women's Movements. What is lost when only one group has the power to decide what kinds of literature or art are 'good'? How can a society morally or aesthetically justify valuing the cultural expression and production of members of some groups over those of other groups? At that point, I wasn't even making enough mental connections to apply my new insights about discrimination against African Americans to my own situation as a woman in a man's profession.

Older men dominated my small graduate program of about twenty active students. There was one other young woman, straight from college like me, who entered the program when I did. Except Sylvia, unlike me, came with star status, a special two-year scholarship that paid all her school expenses plus a stipend. Sylvia and I fell into the habit of plopping down on the stairs of the sociology building in the late afternoon to talk. We just dropped our things and sat, sometimes silent for several minutes, halfway between the second floor and the third, where the sociology statistics lab was located. Classes were over for the afternoon, the building felt nearly deserted. Weak sunlight slanted down on us from a high window. We'd made it through another day but weren't yet ready to climb the last few steps to the lab to start our onerous statistics homework.

"I'm miserable," Sylvia would sigh, leaning back on the step, throwing her dark hair over her shoulders.

"But you're doing so well," I'd say, enviously.

"But I always feel so shitty."

"Yeah," I'd agree, hunching my shoulders forward.

Neither of us realized then how being a woman in a man's world sapped our confidence and self-esteem, how it left us with an entrenched sense of isolation and alienation. We were outside the invisible boundaries for women. We had no women instructors. I'd had no women teachers as an undergraduate either, except for gym. There were also no role models in our reading. Our sociological books and articles were written by men, mostly about men. We studied 'mankind.' The use of male nouns and pronouns to refer to everyone was the norm, the acceptable way of writing. We wrote that way too. It would be another ten years before two feminist editors, Casey Miller and Kate Swift, raised the topic of gender-neutral language in their article "Desexing the Language" in the first issue of MS Magazine in

December 1971. It would be many more years before researchers would suggest that when readers saw masculine pronouns they actually visualized males.

Sylvia and I could not find images of ourselves anywhere. We didn't understand the impact of that then. All we knew was that we felt "shitty," not good enough, not taken seriously, like outsiders. I thought my graduate school struggles were because of my difficulty concentrating, lack of ability, and wavering commitment to sociology. We were in a world in which sexism was in the air we breathed, so familiar that none of us, male or female, recognized or questioned it. I would have said at the time that I faced no obstacles as a woman in a man's profession.

Although Sylvia and I shared the status of being women in a man's world, we were not especially close. Her life was still tied to her family and friends, and she went home often. My life, for better or worse, was at Northwestern. My closest friend, actually my only real friend in the sociology program, was Shig, a small boned, wiry, Japanese Hawaiian man in his thirties with a lined face the color of a walnut and a voice gravely from years of smoking. He had been sorting mail at the US post office in Chicago until Aaron Cicourel, one of our professors, had recognized his intelligence in a night class and convinced him to start graduate school on a full assistantship.

Shig aced every class and was included in the inner circle of the brightest students, but in some ways he didn't fit in the department that first year much better than I did. Even though he worked hard to 'talk like a sociologist,' he would occasionally lapse into phrases like, 'that cat doesn't get it.' He always called me 'Babe.' I'm sure he would have stopped if I had complained, but I liked it. It was an authentic part of who he was and somehow communicated his affection, appreciation, and respect for me. There was never any romantic involvement between us, but we often sat for hours talking about sociology, life, and the peculiarities of academia. He always had my back, always valued my intelligence and ideas, always kept me informed about what was going on in the department and among the other students.

Many days that first year I despaired of ever becoming a 'real' sociologist. I could find little sense in the turgid prose of the famous theorist Talcott Parsons, who was considered to be one of the greatest American sociologists of our era. His paragraph-long sentences seemed to have no meaning when I finally unraveled them into everyday English. What was I missing? Why wasn't I smart enough to grasp his great thoughts? Yet on other days, studying alone in my room, I was happier than I had ever been in my life. I liked wrestling with abstractions, theories, and research problems, and felt challenged intellectually, as I rarely had been before. The pleasure was especially keen when I engaged with the ideas of Alfred North Whitehead in *Science and the Modern World,* one of our assigned books for methodology class. Whitehead opened me up to new ways of thinking about the world and what we were trying to do as social science researchers. He also wrote with clarity. It was possible to think big and still write well!

I got excited as I began to work on my research project for our important year-long research methods course in which we had to conceive, design, and execute a small research project. In line with my practice of trying to combine English and sociology I decided to look at whether creative individuals were more tolerant of mild deviance than students who were not engaged in creative writing or art. To explore this hypothesis, I interviewed members of a creative writing class and a small random sample of other Northwestern students who described themselves as neither writers nor artists. Once I pushed myself beyond my inherent shyness and fear of being pushy, I discovered that interviewing was fun. Talking to creative writers, even in a brief interview, seemed lyrical after months of conversing almost exclusively with sociologists. The sources I read to help me frame the study were fascinating, and I relished the detective work of organizing and analyzing the data.

The study, which suggested that creative writers were indeed somewhat more likely to tolerate small deviance than those who were not artists, was small and not very scientific, but for the first time I felt a little bit like a real sociologist. That came through in my final oral report to the class. Aaron Cicourel and Gresham Sykes, our two professors, and the other graduate students responded enthusiastically to my presentation.

"Hey babe, you really wowed them yesterday," Shig exulted the next day. "Everyone was really surprised, said you did a great job, that you'd really come out of your shell. Cicourel thought you were great."

Professor Aaron Cicourel had very high standards and his praise was coveted by the graduate students. It seemed like my colleagues took me a little more seriously after that, especially when the word leaked out that I had received one of only three A's in the class. I felt a tiny burst of confidence, pleased that I had finally publicly vindicated Shig's year-long confidence in my intelligence and ability as a sociologist. At last I felt I had in Aaron Cicourel what every graduate student needs, a professor advocate.Unfortunately, he left Northwestern at the end of that school year to teach at another university.

CHAPTER **3**

First Love

I HAD NEVER camped out before, never seen the United States west of Chicago. Neither had my college roommate Penny. So as soon as she finished her first year as an art teacher and I finished my classes at Northwestern we bought a teeny, tiny tent, packed up 'Wolfgang', Penny's VW bug, and headed west. We were good travel companions, could break camp in ten minutes, and for the first time in our lives were truly on our own, away from our families and others' expectations.

We started in Ohio and camped partway across the U.S. by way of Indiana, Illinois, Missouri, Oklahoma, Texas, New Mexico, Arizona, and Utah, then circled back to Boulder, Colorado in late July. There we settled for five weeks in an apartment across from the University of Colorado where Penny planned to take an art workshop in scene design. I hung out reading sociology and writing poetry, and we both took advantage of the plethora of activities available on campus. About halfway through our stay in Boulder, we signed up for a University sponsored mountain hike and steak fry. While I milled around at the top of the hike eating my steak, which turned out to be a small hamburger, I caught the eye of a man about my age standing alone. He waved me over to him, laughing and brandishing his empty paper plate.

"Guess hamburger is all we can expect when the cost for the hike is so low."

I laughed too. We introduced ourselves; Eli was a Ph.D. student in physics from Columbia University, in Boulder for a summer workshop. Talk flowed easily. Eli was medium height and a little stocky. His forehead was high, framed with dark hair, damp now from the climb. He had an open expressive face, brown eyes, and wore dark rimmed glasses. I liked the way he looked standing with the setting sun slanting briefly on his face.

"How about stopping somewhere for a pizza to fill us up?" he asked as he, Penny, and I trudged back down to campus. "I'll call my friend Larry and we can all go out together." Larry had a car, and over the next two weeks the four of us explored Colorado together.

Eli quickly tried to get romantic, but I resisted his advances. I wasn't ready for that. It was 1960. As soon as a woman fell in love she supposedly forgot about everything except settling down with her man and having babies. Everyone said that would happen, even my professors, like the chairman of the English department who handed me the Creative Writing Award I won at Kent State University. When I told him I was planning to go to graduate school he chuckled, "Well you'll meet someone and fall in love and that will be the end of that." I sat stunned, silenced by his certainty and his laugh, as if I had made a joke.

My relationship with Eli changed a few nights after the Boulder steak fry when he and I had driven with Larry and Penny to a tiny pizza place in the mountains. The spicy aroma of pizza piled high with pepperoni and fresh mushrooms wafted around our table. I filled and refilled my glass with the full-bodied Ruffino-Classico Chianti. The red checked tablecloths, candles in bottles, dim light, and good conversation all left me feeling deliciously mellow.

When Eli kissed me in the back seat on the trip home to Boulder something inside let go. Instead of resisting his advances, as I had done previously, I kissed him back with an intensity I didn't know I had. As I relaxed into his caresses, my carefully constructed defenses against emotional involvement crumbled. Two days later Eli became my first lover. The event left me surprised, startled at how quickly I had succumbed to love, or at least to sex, and how delightful it was.

I had no personal moral qualms about sex outside of marriage. My parents had always encouraged me to read, think, and act independently. As a teenager I avidly read the *Reader's Digest,* which at that time included several articles about birth control. After some thought I had decided that making love with someone I cared about was okay, as long as I used contraceptives and took responsibility for my actions. Given this perspective, I had not expected my new behavior to sharply shift my worldview. But it did. Doing was different from thinking and talking, more so than I'd comprehended before crossing the line. As a resident counselor I was supposed to be a model of morality and help keep my undergraduate charges on the narrow path of virtue. My life had always been an open book; now I had secrets and suddenly registered the reality that other individuals probably had secrets too. The assumption restructured my whole world view.

For the next two and a half weeks in Boulder Eli and I spent all our free time together camping, hiking, and talking. When I showed him my poetry, he read with appreciation. He was the first person I had showed it to who took it seriously enough to occasionally make a suggestion or ask a question. As we rested under a pine tree after one of our hikes in Rocky Mountain National Park he pulled a gift for me out of his daypack, *Collected Lyrics* by one of his favorite poets, Edna St. Vincent Millay. I had never read her work before. Side by side, surrounded by mountains and sky, we read her poems aloud to each other letting the music of the language, first in my voice, then in his, engulf us. I'd never experienced this kind of intellectual and emotional closeness with anyone before. I was profoundly different than before I'd met Eli. It wasn't just that he was my first love. He had awakened in me a longing for a kind of closeness and connection I'd not had before with anyone.

I began to hope that we might see each other after the summer was over, but Eli made it clear that our time together was nothing more than a delightful summer romance. He was Jewish, he said, and could not envision himself in a long-term relationship with a woman who was not Jewish.

On our last night together Eli and I lingered on the small white porch of my apartment house, sitting straight on its little bench. I kept pressing offers of food or drink, starting conversations, asking questions that required long answers and a smile. He obliged, until finally we stood up. We leaned together, laughing so as not to cry, as our hands held tight, then slowly let go. Reluctantly I went inside, closed the door, and watched him down the street and out of sight.

I was different when I returned to Northwestern in September 1960 for my second year. My summer experiences had left me with a much wider and more complex world view. I was trying to figure out who I was and who I wanted to be. Before my summer adventures, I had only railed against middle class values; now I actively violated some of them. It was a different way of being in the world. I was searching for an identity that felt right, but the process was scary. There were no easy answers anywhere.

The environment I returned to at Northwestern was static. In the spring I, like all my colleagues, had applied for a sociology graduate assistantship for my second year. The department had not awarded one to me and, to my chagrin, I had to continue as a dorm counselor in order to support my second year. Mrs. King and I were moved together, to my dismay and probably hers, to a larger dorm that employed six resident counselors. My tolerance for the *in loco parentis* system that dominated college policies toward women students, which I'd accepted without question in college and even somewhat the previous year at Northwestern, had fallen close to zero. There was an almost religious fervor in the attempts of old-guard administrators and housemothers to protect the morality of their female charges. That I was a cog in that system now rankled in a way it had not before. When a college took the role of parent, it seemed to me, it kept women from growing up.

Although we six resident counselors were a fairly congenial group and usually ate dinner together in the dining hall, only one of the other five, Lois, became a good friend. She was an English major with honey colored hair and a slight southern accent from growing up in Atlanta and attending college in New Orleans. I quickly discovered she was wise, adventuresome, and a Democrat. We cemented our relationship the night of the Kennedy/Nixon election, the first in which I could vote. She suggested we avoid the TV sets in the dorm lounge, surrounded by Republicans, and go to a bar in Chicago, where we could watch election returns among Democrats. We bonded in despair when we came home that night, convinced that Kennedy had lost. The next morning at breakfast we took one look at the morose face of Mrs. King and knew that Kennedy had won the election. We tried not to look too exuberant as we joined her for breakfast.

Monthly counselor and housemother dinner meetings became almost unbearable. I'd hesitate in the doorway of our special dining room with its silver teapots and gaze at the blue haired, corseted housemothers in pastel suits surrounded by obsequious resident counselors. They all smiled and chatted nicely together, finding chairs, offering them to each other. It was a murmuring sea of banality in which I felt an intense sense of loneliness and a nearly irresistible desire to flee. But I walked in. Slowly. Found a seat on the edge of the group. Smiled like I belonged. But I knew I didn't, and desperately didn't want to.

CHAPTER 4

Love Is Essential

EARLY IN THE fall, Eli sent me a postcard and we started to write to each other. In late October he called to ask me to come to New York for Thanksgiving break.

"I want to show you my city."

"You said it would never work for us because I'm not Jewish."

"I know, but please come."

I focused on the last two words and made my plane reservation.

We made small talk in the taxi to Eli's place and managed to keep it up as we climbed the four flights of stairs to his flat and passed through the kitchen into his bedroom. There he dropped my suitcase with a thud, and we stood looking at each other awkwardly. I suddenly realized that we hardly knew each other. What on earth was I doing here? I had no idea how to act. Then we simultaneously reached for each other in a tension breaking, rib straining hug, followed by a long kiss. It was like we'd just parted yesterday on that little white porch in Boulder.

That first evening at twilight he took me to a viaduct overlooking Harlem to share one of his favorite scenes--thousands of raucous starlings swooping in to settle for the night in shifting, sloping strands of black along the gray roofs. It was the kind of special experience that I loved. In the morning Eli introduced me to bagels and lox. We ate at his scuffed kitchen table gazing out at grimy windows laced together by lines full of flaccid clothes. After breakfast we hurried to the subway station in Harlem at West 125th Street to go to the Thanksgiving Day parade. I pressed my body close to Eli as we pushed ourselves into the train to hurtle downtown buttock to buttock with strangers. The subway was a poem of sound, the clickity clack of wheels on tracks, sheeh-sheeh clumb of opening doors, the noisy sigh of exodus. We emerged from the 59th Street subway station into a river of color, swirling toward the parade.

The huge bird lumbered above Broadway, wobbling uncertainly between the skyscrapers on each side. Two men in white suits jumped about anxiously, hollering orders, their hands stretched out, in, waving to the small army of balloon handlers in bright blue uniforms who struggled to keep it on course. Eli and I grabbed hands as we laughed and cheered. I was 23; he was 26. The New York day was brisk and sunny, perfect for the 1960 Macy's Thanksgiving Day parade.

"Oops, Snoopy almost went off course," shouted Eli pointing up the street to a group of straining handlers trying to reorient the wayward dog.

"Do they ever get away?" I asked. Part of me hoped a balloon would break free, go off its prescribed path, like I wanted to break free.

"Too many strings attached."

We hugged each other and waved as the parade wound on and on, like forever, bands, floats, clowns, and balloons with their entourage of nervous managers, until Santa Claus rode down the street in his sleigh, with his ho-ho-ho, eight tiny reindeer and Rudolph. The crowd roared. Then suddenly it was over, with just a few policemen on motorcycles, trailed by an army of streetcleaners and slow-moving cars. We stood disoriented, then turned from our spot in Columbus Circle and walked east along Central Park toward Fifth Avenue.

"What's that delicious smell?" I asked lifting my nose, suddenly focused.

"Roasted chestnuts, want some?"

We stopped at the brazier of a wizened seller with an old red knitted cap. He picked out six for each of us, moving his tongs with deliberation through the steaming pile.

I watched Eli as he waited to pay. He stood patiently in his dark blue jacket and the light blue pants he said he bought for a dollar at the discount store on Harlem's West 125th Street. I was his opposite, thin, though not as thin as I would have liked, with short blond hair, glasses I hated, blue eyes, and fair skin. I looked like a WASP (white Anglo-Saxon Protestant), which is what I was—a mix of English, Scottish, Dutch, and who knows what else.

Eli had grown up in the New York area. I had grown up in a small town, Linesville, in rural Western Pennsylvania. It had a two-block main street of small shops that provided everything its thousand inhabitants needed. The town was so quiet that people said you could hear the grass grow. My roots there went deep. My parents and several generations of my relatives had grown up there. Amos Line, the town's founder, was one of my ancestors. I had assumed that everyone's family was like mine until I went to Kent State University in Ohio, where most of my friends came from families of recent immigrants from Eastern Europe. I was jealous of their ethnic food and customs—the sweet poppy seed kolaci their mothers sent back to the dorm with them on Sunday nights and the lively polka bands at their weddings. I felt sad to have no distinct ethnic heritage.

"You eat them like this," Eli said as he turned back to me and handed me one of the two steaming bags and showed me how to peel off the outer husk of the chestnut. I cradled the hot paper bag against my cold hands, extracted a dark brown nut, peeled it, then bit into its tan crumbling center, savoring its smoky, nutty taste, like nothing I'd ever had before.

We turned on to Fifth Avenue and wandered into the Central Park Zoo, weaving around white-clad nannies navigating shiny blue baby carriages like small ships through the crowd. We laughed at the elephants trying to snatch bags of peanuts from onlookers and the polar bears cavorting in their pool, posing for visitors. As we strolled in companionable silence up the hill to the carousel we stopped to watch the multi-colored swirl of excited children riding up and down on exotic animals.

"Mommy, Mommy Up. Up. Ohh," screamed a red-suited toddler as he let go of his yellow balloon to wave to his brother passing by on a zebra. Tears streamed down his face as he stood watching it become a golden dot against the blue sky. I stood gazing up too, feeling both the child's loss and the exhilaration of the balloon's unconstrained flight. I was flying high. I was in love. With the city? With Eli? I wasn't sure, but I was deeply happy. Big cities had always fascinated me. I wanted a wider world than the small town where I'd started my life. Eli was giving me that in ways I could not have imagined. Our playfulness with each other was a new experience. As an only child I hadn't had much of that when I was young. I knew my parents loved me, but there had always been a cloud of loneliness and seriousness in my home.

Eli and I continued walking, onto a path that took us back toward Manhattan's West Side and Broadway where we could catch a bus to his place. The wind came up and we picked up our pace. Parents hurried by pushing strollers with bundled children. Eli grew silent. I sensed a different quality in his silence now, more withdrawn. Perhaps it was just my own mood shift in response to the sudden weather change. I took his hand. He left it in mine, but the grasp was limp and after a minute he let go.

"What are you thinking?" I asked.

"Nothing much."

Eli's apparent disengagement as we walked through Central Park toward the West Side unsettled me. I felt a chill that went deeper than the impact of the rising wind. I'd taken risks in coming to New York. In 1960 it was not acceptable for a nice girl to travel across the country to spend a holiday weekend with her boyfriend. I could probably lose my job as a dorm counselor. That reality had suddenly come home to me when Mrs. King appeared in my room to chat just as I was packing to leave, something she had never done before. "And where are you staying in New York?" she asked as she settled into my one comfortable chair for a chat. Yet it was not so much the social consequences of visiting Eli that concerned me most. It was the emotional risk. I'd kept my emotions cordoned off for a long time. Now they had broken through and since I had arrived in New York they were intensifying by the hour. I was like the little boy's yellow balloon rushing toward the sky. I knew what happened to balloons when they flew too high.

Eli had chosen several plays for us to see during my visit, all ones I would have picked myself. I was impressed by our similar taste. The night after the parade we saw *Taste of Honey,* a new Irish play by Shelagh Delaney, and I sensed again, our closeness. Or so I thought... until later that night when Eli began to talk about his former girlfriend Sarah. He described her in loving detail, as if no one else could ever fill her royal shoes. I pulled away from him. I didn't want to be second best. This beautiful world I'd thought we were creating was all my own fantasy.

"Why are you telling me all this?" I asked, pulling on him, trying to make eye contact.

"I wanted you to know about me, so you would understand."

"Understand what? I don't understand anything. You started up our relationship again. You invited me here. Why?" I shouted. Anger momentarily overcame pain.

"Because I wanted to be with you."

I stared at him blankly, trying to make sense of what he said.

We didn't mention that conversation during the next two days as Eli continued to enthusiastically introduce me to New York City. We had fun together. I got an idea of what love might be like, and I now knew, absolutely, that I wanted love in my life. To be complete, whole, I needed both love and work!

The last afternoon of my visit we began to talk about us.

"I really like you, but I can never love you," Eli said slowly, head down, his voice flat, final.

"I don't want a relationship that can't go anywhere."

There wasn't much else to say. We decided not to see each other again. I ran into Eli's bedroom, shut the door, and jammed a pillow over my mouth to try to stifle the sound of my sobs. My emotional awakening had been shut down with two words that reverberated in my head like the sound of a large hammer. Never love.

At the airport the next morning I learned that the Chicago airport was closed, and we would be delayed. Travelers rushed to the phone booths. I strained toward the phones too. I wanted to call someone, attach somehow to a person who cared that I would be late. But I had no one to call. As a member of the silent generation I had learned early in life to accept the way things were. We all tried to 'make do,' make the best of whatever situation came our way. As I sat numbly on the airplane, finally on my way to Chicago, I tried to convince myself that the kind of comradeship I had with Eli was not for me, that my mother was right when she said I wanted too much, was too independent for a man. Still I ached with the loss of the intimacy I had just discovered and desperately wanted.

CHAPTER **5**

Smiles and Games

IT WAS DARK by the time I got back to Chicago and my dorm at Northwestern. As the elevator door opened on my floor I heard a phone ringing down the corridor. It sounded like mine. My dad had had a heart attack a year ago. Had he had another? I ran toward my room dragging bag and purse, got the door open, and groped unsuccessfully in the dark for the light switch. Dropping everything, I felt my way to my desk beside the door, fell into the chair, and fumbled for the phone.

"Hello."

Not my mother's voice. Eli's voice. Saying what?

"I think it's silly for us to stop seeing each other."

What was he saying? I tried to push my coat collar aside so I could get the receiver closer to my ear.

"Are you there? I think it's silly..."

"Yes," I said almost inaudibly, still breathless after my dash down the hall. "It doesn't make sense."

I sat in the dark, suitcase tilting against my partially open door, half in my chair with one of its arms digging into my lower ribs. Disoriented. Emotionally backpedaling.

"You look like a girl who's never tasted borscht. I've only associated with Jewish girls," he said in a rush. "It's hard not to think of you as a stranger, but my feelings for you are growing. I want to get to know you better."

What did I feel? Confusion? Anger? Relief? All of those things. Mostly relief, but it was hard to turn my feelings on and off like the peal of a telephone.

"Let's take our chances," I said.

It was all I could muster as I tried to rearrange, for the second time in 24 hours, my perception of our relationship. I hung up the phone, located the light switch, pulled my suitcase inside, and shut my door. Then I sat down, the right way this time, and didn't move for a long time. I'd been so high, had dropped so low. Could I ever go that high, that low again? Had something been inextricably altered inside?

If we were going to try to continue our relationship, we would need to see each other over Christmas. Going to New York then would be a hard sell to my parents, but I had no time to dwell on that. I needed to focus on completing assignments and my thesis proposal and also manage the two disparate roles in my life, dorm counselor and sociology graduate student. Every day I felt more like a misfit in both.

My role as a dorm counselor was feeling increasingly uncomfortable. I disliked being a part of an institution that controlled women. As someone who had just returned from spending a weekend in her boyfriend's apartment, I also felt like a hypocrite. Were there other counselors like me, I wondered. Women with secrets? I tried to imagine, in a hopeful moment, that there was an undercurrent of impure thoughts, passions, and desires flowing beneath our insufferable counselor meetings. But my imagination, usually so thriving when I read about disasters in the newspaper, utterly failed me. The 1950s and early 1960s were years of women's bright smiles and unruffled surfaces. We had learned to put on our cheerful faces, no matter what. We all acted our parts so well that there was rarely a sniff of possible impropriety or inconvenient reality like abuse, rape, alcoholism, or betrayal. Discontent was buried so deep inside most of us that we didn't even know we had it. Our questions and anger would roil up soon enough. But not yet. We kept smiling in the face of crimes and indignities, still pretending they didn't happen.

In the sociology department I felt isolated in a different kind of way. Sylvia, the only other graduate student like me, hadn't come back to finish her sociology degree after her first year. She just threw over that prestigious, lucrative fellowship and her good grades. I felt a sense of pride that I *had* returned, but I missed her. Because I had finished all my classes and was working alone on independent studies and my thesis, I had little contact with other graduate students. My friend Shig was my main link to the department. As part of the inner circle of brightest students and faculty members he was a good contact. He picked up all the departmental gossip and became a sort of mentor, as well as a close friend. He lived directly across from my new dorm and we often sat talking for hours in his landlady's small, doily-covered living room.

If Aaron Cicourel, who responded to my methodology seminar paper so positively at the end of my first year, had remained at Northwestern, I would have asked him to be my advisor and I might have had an advocate and been convinced to somehow expand my successful first year seminar paper into a related master's thesis. Instead I struggled stubbornly on alone, insisting on doing my thesis on creative artists, a topic that was nebulous and did not mesh with the sociological interests of any faculty member in the department.

I chose Dr. Noran to be my thesis advisor because he was a poet, although his field in sociology was social organization, very different from the topic of my research. Dr. Noran's free-spirited and poetic nature, though interesting, made him difficult to track down through his three different phone numbers. Sometimes it took me a week to get an appointment and I agonized over each phone call. I needed to be more assertive to get ahead as a graduate student, but my mother had taught me the dangers of being 'overbearing.' Overbearing meant pushy, demanding, trying to get your own way, not nice. It was one of the worst things a woman could be.

Shig kept urging me to become more active at our monthly sociology gatherings in which a research talk by a faculty member was followed by a lively social gathering with lots of wine, food, and sociological discussion. I found it even harder to speak up at these social events than in classes. Ideas and arguments flew between faculty members and students like bouncing balls. Everyone but me, it seemed, vied for attention, tried to sound erudite, and held forth in long sentences.

Christmas festivities were big at Northwestern. The party for resident counselors was scheduled for several days after I got back from my Thanksgiving weekend in New York and the sociology department's party was a few days after that. Both posed problems. I would be expected to smile all the time at one and play the one-upmanship games of men at the other. I was lousy at both.

I decided that one way to produce the requisite happy counselor smile was to remember that I owned a diaphragm. In particular I would focus on the satisfaction I felt on the November day just before my trip to New York when I brought it home to the dorm from the gynecologist's office, right under Mrs. King's nose. I had hoped Mrs. King wouldn't be in her office just outside the back elevator when I came in, but there she was, staunch keeper of morality, waiting for someone to talk to.

"Good afternoon Anne," she chirped, "been shopping?"

"Just a little," I replied cheerfully as I clutched the box, which was pretty big, quite noticeable actually. Were there any pictures or printing on the outside I wondered. I couldn't remember and didn't want to draw attention to it by looking. I hastened to the elevator and pressed the button five times, hoping for a quick deliverance before Mrs. King called me back into her office for extended chit-chat, as she sometimes did. Open and closing sounds above me sounded like someone might be moving--please don't let it be a mover, that could take an hour. But then the elevator arrived with a thump. I ducked inside and took a deep breath.

My strategy at the party for the counselors worked well. I smiled happily through the oohing and aahing over the table decorated with alternating red and green napkins and a big flower arrangement, surely used for numerous gatherings over the holidays. I smiled as women exclaimed over presents from the gift exchange we were supposed to have, that I'd totally forgotten.

"It's lovely isn't it?"

"Oh, that's so cute."

"You made it yourself! How did you ever find the time?"

"Why," I asked my counselor friend Lois after the party, "are these dorm gatherings so awful?"

"They feel phony. A room full of fake intimacy."

Fake intimacy. Yes. None of us knew each other really. But we acted as if we'd grown up together. I hoped there were some women in the room that day, who like me, understood that they were more than the face they put forward, who recognized the difference between fake and real intimacy, who were plumbing their depths, as I was plumbing mine, to figure out who they wanted to be.

I hadn't realized how crucial the sociology Christmas party might be for me until a few days before the event when Shig looked solemnly across the room at me as we were sitting in our customary places in his landlady's living room.

"You need to talk more at the Christmas party this week," he said. "The professors aren't sure how committed you are to sociology."

He didn't even preface his statement with 'Babe,' so I knew he was really serious.

"I'm not sure how committed I am, either," I said, tossing my shoulders defiantly.

"None of us are," he replied, "but you gotta play the role. You know what to do. You've been reading the same books as everyone else. You know Goffman's theory that social interaction is a series of roles people play, that we're all actors on a stage. Stroke the professors' egos. Show interest. Ask questions. Play the game."

I stumbled over my words as I tried to explain that I was searching for some core that was *me*. I couldn't deal with games.

"I don't want to play a game, I want to be myself," I finally summarized, trying to keep the tremor out of my voice.

"That's what I like about you babe. You're real. But I'm telling you, getting your degree is going to be hard if you don't start acting like a sociologist."

I took what he said seriously but didn't know whether I could do what he suggested. The night of the party I faced my closet and stared at the small selection of utilitarian clothes: skirts, slacks, sweaters, and a couple tailored dresses left over from when I was on the debate team in college. Everything looked dreary, dumpy, worn. I pulled out one of the dresses, blue and red, the brightest thing I had. Eli would probably say it looked mid-western. I slipped it on, slapped on some lipstick, adjusted my glasses vowing that if I ever got a job I would get contact lenses with my first paycheck, and stared disapprovingly at myself in the mirror.

A short time later I stood in a narrow, smoky apartment sipping wine, trying to act like a sociologist. I made sure I stayed far away from the cluster of faculty and student wives, to whom I had occasionally allowed myself to gravitate at earlier events. The tangles of conversation around me seemed impenetrable. I edged myself into a huddle of colleagues around a professor, but even if I could think of something to say, I wasn't sure how I could insert myself into the conversation. The men, with voices lower and louder than mine, just butted in. They didn't even wait for a speaker to breathe.

None of us recognized in 1960 that men and women in that era had learned different communication styles. In graduate school, our male teachers expected and rewarded male modes of communication that involved one-upmanship, certainty, confidence, and jumping into the action. It was not until the 1980s and early1990s that sociolinguists like Dr. Deborah Tannen, in her book *You Just Don't Understand: Women and Men in Conversation*, began to explore differences in the ways males and females communicated. She actually referred to the variations she discovered as "cross-cultural communication." She argued that men and women of that time period differed from each other in verbal style and subtle understandings of words or gestures, just as individuals from diverse cultures do. We now know that minority members of a group, whose communication patterns differ somewhat from the majority, can face discrimination without anyone, including the minority members themselves, realizing it is occurring. In graduate school in 1960 I didn't understand any of that. I understood only that I was having trouble 'acting like a sociologist,' and was failing to meet the expectations of my professors. I might never get to be a sociologist.

At the counselor party all I had to do was smile and be pleasant. I'd been taught how to do that all my life. At the sociology party I needed skills in game playing, one-upping, assertiveness, and sounding knowledgeable even when I doubted what I knew. Those had not been part of my girlhood education.

As I walked back to the dorm after the sociology party I was struck by how similar the two parties had been, even though the behaviors were strikingly different. Both called for facades. I wondered if being a real grownup was just about playing games, an endless series of events for which we put on the right faces and planned our strategy. If so, I didn't want to grow up. I was more than my smile or my game. I wanted to discover and hold on to some part of myself that was genuine and fixed, a core that I knew was me, but I wasn't sure what that was or how I could find it.

What I really wanted was to be with Eli. Some days the only thing that kept me going was the prospect of seeing him. He had invited me to New York for Christmas, and I visualized festive Fifth Avenue, decorated store windows, and the tree at Rockefeller Plaza. But my parents resisted, as I had suspected they might. They hadn't seen me since September and wanted me home for the holidays.

"Why don't you invite Eli here?" my mother had written with her big loopy Ls and Hs in the green ink she always used.

I had stared at my mother's letter for a long time. The potential visit seemed fraught with difficulties. Eli had never celebrated Christmas.

34

His visit would only accentuate the differences between us when I wanted to minimize them. My hometown, Meadville, Pennsylvania, where I'd lived since I was twelve, was small, about 35,000 people. It didn't have many sights, especially in winter. What would we do? What kind of privacy would we have? But desperate to see him, I had broached the subject in a letter and was waiting anxiously for a reply.

CHAPTER 6

Don't Do It If It's Too Hard

ELI CALLED ABOUT Christmas the day after the sociology party.

"I've been hesitating," he said. "It's scary. Then I talked to my friend Marilyn from downstairs and she said, 'how nice, a new experience' and I thought yes, why am I afraid of a new experience?"

"So?" I asked.

"So, I've decided to come to Meadville for Christmas."

Once the decision had been made, I began to get excited about showing Eli where I had grown up. I explained repeatedly to my parents in phone calls and letters that we were *not* contemplating marriage, that this was not a 'meeting the folks' visit, that my mother didn't need to fuss.

I headed home on the December 19th night train on the Erie Railroad, which had tracked the outward surge of my life since I'd started college. The rail line extended from Chicago, through Kent, Ohio, through Meadville, to Bayonne, New Jersey, across the river from New York City, where Eli would board the train in a few days to come visit me.

When I got home my mother was in a tizzy. In spite of my efforts to answer all possible questions, she hadn't seemed to register anything I'd said. I tried to convince her that Eli was my guest and that I would take care of him, but she remained wracked with anxiety. She had little confidence in her ability to manage an event, but she always rose to the occasion. My mother was forty-four, nine years younger than my dad, with blue eyes and graying hair that she wore in a sort of curled upsweep. My friends always commented on how pretty she was.

Dad was in his mid-fifties with blue eyes and thinning hair, and now after his heart attack a year ago, very trim. I knew Eli and Dad would get along. Dad met everyone with a sense of interest and respect that made each person feel important and comfortable. He was a wonderful teacher, whether he showed me how to fish or do a math problem. I wanted to be like him, ever willing to keep my mind open to new perspectives, always ethical, always kind. I wished sometimes he had sought more for himself, but he was not the kind of person to push himself forward. He had worked since he was 30 in the accounting office of the American Viscose plant that manufactured rayon. His paycheck was regular, but always too small to allow building any financial reserves. I would have had a hard time going to college, much less graduate school, if he and my Uncle Mike hadn't jointly inherited an orange grove in Florida from my Great Aunt June when I was a senior in high school.

I met Eli's late evening train and showed him around Meadville to give us the chance to reconnect before we had to face my parents. There wasn't much to see—four blocks of Main Street with Diamond Park at the top. Facing each other across that park were the two most important institutions of my adolescence, my high school and the historic Unitarian Church with its wide steps, Greek pillars, and big portico now decorated with evergreen boughs. When I was 14 my agnostic parents and I had been introduced to this church and its minister Rev. Robert Smudski. Its emphasis on love, social justice, and the freedom of belief suited us all. I explained to Eli how the church had centered me in my 1950s adolescence and encouraged me to try to become who I wanted to be. Did he understand? I wasn't sure, but he said he found it all fascinating, so different from his own urban growing up.

My folks and our one-eyed, black and brown mutt Nicky were all in bed when we got back. We managed some stealthy love making on the pullout couch where Eli slept in the guest room, next to my parents' bedroom in our small house. I held on to him tightly, breathing in his closeness, glad to be with him again. We thought we had handled everything discretely until I noticed the next morning that I had left my shoes beside his bed. No one mentioned them. I introduced Eli and my parents at breakfast, and all seemed to go smoothly. Nicky sniffed him, wagged his tail and then sat down to get his head rubbed.

After breakfast Eli and I took a long walk through Waterworks Park, a huge wooded tract across the street from my house. It had been my sanctuary of low hanging trees, narrow winding dirt roads, and bird trills during my adolescence, the place I always went for refuge and renewal. It was there that, as a freshman in college, I had put away my first pack of cigarettes and decided never to smoke because of my asthma. We walked back through the still woods, past the swamp, its fall color buried now in snow several inches deep. The day was all winter, no foolishness or pretense. I felt calmed, replenished, back in touch with who I was.

As we stopped to watch a bird sidestep lightly along a snow-covered branch, loosening bits of powder as he moved, I told Eli about an intense experience I'd had in these woods when I was fifteen. I'd sought the solace of the park on a damp cloudy day and stopped at a spot I especially liked, where two roads converged close to the swamp. As I looked up at the sky, stood listening to water dripping through leaves and a single bird chirp, woods, sky, sounds, the world and I became one. I felt complete, unified with everything. I didn't believe in God, hadn't read much about meditation, and struggled to describe an experience that was simply beyond words.

"I wanted that feeling forever, but it faded away like a rainbow," I whispered.

We turned and trudged silently back home through the snow, holding hands.

In the afternoon we decorated the tree. After dinner my parents thoughtfully removed themselves to their bedroom and we snuggled together on the floor.

"Shall we make love under the Christmas tree? Eli asked.

"What if we knock it over?"

"We'll be careful," he said as he ran his hand along the inside of my waist band.

His kiss on my stomach and then my mouth stopped all further conversation. We curled together. The colored lights and shimmering balls reflected in our eyes and against our skin, shifting like a kaleidoscope as we moved. Tinsel icicles caught in our hair.

The highlight of Christmas day for Eli and me was a walk in the clear sunshine along a deserted, rough fisherman's road beside French Creek, which ran a few hundred feet behind our house. Winter shone in its perfection. Sun, in a sky mottled with white clouds, glanced off the smooth ice on the creek. For the moment life seemed easy, simple.

We had both worked to keep Eli's short visit light. When he left we expected to see each other again. After I'd taken him to the train to go back to New York I felt empty and lonely and sat down at the kitchen table to visit with my mother as she puttered around cleaning up after lunch.

"I really like Eli," I said, hoping she would encourage me to talk about him, so I could bring him back for a few moments in words.

"It seems warmer this afternoon," my mother replied as she looked out the window over the sink.

"Eli and I have good times together. We always have things to talk about. We share a lot of interests."

"There really aren't many dishes," my mother said as she pulled dishes from the white drying rack and started to put them away.

"He really appreciates my poetry and keeps encouraging me."

"Henry sounded so stable," my mother said, her back turned to me as she reached to put a plate up in the cupboard. Henry was a man in Chicago I'd dated briefly during early fall and had mentioned in a letter to my parents, noting that he was about to finish his Ph.D., also in physics, and that I had tried to get interested in him, but just couldn't.

I sat stunned, cut to the quick by what seemed to be a total de-nial of Eli's recent presence and what I was trying to tell her. I felt betrayed. Eli had been a good guest, pleasant, well-mannered, appre-ciative. My parents had appeared interested in him and at ease, just as they always were with my friends. It seemed like everything had gone well. Where was this coming from?

I fled the kitchen, slammed the door to my room and lay down on my childhood bed with its white coverlet and dark wooden frame that used to seem so high but now felt low. I didn't cry, just lay there silently, feeling the hurt in every cell, trying to understand. In recent years I had rarely opened myself up to my mother about things that mattered to me. I'd learned that she usually didn't understand. But that day, in my eagerness to talk about Eli, in my desire to share my happiness about being with him, I had attempted to engage her. She had been so concerned about my finding a husband I thought she would be happy, would want to talk about him.

As I began to think about my mother's reaction I remembered that when I was young she had used phrases like "he's sort of foreign look-ing" as a warning about someone. In fact, the description of some-one as dark, swarthy, or foreign was code in popular literature of the '50s for someone who was untrustworthy. Such individuals appeared regularly in the Nancy Drew mysteries I read avidly in fourth and fifth grade. Without consciously registering the words you knew that this new character was going to cause trouble. Eli fit the description with his dark complexion, dark hair and eyes. He spoke with a slight New York accent, and used his knife and fork like a European. My mother prided herself on not being prejudiced, but she was.

As I lay on my bed staring at the ceiling of my childhood room, I remembered how my mother had always tried to pull me back. In high school she always urged me not to take on too many activities, stay up too late, or work too hard. Her most dramatic attempt to lim-it my forward momentum occurred shortly before I graduated from Kent State, when I mentioned something about my progress toward choosing a graduate school.

"Oh Anne, you're not going to graduate school!" she exclaimed, looking up at me with her eyes wide and her mouth in the shape of a big O.

I looked at her startled. I'd been talking about going to graduate school for months. "Yes. How else will I get to be a college professor? I need a Ph.D."

"A Ph.D.! Oh Anne."She said those last two words the way she always did when I'd said something she thought was particularly disquieting.

"You never listen. You go on about how wonderful I am, but you never listen when I talk to you because you don't really care."

"It's time for you to get out in the world and face reality."

"What do you think graduate school is? A playground? It's real."

"I mean real reality, getting a job, getting married, being responsible for yourself."

There it was again, 'getting married,' very important for women in 1959. I was about to graduate from college without being engaged. I hadn't even dated anyone seriously. The anger hit me in the pit of my stomach, where it always went when I was most upset.

"I don't want to get married yet," I responded in a sort of sob-shout. If I get married I'll never be anybody, I'll never get to school."

"You'll get so much education no one will want to marry you."

"Maybe we should let this all go for now," suggested my father who had been hovering worriedly around the edges of our fight. Night had fallen. The living room was dark, the wall behind the fireplace, painted dark teal, absorbed what little light there was from the nearby kitchen overhead fluorescent, leaving a half-lit nightmarish quality over us. Emotions were so strong they were almost visible.

I knew my dad supported my going to graduate school. I knew I was going to go, regardless of what my mother said. The battle was really about something much deeper, but I wasn't sure what.

Now, almost two years later I was in graduate school, hoping to finish up my M.A. degree, but I still felt the sting of that night. I knew

I would feel the sting of my mother's response to Eli for a long time too. Loneliness rolled in like a heavy fog. I recognized this loneliness. It had floated in the silence that had drifted through my childhood, not the won't-speak-to-you kind of silence, but an indirect, everyday avoidance of connection and emotion. It was part of what I was fighting against when I resisted the smile self, the game self, all the ways individuals tried to hide from each other. Grudgingly I accepted the reality that my mother did not, could not, would never understand who I was trying to be, what I was trying to do with my life. It was the end of a hope. A piece of growing up.

Before I went back to Northwestern after Christmas break my mother took me aside.

"You don't have to finish your degree, dear. Don't do it if it's too hard."

"I want to finish, Mom."

"But you don't have to. We'll love you just as much if you don't."

My family stories, the few that we had, mostly from the Great Depression, were not about pushing forward until we succeeded. They were about clipped dreams. My father had been called home from Philadelphia in his second year at Temple University to become head of the family when his father died suddenly. It was 1928. The Great Depression hit, and the family drug store failed. Nearly ten years later, he helped dig Pymatuning Lake near Linesville on a Federal work program and made enough money to take correspondence courses in accounting. With those skills he got the modest job in the accounting department that he kept for the rest of his working life. My mother had gone into nursing school right after high school, the only girl in her class to leave Linesville and attempt a career. She left the training program halfway through. Had it gotten too hard? Had she chosen to leave or been dropped from the program? She never said, but her nurse's training remained essential to her identity, to her liberal approach to raising me, and to her care of me as a sickly, asthmatic child. It set her apart from her friends who had not attempted a career. Yet in the end, hers was the story of an *almost-nurse*. She was a housewife in her small hometown like her high school classmates.

I didn't want either of my parent's stories to be mine!

In telling me that I didn't have to finish I knew my mother was assuring me of her and my father's unqualified love. I had always known absolutely that they would be there for me, no matter what. That knowledge gave me a rock bottom security. But with that un-conditional love, I wished my mother could have offered encourage-ment, a sense of confidence that if I worked hard I had a chance for success. The idea of quitting was already a possibility that hovered in dark places in my consciousness, like a bird of prey waiting to get me. I'd never attempted anything before in which I felt so unsure of my ability to do what was required.

CHAPTER 7

Survival Mode

"WHAT YOU REALLY should do," my advisor Dr. Noran mused, his long face breaking into a delighted grin, "is take another master's degree in art or aesthetics, then come back and get a Ph.D. in sociology and be the world's expert on the sociology of creativity." I sat across the desk from him in January 1961, just back after Christmas break, my gut suddenly buzzing with distress, mouth open, lungs pulling for air that I couldn't seem to draw in. He glanced up and caught the look on my face.

"Guess it's a little late for that," he added, his grin fading.

"Yes," I breathed.

His comment was probably meant as a compliment, an indication that he thought I was capable of doing interesting academic work. I took it as a concern that my topic was impossible and that I might never finish my thesis. My anxiety level shot up higher than it already was. I had five months to complete my thesis before the beginning of June. What I needed now from my advisor was some good, concrete guidance, not a long-term, multi-degree dream plan.

Over the next few weeks, I tried to stay centered by getting outside and taking long walks. Evanston was bordered by curving shoreline and a long stretch of park with a pond that was used for ice-skating in the winter. Sometimes I ice skated in the evening for half an hour. The wind blowing in from Lake Michigan nipped my nose; snowflakes glistened in the beam of light thrown from a single pole beside the deserted warming hut. My senses, dulled by days inside, came alive. I breathed in the natural world, felt momentarily unencumbered, the free spirit I used to believe myself to be.

The start of winter semester brought the beginning of one of my most memorable experiences at Northwestern, my first exposure to a woman academic. German American philosopher and political theorist Hannah Arendt came to the university as a one-semester visiting professor and, among other activities, gave a weekly public lecture series. What a role model she was! Although Jewish, she had done her dissertation in 1929 on the concept of love as articulated by St. Augustine. Her first book *The Origins of Totalitarianism*, published in 1951, described and analyzed Nazism and Stalinism political movements. Her newest book, *The Human Condition*, just published in 1958, explored the issues of diminishing human agency and political freedom. I had never been in the presence of such an intellect. She thought outside the box, was open to ways of looking at the world that weren't necessarily popular, and expressed herself so clearly that, even though I had little background in most of the topics she discussed, I could follow her talks easily. Her lectures gave me a burst of energy each week. I loved being exposed to so many big ideas! Although I did not know it then, she would come to be classified as one of the most important political theorists of the 20th century.

Otherwise my life contracted to my desk in my square bland room with gray and brown walls, drapes covered with maze-like squares, and a green overstuffed chair. The thesis stage of finishing my M.A. degree consisted of several steps. First I read extensively on the topic I wanted to study and wrote up a review of relevant literature. I had already done a lot of work on that. In January I developed my research proposal. This had to be passed on by my advisor, but when he returned my approved draft, I sensed he was not satisfied with it, even though he offered few suggestions. Feeling the need for more feedback I asked Shig to read it. After Shig had a chance to go over it we sat together in his landlady's living room.

"Babe, I'm not clear what your main goal is here," he said gently, oh so gently. "Maybe you could spell that out a little more in the beginning of your literature review."

I listened stony faced. Actually, I was not clear about my main goal either, but more importantly I wanted him to say it was wonderful. That's what my mother would have said. But then I would have been angry with her for not really engaging, not thinking about what I was showing her. Shig took me seriously and gave good thoughtful feedback. I hadn't had much of that in my life. It was hard to take.

After talking with Shig I raced back to my room and collapsed in tears on my bed. Maybe I wouldn't make it after all. I had never before been pushed this hard. Words like hopeless, can't, impossible, never, batted like trapped birds in my brain. Was it all over? The life I'd dreamed for myself? Had I tried to fly too high? Failure was possible. For the first time I acknowledged that it could happen to me.

As I calmed down I realized my choice was simple. If I wanted to be told my work was wonderful I could go home, and my mother would surely oblige. If I wanted to be a sociologist, an academic, or a poet, I had to seek serious critique, learn to take it, and use it. It was time to grow up. I got up, put on my glasses, sat down at my desk, and opened my proposal, its margins filled with Shig's spidery handwritten comments.

After reworking my proposal, I moved on to the collection and analysis of information I gathered from a questionnaire I administered to a group of college students. Analyzing the data was interesting and I realized I was learning a lot about research. Still, I continued to struggle to articulate the theoretical point of my project. Through the process of research and writing, my moods bounced like a flat ball, down with a thud and never very high. Sometimes I got excited about something I was reading or my ability to articulate a complicated idea. Other times I was more depressed than I had ever been in my life.

"Would you like a tranquilizer?" asked a fellow counselor one evening at dinner when I mentioned how stressed I felt. "I have lots."

"I've got some too if you need them," added another.

Tranquilizers! The other counselors were taking tranquilizers! The thought of taking a tranquilizer had never crossed my mind. I didn't want to need tranquilizers. Avoiding them became one of my motivations for trying to work smart, for keeping myself together.

As spring approached the other counselors began to talk about job possibilities. I had no prospects. Everything in my life was up in the air, except for one thing. I had *not* applied to stay on in Northwestern's Ph.D. program for the next year. My goal remained what it had been when I started Northwestern -- to get an M.A. degree, find a job, and then go back to school in a couple years for a doctorate. My fellow graduate students found this unnerving.

"Please don't stop now, Babe," Shig pleaded. "You'll never come back. We all have to keep going or we'll never get the degree."

"If I really want a Ph.D. I'll go back. If I don't want one, then why should I stay here and be miserable?"

I wasn't clear about what I wanted to do next, but I was sure of one thing. I *had* to get out of graduate school into a larger world that was more hospitable to the person I was trying to become.

New York kept calling me. In my brief time there I had fallen in love with the city. I was curious about where my relationship with Eli might go. Lois, my closest friend in our resident counselor group, had decided to move there to work in a publishing firm after she finished her M.A. in English in September. We asked each other if we wanted to share an apartment in New York and decided we did. We got along well, liked to do off-beat things, enjoyed hanging out talking together, and were both independent. The chance to room with Lois clinched my decision to move to New York and I began to explore employment possibilities. The ugly truth about jobs for sociologists emerged quickly. Sociology students kept going to school for the Ph.D. because there was little work for those with a master's degree. I looked for every kind of job I could think of including research, teaching in junior college, social work, and, given my undergraduate English literature background, working in publishing. Nothing. I began to panic.

"Have you asked Aaron Cicourel to help yet?" inquired Shig, who had kept in contact with him after he left Northwestern at the end of our first year. "Remember how impressed he was with your seminar paper last year. He'll help you."

"He probably doesn't even remember me. Besides he's in California, he won't know anyone in New York."

"He helps people," Shig said simply, "and he knows people everywhere."

Shig insisted on writing out and giving me Aaron's address. I wrote to him and got a brief reply, "let me know when you are getting ready to go." It seemed like a brush-off.

Communication with Eli had fallen off sharply after Christmas break. In his infrequent letters he sounded depressed, and after weeks of broken equipment and false starts on his dissertation project, he had given it up and was trying to find a new one. I felt disconnected from Eli, as well as from everyone else, and was ambivalent about going to see him in New York over spring break. In the end I decided to go on the train, after a brief stop at home. The moment I saw Eli waiting for me on the train platform all my doubts about visiting him vanished. How could I have been so silly as to want to stay away? Eli said that our being together felt like one continuous time and I agreed. When we were apart I worried, but when we were together I felt happy, content, and whole. Besides, getting away from Northwestern was like a tonic. I sat mesmerized in the Circle in the Square Theater floating on the exquisite language of Dylan Thomas' play *Under Milkwood*. I had been so immersed in my world of sociological jargon I had forgotten how beautiful the English language could be. On our way home from the theater we stopped to buy a copy of the play. I was under the spell of its words for days.

There were aggravations during my New York visit that I hadn't noticed on my previous visits. Why did Eli have to act like he was right all the time? He also told me that my "new" hairstyle looked silly and asked me why I didn't wear it long "like other women." The comment sliced deep. My super-fine hair that just didn't get long had been a source of distress all my life. When I was a kid, my mom insisted on taking me to the local barber to get it cut. Back then barbers weren't unisex; they were just for men and me. Kids teased me because I looked like a boy. As I got older she insisted on giving me home permanents and it got so curly everyone called me 'Fuzzy.' She continued to urge me to get regular permanents. My most recent was what Eli had called silly. I worried that I could never be a real woman because my hair never got long. It was one more strike against me.

The evening I got back to Northwestern from New York Shig turned up at the dorm with Aaron Cicourel, who was visiting from California.

"Have you found a job in New York yet?" Aaron asked.

I shook my head. "Just got back. Nothing."

"I've got some friends in New York. I'll see what I can do."

"He'll find you a job, " Shig assured me excitedly the next day. "When Aaron says he knows people, he knows people."

Aaron's interest in me and confidence that jobs existed briefly buoyed my spirits, but soon I was back in my shell. There was nothing in my life but the thesis. Occasionally I had moments of triumph when I thought I couldn't figure something out, and then did. The satisfaction was sweet, though fleeting. Sometime in early May, in the middle of my worst thesis angst, the phone rang.

"This is Herb Sturz from the Vera Foundation in New York. I understand you are looking for a job in sociology. The project we're starting involves the sociology of justice. Is that a specialty you're interested in?"

"I don't think we have a specialization like that in sociology," I replied, wondering why he didn't know.

"Then we'll create one," he responded confidently.

Who was this guy? He sounded very formal, but seemed vague about the job, the project, and what the Vera Foundation itself did, except that it involved the criminal courts. That part I could relate to. I had an excellent undergraduate background in criminology.

It seemed like a long shot, but I told him I'd send a resume and references. The next week I came across a job listing for a sociologist at The Russell Sage Foundation, a major social science research center in Manhattan. The position had already been filled by the time I called, but they told me there might be another one coming up and to phone when I got to New York. The two encounters left me feeling slightly encouraged about jobs.

The final stage in my M.A. work was an oral defense of my completed thesis before a three-person faculty committee who read and critiqued it and then questioned me extensively about my research. At the end of the exam they could give me a Pass, a Pass with Revisions (the most common result), or a Fail. After that, I had to finish everything, including revisions, which I would surely have, and then get the thesis professionally typed, approved, and the final version deposited in the Graduate Dean's office before I left Northwestern in early June.

At the beginning of May, after fighting with correction tape and four carbon copies, I finally finished typing my thesis and distributed it to my advisor and Professors Jones and Kaito, the two other members of my examination committee. I had had a class with Jones but knew little about Kaito. He had been my advisor's choice for the committee because he had done innovative work in areas relevant to my thesis. I had always avoided Kaito, even though he might have been able to help me formulate the direction of my research, because he seemed unapproachable and had barely acknowledged my presence during my two years in the department. I dealt with my upcoming oral defense in the same independent, go-it-alone approach that I had adopted throughout my time at Northwestern. I didn't talk to anybody to get a sense of what an oral exam was like and made no attempt to have a friend with me after it was over. In fact, I didn't even tell anyone when my exam was scheduled.

The exam was psychologically shattering! I have no memory of what went on in it. The first thing I remember is standing in the hall outside the examination room afterwards, waiting for what seemed like hours while my committee members deliberated about my thesis and performance. I kept reassuring myself that this long wait was routine. When the departmental secretary, who worked across the hall from where I stood, brought me a chair and commented that it was cruel for the examiners to keep me waiting so long, I realized that it was not routine. I tried to act nonchalant, embarrassed that she was a witness to what was beginning to feel like deep humiliation and failure.

Finally, they called me in.

"You have passed with revisions," my advisor Dr. Noran announced.

This was good. But the atmosphere in the room didn't *feel* good. It felt like major failure. The discussion about revisions was long and painful. Professor Kaito was vocal and demanding. He was asking for what sounded like a total rewrite of my thesis, which would take months. I didn't have months. I had to be out of the dorm in three weeks. After the long, agonizing discussion about revisions led by Professor Kaito, my advisor Dr. Noran noted that the committee would put a note in my file indicating its support for my going on for a Ph.D. in the future. I had heard that sometimes a committee noted that a student should *not* go on and awarded what they called a 'terminal M.A.' Given the discussion that had just ensued, I couldn't believe that they could possibly recommend my continuing for a Ph.D. I stared at Dr. Noran open-mouthed.

"You're saying you think I have the ability to go on for a Ph.D.?" I asked incredulously.

"Yes, but we think it would be good for you to work for a couple years first."

At least we agreed on that.

In spite of the pass and the committee's endorsement for further graduate work, the long wait and sweeping criticisms of my thesis by Professor Kaito left me so devastated that I felt like I had failed miserably. I slipped unobtrusively up the back stairs of the dormitory to my room, where I cried hysterically for a long time.

For two days I avoided everyone, pulled the covers over my head, and sobbed. I desperately wanted contact and support, especially from Eli, although I was sabotaging any hope of that by refusing to answer the phone or make any calls. The more I orchestrated my life to avoid contact with anyone I knew, the more depressed I became because I felt no one cared. I sensed how easy it could be to just keep going down. My hold loosened on the rationality that I had always relied on, the self-talk that should tell me that the alienation I was experiencing was of my own making. I was acting like my mother when she went into one of her withdrawn, depressive spells, those awful times when Dad and I did everything possible to make her feel better, but never could.

The recognition that my behavior was like my mother's registered like a smack. I lay for a moment, letting that idea sink in. That was not who I was! Not who I wanted to be! I sat up.

"I passed," I told myself. "Passed. I am going to get my degree. Why am I so distraught? It doesn't matter how I *feel* about the defense. What matters is that I *passed,* that they recommended me to go on."

As that began to sink in I pulled back the covers, swung my legs down and felt the pile of the gray rug on the bottoms of my feet. I moved toward the window, opened the curtains, and took in the sunlight and green of spring. Slowly, deliberately, I showered, put on clean clothes, and made my bed. "I passed. I can go on." I repeated. I sat down at my desk, dialed Shig, and told him I passed. It was dinner time. I headed down to the dining room. The other counselors all waved me over to their table as soon as they saw me.

"Didn't you take orals recently?

"Yes. I passed." The word reverberated through my head. Passed. Passed!

"Congratulations." they all exclaimed. "We were all worried because we couldn't find you."

As I struggled with revisions there was some good news. Eli's old roommate, who was now in his own apartment, wrote to say I could sublet it for six weeks from mid-June to the end of July while he was out of the city. I had a place to land in New York when I arrived! No such good news about jobs, however. A secretary from the Vera Foundation called and announced in a rather cold voice that they were rethinking their staffing needs, but I might want to check in when I got to New York.

After day and night work on revisions, several meetings with my advisor Dr. Noran, and just three days left until I had to move out of the dorm, I took to Dr. Noran what I thought was the final version of my thesis. He flipped through it quickly, made a suggestion in direct opposition to one he had made a few days earlier that I had worked many hours to address, and tossed it on a pile of papers.

"I'll have Kaito look at it tomorrow. Then we can talk."

Anger that I had been holding down for weeks growled up from deep inside. He acted like we had all the time in the world. I'd lined up a typist to do the final retyping and was trying to pack up my things to be out of my room in three days. I argued, not too calmly, that we needed to get it resolved right away. I think my mother would have described my behavior as 'overbearing.' He agreed grudgingly to look it over that afternoon. I re-entered his office a few hours later with my stomach churning. Could I stay calm? Make my case? Avoid crying?

"I guess it'll do," he said as he scribbled his signature on the form for advisor's final approval at the front of the thesis and handed the package back to me, "though it could still stand a lot more revision."

I felt relief, but also anger. Graduation was supposed to yield a sense of accomplishment. With one phrase he had denied me that.

My last night at Northwestern Shig took me out to dinner before I settled at the front desk for my final night of duty as a resident dorm counselor. He came over later with brownies and coffee to keep me company in the ghostly quiet, dorm lobby. I gave him my complet-ed, typed, and approved thesis to turn in to the Dean's office the next morning. Our conversation, usually so animated, was sporadic, subdued. We'd been like two soldiers together in battle, had shared

53

pieces of our lives we hadn't shared with anyone else. As the campus security guard got ready to close the dormitory doors, we stood holding tight to each other.

"I'll come visit you in New York Babe."

I watched him go slowly down the walk and across the street, registering deep inside that Shig was one of a kind, that I'd never again have a friendship quite like ours.

Early the next morning I caught the train to Meadville. After a few days there to unpack and repack, I would travel on to New York City. I was on my way!

Part Two

Vera: A Solid Foundation

CHAPTER **8**

An Experiment in Criminal Court?!

"BE CAREFUL," DAD said with a smile as he backed down the train steps after hoisting up and storing my suitcase and overstuffed khaki duffle bag. There was a world of love, care, and wish of good luck in that simple caution. I knew he understood my eagerness for adventure and exploration. My mother stood beside the train waving; her face distorted by her effort to not cry. I was on my way to New York, finished with all the packing and unpacking at Northwestern and home. By the end of this day, Wednesday, June 21, 1961, I would be a resident of New York City.

I settled into my window seat, feeling the scratchy rose-colored upholstery against the back of my calves as I leaned forward to wave, eager to get past the goodbyes with Mom and Dad, glad the stop was so short. This was a momentous leaving because it had no demarcated return point. Always before when I clambered up the steps of an Erie Railroad car I was going away for a defined period, until the end of the quarter at Kent State, until Christmas, until I finished my M.A. in Chicago. This trip was open-ended, had none of the clear markers by which I measured my life as a student. It turned out to be the last journey I ever took on the Erie Railroad.

I had a twelve-hour interlude on the train before my life as a New Yorker began. After so many hectic weeks it was hard to remember back to when life had been normal. I felt a surge of jubilation as the train gathered speed in the early morning light and cleared the boundaries of Meadville. That diminished quickly. It had been drizzling when I got on the train and as we progressed the clouds sank lower, dragging the train mile after mile across the dreary gray Pennsylvania landscape, dampening my spirits. I gazed out the window disconsolately wondering why I had chosen to go, jobless, with only a short-term apartment, to add one more body to the teeming mob of human beings already crammed into Manhattan.

I'm going to New York because I like the city, I had told myself and everyone else. As Lois, my soon-to-be apartment mate, explained, it was like going to Paris from the provinces to get polished. When I let myself think honestly about my decision, however, I knew I was going mostly because I wanted the relationship with Eli to work out. I had thought a lot about marriage and was very clear that I wanted a partnership kind of marriage, in which my husband and I both engaged in work we loved and raised a family together. I wanted *both* work *and* love at the same time, not the norm for a woman in 1961. To do that, we would both have to shake free from traditional assumptions and expectations. Was I liberated enough and strong enough to move beyond the boundaries drawn so clearly for women? Was Eli?

Most of my friends in high school and college seemed to accept the way things were, that finding a man and getting married was a woman's most important goal. I railed against those expectations. I had known, since eighth grade, when I looked around and saw the narrow lives of my mother and the mothers of my friends, that I wanted more than bearing children who grow up to bear children in an endless cycle. I wanted kids, yes, but I wanted other work too.

My friends didn't understand why I wasn't satisfied, why I wanted something different, why I loved the songs of Pete Seeger and worried about social justice and inequality. They good-naturedly called me 'Communist Annie' and 'Radical Rankin.' I took secret pride in the nicknames. I knew I wasn't anywhere close to communist or radical, but the teasing was recognition of my difference, who I was. I had purposely stayed away from anything to do with an education major, the major of all but two of my friends, so I would never be tempted to settle into a traditional woman's profession. Sometimes I worried I might end up with nothing. It was scary to try to be different, step outside the circle of expectations that surrounded me as a woman. Did that make me less of a woman? Less likely to ever find love?

As I gazed out at the bleak world, I tried to feel optimistic. The motion of the train briefly lulled me, but tired as I was, sleep never came. When I tried to read, I remembered nothing from the previous page. I hovered between two worlds: one known, one unknown.

When I spotted Eli's stocky figure on the platform as the train pulled into the terminal in Bayonne, New Jersey my optimism returned. He jumped on board to help me with my bags and gave me a big hug. Steve, whose apartment I was going to sublet for six weeks, stood just behind him. We went straight to the apartment where we set my duffle bag beside the trunk I'd sent ahead from Northwestern. The place was a spacious one-bedroom on the 18th floor at the corner of West 99th Street and Broadway. It was an easy bus ride or walk from Eli's place, light and airy, with a huge terrace and full view of the city. I was delighted, but worried that it would set too high a standard for my own apartment search.

"You can move in Saturday," Steve said as he handed me the key.

In just three days. Until then I'd stay with Eli.

Eli and I headed up Broadway to one of our favorite restaurants, the Szechuan Inn. With my suitcase propped beside me, I let the warmth, color, and bustle brighten my mood. After a couple beers and a dinner of spicy beef with snow peas and chicken with pecans I felt euphoric.

"Tomorrow I'll start looking for jobs. I'm in New York to stay this time," I said beaming at Eli.

"Yes," he said as we clinked glasses.

Did I hear less than full enthusiasm in his voice?

It was 10:00 a.m. Thursday, June 22, 1961, sixteen hours after I'd arrived in Manhattan. I sat in shorts and sleeveless shirt, propped up by pillows on Eli's bed beside his phone, ready to start my job search.

My first call was to Mr. Herbert Sturz, Director of the Vera Foundation, who had contacted me over a month ago about a possible sociology position. The job he described sounded vague, and his secretary had not been encouraging in a follow-up communication, but she suggested I call when I got to New York. I had pretty much written Vera off, but it was worth a try.

"Can you come in for an interview this afternoon?" Mr. Sturz asked.

"Yes," I said as I climbed out of bed.

I reached for my city map and begin to paw through my suitcase in search of something suitable to wear. Eli had left earlier for his lab, where he was working on a new dissertation project. I was on my own to figure out how to get to the Vera office.

Three hours later I sat in the waiting room of the Peter J. Schweitzer Division of the Kimberly Clark Corporation in a skyscraper on Madison Avenue. It was not the atmosphere I had anticipated for a small nonprofit. Mr. Sturz led me into a large conference room with padded armchairs and a long, highly polished mahogany table. We huddled at one end under a single set of lights, the rest of the room in darkness.

Herbert Sturz was younger than I had thought he would be, a tall, gangly, good-looking man, probably in his early thirties. He had black hair, dark eyes, a wide smile, and gesticulated with animation as he talked. Initially he had appeared somewhat guarded, even a little awkward, but as he began to talk about the Vera Foundation his eyes lit up with enthusiasm.

"We're just here temporarily," he explained, waving a hand toward our surroundings. "Mr. Schweitzer is supporting Vera for the first year and it's up to us to get more funding after that. Now our office is in his ham radio cubical off the secretary's office, but we'll soon move around the corner to space of our own."

Cubical? Radio equipment? Maybe this organization was a little too new, too amorphous for me.

Mr. Schweitzer, president of the company in whose offices we sat, was a philanthropist who had been born in Russia, from which his family had fled anti-Jewish violence in 1899 and soon afterwards moved to the United States. This family background had left him with a strong appreciation for the American Bill of Rights. Recently he had learned, to his dismay, that despite the U.S. Constitution's Eighth Amendment prohibition of excessive bail, New York City had, in the previous year, held over 120,000 men and women in jail for months awaiting trial. Surely if 120,000 individuals were unable to raise even a minimum bail, their bails had been excessive, and their Eighth Amendment rights violated.

Mr. Schweitzer decided he had to do something. He recruited Herbert Sturz, a journalist who had recently published a widely circulated brochure on the Bill of Rights, to help him develop the Vera Foundation for Justice. The foundation was named in honor of his mother Vera, who had devoted her life to social service and helping the vulnerable. The Foundation's purpose was to "to seek and further the equal protection of the laws for the indigent by research into neglected aspects of court procedures, law enforcement, and the nature of crime." I began to understand why Mr. Sturz had been so vague about everything in his May phone call to me at Northwestern and why he still had difficulty describing the job for which he was interviewing me. The Vera Foundation was brand new! Mr. Schweitzer had created it and hired Herbert Sturz as Director in January 1961, less than six months earlier.

Concern for social justice and protection of the "little guy," ran deep in my family and in my Unitarian background. That was one reason I'd been drawn to sociology. In spite of the project's amorphous nature Mr. Sturz began to pull me into it, get me interested in addressing the injustice of how the bail system worked in practice. But I was still puzzled about where I might fit in.

"We finally decided, after looking at lots of options, that we need to change the bail system," Sturz explained.

I sat up, startled. Just how did this new, untried, seemingly unsophisticated Vera Foundation plan to do that?

"We're going to do a controlled experiment in the courts," he continued, leaning across the table excitedly. "We want to find out if more indigent defendants can be released under a rarely used New York statute that permits release without money bail. We want to do interviews so we can provide and make verified information about a defendant's character and community roots to the judge."

"You're what?"

"We finally decided," Mr. Sturz reiterated, "to do a controlled experiment in the Manhattan Felony Court, a research/demonstration project."

It was a wild scheme. An experiment made sense as a way to show the impact of a change in an organization. But not in a court! Nobody did controlled experiments in courts. Courts were circumscribed by laws, precedent, accepted ways of doing business, boundaries that no nonlegal entity could cross, especially a small, newly formed entity that no one had ever heard of.

"That's what we need a sociologist for," Sturz explained, "To help us work out the details."

The interest I had started to feel about this job possibility plummeted. He was interviewing me for an impossible task.

"Two of the social scientists Mr. Schweitzer and I talked with about helping pretrial indigent defendants stay out of jail suggested the experiment. They recommended we hire a sociologist. One of them gave me your name," explained Mr. Sturz, "said a colleague had just written recommending you."

Aaron Cicourel. He said he would help me get a job and he had. In the midst of my shock at the audacity of the Vera scheme, I felt like crying. My former professor's recommendation was an unbelievable gift of confidence and care.

But the job sounded impossible. I knew enough about courts and controlled experiments to believe that the two could not exist together. A court would *never* allow a controlled experiment inside its walls. Courts were among the most closed, change-averse institutions in American society. The project was not feasible. Even if it were workable, did I have the necessary skills and experience to take responsibility for setting it up? There were very strict methodological rules about how you did experiments.

"I'll be back in touch the end of next week," Mr. Sturz said as he walked me toward the lobby.

CHAPTER 9

Anything Is Possible

THE NEXT DAY, Friday, I interviewed for another job at the Russell Sage Foundation, a prestigious social research institution that would look good on my resume. Russell Sage was looking for a sociologist to code research data, basically a data entry job, not very exciting, but appealing because it was something I knew how to do. Working with several well-known sociologists should be educational. However, the job's downside was substantial. It was unlikely to be full time and would probably last just a few months. How could I sign an apartment lease without the security of a regular paycheck over at least a year? Still the pull of the known and familiar was strong at a time when everything else in my life was in flux.

On Saturday I packed my suitcase yet again and we lugged it over to Steve's apartment, where I spent the day unpacking and trying to make the bare apartment more homelike. Suddenly I sat down, so drained I could barely move. Even though I said I was too exhausted to go anywhere, Eli talked me into visiting the Cloisters, the Medieval branch of the Metropolitan Museum of Art, to listen to ancient choral music. We sat close together on a stone bench in a garden enclosed by vine-covered stone walls, inhaled the odor of basil and thyme, and let the ancient chants wash over us. I felt close to Eli, breathed in his smell mixed with the herbs, and relaxed against him. After weeks, I began to slow down.

I was still dozing on Monday morning, in that delicious half awake-half asleep state of not having to get up for anything, when the phone rang. Herb Sturz wanted to talk to me again about the job. Could I come in that afternoon? He'd told me he would call at the end of the week. First thing Monday morning seemed encouraging. We sat again in a pool of light at one end of the long table. This meeting was more substantive, but still vague about what I would be doing if I got the job. Herb and I were on a first name basis by now. He gave me a questionnaire to revise, and a few law journals with articles to read about bail in the criminal courts.

"These articles by Beeley and Foote are about all the research there is on bail," he said, as he dropped them in front of me.

"Come on. There has to be more than that," I exclaimed, "there must be millions of bail settings a year."

"Of course. But hardly anyone cared enough to ask questions."

I understood. Poor individuals rarely got attention in the courts or anywhere else. Institutional power was part of what sociologists studied, especially how our society benefited the affluent while it used, then threw away the poor. Bail was a good example. Poor defendants sat in jail for months or years. Individuals with money, especially professional criminals, could pay and got out right away.

I could feel myself being drawn into the Vera job by Herb's optimistic, "anything is possible" attitude and his conviction that we could make a difference in individual lives. Though still dubious about the feasibility of a controlled experiment, it ceased to matter that my role was vague and that the study Vera planned to do was wild. I wanted to be involved. I forgot all about the job at the Russell Sage Foundation.

I don't think Herb at that point had much of an idea what I would be doing. He cared about fighting injustice and was appalled by Mr. Schweitzer's story of human beings sitting in jail simply because they were poor, just as I was. He was committed to doing something about the problem but was still winging it himself. Vera had received a grant from the National Council on Crime and Delinquency to hire a sociologist and a secretary to work on the project. Herb knew he couldn't afford to make a mistake, but he couldn't tell me exactly what the job I was applying for entailed because he wasn't sure himself. I sensed that if I got the job I'd have to make my own way. That was what scared me.

"Can you meet me downtown tomorrow morning at 9:00 a.m. at 100 Centre Street to visit the criminal courts?" Herb asked. I said yes.

At first glimpse the courts seemed to be in total chaos. Every courtroom we visited swirled with color, movement, noise, and a sense of desperation and fear that was almost palpable. Rows of scuffed brown wooden benches lined the large, bare rooms overflowing with defendants and their families. Children fussed, women cried, everyone looked worried. The judge sat on an elevated bench in the front, flanked by an American flag. The floor space between the judge's bench and the spectators was alive with court activity.

The 'bridgeman' who stood below the judge's bench, bellowed out the names of defendants. The Department of Corrections deputies herded groups of handcuffed men whose names had been called to stand in a line before the judge for hasty bail setting, then escorted them back to holding cells behind the court referred to as 'the pens.' The clerk, who kept the court records, was in constant conversation with participants. Legal aid attorneys conferred hastily at the side of the courtroom or in hallways with defendants who did not have their own attorney. Prosecutors leafed through criminal arrest records and conferred with defense counsel and witnesses.

Those in charge, the white men in business suits or uniforms, the regulars, knew the ropes. The mostly poor individuals who crowded the halls and courtrooms--defendants, victims, and family members who faced life-changing events--had to depend on them to understand what was happening, what to do. That is, if they could find a regular to help them. Watching, I became even more aware of the injustice of pretrial detention.

Herb said he would make a definite decision about the job on Friday. If I were hired I would go on the payroll in early July. I *really* wanted the job but was afraid to hope. When he called Friday afternoon to offer me the position I accepted immediately and became Vera's second employee after Herb. On my first day of work, July 5, 1961, Herb and I stood surveying the tiny anteroom that was his office. We had to admit that it was too small to install even a chair for me. His adage that anything is possible had limits. Until Vera moved into its own space, I could work in the conference room where we had first interviewed, which Herb assured me was rarely used. One part of my job was to occasionally help Mr. Schweitzer's personal secretary, who was doing all the secretarial work for Vera until we moved into our own office. She was a short, bouncy red head in her thirties with a good sense of humor. I thought we would do well together.

After Herb filled me in on more of Vera's brief history and our still sketchy plans for the fall when he hoped to start the court experiment, he gave me some additional reading on bail and courts and left me alone. I wondered if I could manage this lack of structure.

Eli had settled in with me at the West 99th Street apartment. At Northwestern I had been on my own schedule, working mostly in my dorm room. Living with someone else and getting up to ride the stifling subway to work five days a week from nine to five was a challenge. So was the adjustment to living without dining-hall meals. I suddenly had to think about making dinner for Eli and me when I got home. I had no cooking experience. There was no cookbook among the stack of books I'd brought to New York. We existed on tough, undercooked pot roast, canned spaghetti sauce, and way too much hot sausage, rice, and chicken livers, Eli's mainstay recipe.

We spent all of our spare time together and there was an undercurrent of tension. In order to try to understand what was going on between us, we launched into 'let's try to understand each other and communicate better' conversations that often ended up on the topic of Eli's old girlfriend Sarah. I had hoped that once we were together on a regular basis he would stop obsessing about her, but she remained part of our lives, just under the surface.

At the end of my first week at work, the stresses of the previous two months, worry about my relationship with Eli, and the pressure to find an apartment for Lois and me before Steve returned descended upon me like the furies. I lay dripping tears, head buried under a pillow, trying to shut out my demons--feelings that I was a fraud, unlovable, lazy, not smart enough, unattractive, and incompetent. I had pushed myself as far as I could and was hysterical. Eli had no idea what to do to help. Eventually I managed to pull myself together enough to tell myself, 'You have accomplished a lot. You need sleep.' It was a mantra to which I rocked myself until finally I slept. The crisis signaled a turning point, and I began to feel better both physically and mentally.

My Vera job started off slowly, which left me energy to accelerate my search for an apartment. The selection in our price range was abysmal. I continued to hold out for my minimal requirements, good natural light, location near a subway stop, a toilet in the apartment rather than down the hall, and affordability. I wanted a place in which Lois and I could feel safe and happy, invite in friends, and curl up with a book. Captivated with Greenwich Village's history as a literary and artistic center, I started looking there first, but quickly gave up. Everything I saw was expensive and had other limitations like a bathtub in the kitchen, a toilet down the hall, or neighbors who sounded like they were having orgasms against their apartment door. Apartments in the Upper West Side, where I was staying, were reputed to be somewhat cheaper and larger, but appeared equally depressing.

Everyone said the Sunday Times was the best place to find an apartment, but in desperation I started checking the weekday adds. There on a Tuesday, I found a good possibility close to where I was currently living on the Upper West Side of Manhattan. I looked at it on my way home from work that day. It met all my requirements and more. It was almost affordable, on the top floor of a well-maintained brownstone on West 106th Street. Two floor-to-ceiling windows flooded the narrow bedroom and living room with light, the kitchen and bath were small but modern, and there was a tiny rounded front balcony that gave access to the outside and a view of leafy Riverside Park. I told Mr. Farmer, the landlord, that I wanted it, but felt I couldn't make a final decision without talking with my roommate Lois. He said he'd hold it for me for a day. Innocent of the ways of New York real estate I walked away without giving him a tip or a deposit.

"You just left it? Without making a deposit or anything?" asked Eli incredulously when I'd told him I'd found an apartment I was really excited about.

I cursed my small-town naivete. What had made me think that an unknown New Yorker would save an apartment for me on the basis of a verbal agreement once an immediate and better offer came along? And surely such an offer *would* come within hours. It was not until late the next afternoon that I got Lois' approval. Eli's words kept ringing in my ears as I hurried up the subway stairs at West 103th Street after work and practically ran the three blocks to West 106th Street.

CHAPTER **10**

First Big Job for Vera

AT 5:58 P.M. Wednesday, just 24 hours after I had first viewed the apartment, I stood in the building entryway of 303 W. 106th Street with a purse full of cash for my deposit and first month's rent. Feeling a little sick in my stomach and cursing my small-town trustfulness, I braced myself for disappointment as I pushed Mr. Farmer's buzzer. He appeared almost immediately, a wide smile lighting up his broad Eastern European face.

"You nice girl. I save apartment for you. Someone come by, offer me money. But I say 'No.' I save for you." Mr. Farmer had small town values too. I relaxed and smiled back.

Two nights later I slept, exhausted, in my own place, by myself. I had finally arrived. The world swirled chaotically around me, but I was home. And just in time.

The day after I moved, my job at Vera suddenly exploded. While I had had my mind on apartment hunting, Herb had been busy meeting with local judges, lawyers, and others in the criminal justice system, including some of the highest officials in Attorney General Robert F. Kennedy's Department of Justice. Herb had discovered that Kennedy was creating a high-level Committee on Poverty and the Administration of Federal Criminal Justice, or the 'Allen Committee' as it came to be called after its Chairman, Frank Allen. Its agenda of poverty issues in the federal criminal justice system, though lengthy, did not include bail.

Herb felt this was a serious omission and got himself an invitation to talk about bail at one of the committee's early meetings. He was not a polished speaker, but his passion about the injustice of bail gave him eloquence. By the end of his talk he had convinced committee members to consider adding bail to their agenda *if* he could provide evidence that there was a bail problem in the federal courts.

"We can provide that," Herb said, always one to take opportunities when offered, even if he had, as yet, no plan about how to deliver.

I had known Herb was going to an important meeting but hadn't paid much attention. He appeared in the office the next day looking excited and a little worried.

"We need to do a study of bail in the New York Federal Court in the next few weeks, using interviews and data collection."

I stared at him nonplussed.

"We have to do it before the end of the summer," he continued, his hands gesticulating wildly.

"That kind of study takes months."

"Well we have to do it in weeks. We can do it. We *have* to."

As Herb began to explain the project I realized that my part was essentially getting information from court records.

"Oh, I know how to do *that*," I exclaimed.

"You do?" he asked incredulously, his hands stopping in midair, a wide smile spreading across his face.

"Sure," I said. "I learned that in graduate school."

"Wonderful! Let's get started."

Within days Herb and the committee established the data they needed. I put together a preliminary codebook for the study of a recent year of federal court records stored in the Federal Courthouse in Foley Square, Manhattan. My job was to look at a random sample of court cases, something like every 10th case, and enter all the relevant information for that individual onto a code sheet with 80 columns. Each sheet had 20 lines, for 20 cases.

The process itself was simple. First I created a codebook that translated the information we wanted into numbers. For example, in my codebook, column 3 was the amount of bail set. For column 3 I created six possible bail settings translated into six numbers:

0   none
1   under $500
2    $500
3    $501-$1000
4    $1001-$5000
5   over $5000

If bail was $500 I recorded a two in column three of my coding sheet. In that way, using 80 columns, I could record up to 80 pieces of information for a case on one line of my code sheet.

It was still in the early days of computer technology. The data on our sheets had to be punched onto 80 column IBM cards, one card for each court record I coded. The cards were then run through computer equipment. One of Mr. Schweitzer's plants, in Lee, Massachusetts, had the necessary equipment and a computer specialist. We planned to send our code sheets up to Lee every few days, where the computer expert would punch the cards for each case and eventually process them all through the computers. While I worked on the coding, Herb planned to interview everyone he could find who was involved with the bail-setting process in the federal court. He also started interviewing key officials in the Manhattan Criminal Court to lay the groundwork for our bail experiment there in the fall.

"Anne Rankin? To look at the records?" the Federal Court clerk asked as he stared at Herb and me across the wooden counter. His guarded expression turned into a broad smile.

"I thought you'd be a lot older," he said, looking at me. "We have orders from the top, and I mean *the top*, to give you whatever you want. I guess you want to see the dockets."

Dockets, I quickly learned, were oversize books, like ledgers, containing court records in chronological order on all the cases that came into a court. In the 1950s all information was still hand entered by a team of clerks, just as it had been for decades. One of the clerks set me up at a small table near shelves filled with books smelling of old leather and plopped one marked January in front of me. Because our project had started so quickly I had had no time to look at the dockets ahead of time, as I normally would have, to make sure we could get the information we needed. With trepidation I opened the book in front of me to the first case.

I sat staring at it with rising alarm. The page contained what looked like random scratchings in different colored inks. I turned to the next page. And the next. All the cases looked equally incomprehensible. How could we possibly get the information we needed from these? We had roughly a month to obtain information on hundreds of cases using these books and they appeared to be written in hieroglyphics. I stared again at a docket page. The cases looked like puzzles, but if court officials and lawyers used them they must be decipherable. I focused on a case and began to trace through it squiggle by squiggle. Patterns emerged and I could begin to formulate questions to ask the clerks. Though I hesitated to bother them, I quickly discovered that they liked having someone interested in the work they did.

The records came alive with stories. Number 2133 never made his $500 bail. He sat in pretrial detention for 100 days until his case was dismissed. Dismissed! After he sat in jail, presumed innocent, for 100 days because he was too poor to post bail! I wondered if he'd lost a job, if his kids missed him, if he felt angry.

Every day I rode downtown on the subway to the Federal Courthouse with a peanut butter sandwich for lunch so I could work 9:00 a.m. to closing time coding cases in the stuffy clerk's office. The only way to break the tedium and have any chance of making our deadline was to devise ways to increase my speed. When my energy began to flag, I remembered Mr. 2133. As coding continued by day, I also began working at home in the evenings on plans Herb was developing for our next project, the experiment in the Manhattan Criminal Court.

In the midst of this work marathon, Shig, my good friend from Northwestern, called to say that he was coming to New York for a few days. I insisted that he stay at my apartment so I could at least see him but warned that Vera was up against a big deadline and we might not have much time together. We didn't and I've always been sorry.

My summer working at Vera had been unexpectedly pressured and all-consuming. Still, the atmosphere in which I worked was very different from the bleak life I'd endured at Northwestern. Herb treated me as a peer, a collaborator in our effort to create change. He made me feel competent and valuable. He had confidence in my, in our, in Vera's ability to do what was necessary to help create change. His mantra "Anything is possible. We just have to figure out how," carried us forward as we faced what legal experts told us were impossible tasks. Herb's bold orientation began to shape the way I too thought about the world. I began to open up, gain self-assurance as a person and a sociologist, at least in my work life.

Although the professional part of my life was flourishing, the relationship side continued problematic. Eli and I still spent most of our free time together. He was getting started on a new dissertation experiment, which cheered him considerably, but he was still often morose and closed off.

"Maybe we should take a vacation from each other for a week," Eli suggested.

I agreed and was shocked at how much I relished being alone.

"I miss you," Eli announced when he called after just a few days, the first to cut our separation short. I took it as a sign that he really cared about me. For a few days our time together was good, but soon I again sensed his emotional retreat. I turned myself inside out in my attempt to be who he wanted me to be, but I always had a sense of not measuring up.

"Yes, she'll be in Lee this afternoon," I was startled to hear Herb say when I walked into our new Vera office, now located in a brownstone at 30 E. 39th Street. I had coded the last case in Federal Court the day before and was waiting to see what would happen next. I hadn't expected a trip.

Herb hung up the phone. "You know more about the Federal Court project than the computer expert does. You've been doing the coding. It's important for you to go up to Lee to help him with the analysis."

The day's pace accelerated. By 4:00 I was on the train to Pittsfield, Massachusetts, a few miles from Lee. A couple hours later our computer programmer met me at the train and took me to a hotel in Pittsfield. I felt a little awkward. Women didn't usually go on business trips then or stay alone in hotels. Early the next morning we settled into the warehouse-like, locked computer facility where we fed all the data we had collected, now punched onto IBM cards, into the massive bank of computers that lined one side of the room. The machines began to whir. Would the results of our study show that the inability to make bail was as big a problem in the federal courts as it was in New York City?

As the tables began to stream out of the printer we saw that the answer was clearly yes. *Over a third* of the accused individuals in our sample had been denied pre-trial freedom when their bail was set as low as $500. A substantial number spent months or years in jail before their cases were resolved. The inability of defendants to afford bail was clearly not just a state or local court problem; it was a major problem in federal courts as well. Our study provided strong evidence that the Allen Committee needed to include bail on its agenda of poverty issues in the federal criminal justice system. We bundled up the tables for me to take back to New York so Herb and I could start writing up the results.

My train ride back to the city gave me a brief, but desperately needed, respite from work. The landscape of a perfect fall day rolled by the windows. I shivered with delight, as I used to do as a child, at the sight of every bush, flower, and tree with changing leaves. Miles of green flowed across hills and between houses in myriad shades, so different from the city-worn grass I saw in Manhattan. I had barely said hello to summer during the frantic months finishing my thesis, moving, and adjusting to New York City. Now summer, strumpet with turned head, was already dancing to command of fall.

We had less than a week to create our final report for Attorney General Robert Kennedy's Allen Committee. I was about to learn that Herb was a stickler for precision in writing and could keep at the task for long hours. He demanded total involvement in the project at hand. That's what we did, how we acted if we cared. No self-aggrandizing academic games here. To make our long working weekend more pleasant, however, Herb and his wife Elizabeth Littleton invited me to their home in Princeton Junction, New Jersey so Herb and I could collaborate in person on the manuscript. They thoughtfully invited Eli to come too and bring his own work so we both had a bit of a holiday break outside the city. When Herb and I finished the report on Sunday afternoon, I carried the finished draft from Herb's breezy suburban home into a New York City that steamed and stank in the grip of a heat wave. The next morning, Labor Day, our secretary and I met in Mr. Schweitzer's office, where we labored all day without air conditioning. We laughed, sweated, and grumbled as we typed, made corrections, retyped, and formatted tables. In the end we had a clean copy of the report to leave on Herb's desk for the next morning. After Herb had reviewed it the next day, we mimeographed, collated, mailed it, and got home before midnight. We made the deadline!

The Federal Court study we had just completed would quickly develop a life of its own. On the basis of our report, the Committee added bail to its list of study issues. It would soon follow up with research in other Federal jurisdictions that showed similar results, and eventually make recommendations for bail reform legislation in all Federal Courts. Five years later, President Johnson would sign the Federal Bail Reform Act of 1966 at the White House, a ceremony to which the entire Vera staff would be invited. Only then would I comprehend the full impact of my first big job for Vera.

Herb and I, of course, knew none of that then. We turned our full attention to the Manhattan Bail Project. But first, Herb suggested I take a couple of days off in compensation for all my extra hours on the report preparation. I took advantage of his offer, slept late, and then sat vaguely staring out the window, not sure what to do with myself after working under intense pressure for so long. With a start I realized the day was my birthday, forgotten in the pressure of getting out our report. It was a big one actually, the first I'd spent in eighteen years that wasn't a prelude to going back to school. Birthdays had always been synonymous with new friends, new beginnings, one more step toward adulthood, toward my future. Each year had been preparation.

My preparation was over now, I realized. I was a grown-up. My future had arrived, and I had what I had wanted, an interesting job as a sociologist and a serious boyfriend. I should feel elated. Instead I felt depressed! What was wrong? I still had this urge toward—what? More? I couldn't articulate or explain the feeling. My friends didn't seem to have this problem. It wasn't about acquiring money or things. My mother saw it as a defect. "Why aren't you ever satisfied?" she asked. I didn't know.

Eli had forgotten my birthday, or perhaps I'd never told him the date because I didn't want to bother him. Summer heat still seared New York's sidewalks. I had a fantasy of going away somewhere interesting by myself, but my fatigue from the intense summer I'd just experienced was too great. Besides I felt guilty that I had given Eli so little attention in recent weeks. I pulled myself together and called him to let him know I could spend some time in the next couple days helping him write a letter for the nuclear disarmament project he had been involved with since early spring. It was a cause he was passionate about.

A day later my roommate Lois arrived from Northwestern to take up residence in our apartment. The day was unbearably hot, as was our top floor apartment, even when we opened the tall windows to catch any breeze that might escape the nearby Hudson River. I could tell by the way Lois's face closed for a moment when she first came into our apartment that she didn't love it the way I did. How could she? She'd just come from bucolic Northwestern University and hadn't seen all the awful apartments I'd rejected. Nor had she had a chance to get used to New York City.

As I registered that thought, I suddenly comprehended what a huge adjustment I'd undergone over the past two months and was still experiencing. In Manhattan I felt confined inside a giant glass jar full of blaring taxi horns, screeching metal wheels on rails, and the smell and feel of sweaty bodies pressed tight against mine. Everything reverberated, multiplied, intensified. The assault on my senses was overwhelming. I loved the energy of the city, the diversity, creativity, color, but day after day its onslaught exhausted me. How would I be able to recharge in New York, track the changing seasons, and stay in touch with the natural world as I had always done before?

CHAPTER 11

The Manhattan Bail Project

THE MANHATTAN BAIL Project was scheduled to start in early October 1961. I had continued to harbor doubts that an experiment in a large city criminal court would be possible. As we moved toward October 1, however, it was apparent that Herb's "Anything is possible" mantra was producing amazing results. Our work on bail decisions in the Federal Court was helping too. Vera's Federal Court Project was garnering positive attention for Vera and demonstrating to the legal reform community what the previously unknown Vera Foundation could do. Vera began to develop a reputation for creative ideas and good work among some of the country's best legal reform lawyers.

The Manhattan Bail Project now had support from, among others, the Mayor of New York, the senior administrative judges of the Criminal Court, the prosecutor's office, the Department of Correction, and the Legal Aid Society. With the agreement of their bosses, the clerks and other court personnel made offices in the courthouse available to Vera, as well as the interview cell we would be using in the detention area. The Ford Foundation had provided a $100,000 grant to New York University School of Law and its Institute of Judicial Administration to provide money for Charles Ares, a Law Professor, to serve as a legal advisor to the project and supervise the hiring of five NYU night law students as project interviewers. The grant also provided for the hiring of a Spanish bilingual secretary. Mr. Schweitzer, who had started Vera, enthusiastically followed the project's development and he and Herb talked about its progress regularly.

The project's goal was relatively simple. The Manhattan Bail Project interviewers would question each defendant who was eligible for our study in the holding cells before he went before the judge for bail setting. In the brief interview they tried to learn about the defendant's connections in the community, including the names of family members and friends, employers, and other acquaintances who might be able to vouch that he would return for his court appearances if he were released without money bail. The interviewers then went upstairs to the Vera office to try to verify the information they had obtained. Defendants with no or minor records for whom Vera could verify information were then considered recommendable by Vera for release without bail.

Herb and I observed the bail setting process and talked with participants in the courts to learn how we could best integrate the Vera interviewers into the day-to-day activity of the courtroom and detention cells. We were worried that during busy times the addition of five extra people jostling among the court workers, lawyers, correction officers, and defendants in the courtroom and detention cells would create almost unbearable chaos. We had approval from the top for the project, but we both knew that approval from the top means little if workers in an organization decide to subvert a program they don't like or that adds too much extra work for them. The success of the Manhattan Bail Project would rest heavily on the relationship between our interviewers and the court staff.

A few days before the Manhattan Bail Project officially started Herb and I visited a nearby second-hand furniture store to purchase inexpensive wooden desks and chairs for our two-room office in the Criminal Court building. The equipment our law student interviewers would use to verify the information from their interviews was already in place—the best equipment of the time—a set of regular New York area phone books, a set of reverse phone books that listed entries by phone number, and three land phone lines.

The holding cells, where recently arrested men in rumpled clothes awaited their first court appearance in Manhattan Criminal court, were crowded. The air was stale and smelled of unwashed bodies and take-out food. Corrections Department deputies milled around the cramped area, organizing forms and moving detainees in and out. It was the beginning of October and Vera's Manhattan Bail Project, the court experiment that I had initially considered an impossible idea, was just getting underway. A big part of my job had been the creation of the research instruments--the interview protocol, verification procedures, and randomization of the control and experimental cases. Although I was not one of the project's regular interviewers, I initially conducted a few interviews in the early days of the project to make sure the process was working the way we hoped it would.

One of the correction officers ushered a tall, muscular man into an empty cell. I followed in behind the defendant with my clipboard, containing his 'yellow sheet,' or criminal record, and our questionnaire. I glanced down at the yellow sheet to note, just as the officer clanged the door shut behind me and let it automatically lock, that the man had been released just two days earlier after serving three years in Sing Sing, a maximum-security prison.

At that moment I was the only Vera interviewer in the detention area and alone in the locked cell with a man I'll call Mr. Doe, who stood defensively against the side wall. Uneasy, I glanced over to see if one of the deputies was nearby, but they were all over by the far door busy checking in a new group of detainees. All the stereotypes about criminals and ex-cons, that I didn't know I had, flooded my brain. I felt a stab of fear followed in quick succession by shame at my response and the realization that I still thought in terms of categories, rather than individual human beings.

I swallowed hard, raised my eyes to Mr. Doe's face, and started the interview with our usual explanation, "Mr. Doe, I'm from the Vera Foundation and want to help you get..."

"Could ya please help me get a job, mam?" he broke in, looking at me with large, sad brown eyes. "That's what ah need more than anything, a job."

His voice cracked with pain and quiet desperation. In that moment I responded to him not as a criminal or ex-con, but as a human being, an individual like me, who wanted the same things I wanted. That flash of profound connection was a lesson I never forgot.

"I'm sorry, we can't help you with a job, but we can try to help you get out of jail without having to pay bail."

"Oh, no way I can pay bail. I ain't got no money."

As soon as I finished interviewing Mr. Doe, I followed the procedures we had worked out for all the interviewers. Speed was essential. We needed to get our positive recommendations to our Vera representative in the courtroom before an individual's bail setting occurred. I hurried upstairs to our two-room Vera office to try to verify the interview information I had obtained by using our phone books. Not everyone we interviewed could provide even the limited facts we needed to help them. Their cases were marked "Not Recommendable" and were not included in our study. Neither the name nor the number Mr. Doe gave me showed up in the phone books although I tried every possible spelling I could think of. As I slipped his questionnaire into the Not Recommendable file, I remembered his pleading eyes and the desperation in his voice and wished I could do otherwise. There weren't many community ties left for most men after three years of prison. That was one reason we wanted to keep individuals out of detention before trial. Individuals in jail before trial seemed more likely to get prison sentences. Jail led to prison to more prison.

Since our study was an experiment, we presented only half of our recommendable cases, our Experimental cases, to the court. The other half, equally recommendable, were classified as Control cases. To determine whether the case was Experimental or Control, the Vera representative in the courtroom checked the number on each interview questionnaire against the random number table we had created at the beginning of the project. Hidden under each interview number on the chart was a sticker that covered either an E for experimental or a C for control. If a case number had been previously designated as E, our Vera representative let the judge know that we had a positive recommendation. When the defendant's case came up, Vera presented that information to the judge. A case that had been predetermined as C, or control, was just as positive as the experimental case, but the Vera Representative let it go through the normal court process without intervening. The Vera project then tracked both **E** and **C** cases through the system.

If Vera's information helped convince the judge to release a person, who he otherwise would have set money bail on and returned to prison, we should find at the end of our experimental year that there were many more released individuals in the experimental group than in the control group. We also hoped that our data would show that the Vera releases returned to court every time they were required to do so during their case. We hoped these findings would encourage other courts, not just the Manhattan Criminal Court, to obtain verified information about defendants before bail setting so they could safely release many individuals who would otherwise sit in jail awaiting trial.

The law students quickly settled into the court routine as the project got underway and coalesced into an effective team. Somehow in that stressful, rapidly paced courtroom the Vera interviewers made the Manhattan Bail experiment happen. They were committed to helping defendants stay out of jail and worked hard to find information that would provide evidence for a positive recommendation for the individuals they interviewed. At the same time, they managed to blend in well with the rest of the court staff, who frequently referred to them affectionately as 'the kids', and often went out of their way to help them. To the interviewers' credit, they adhered to the experimental design, much as they hated to see a 'good' case that they had worked hard on turn out to be in the control group and not recommended. The interviewers were truly the unsung heroes of the Manhattan Bail Project.

Why did the Manhattan Criminal Court let Vera in to conduct an experiment? Even today, legal reformers and historians ask that question. A lot of the credit went to Vera Director Herb Sturz. He had an uncanny facility for making things happen, solid integrity, a deep and motivating sense of caring about others, and determination. I described Herb to friends as having a 'kind of genius.' His genius came with a lot of skill. He was a master at building coalitions, with a knack for finding common ground between individuals and groups who seemed to have nothing in common. One of his greatest talents was introducing potentially key players to a project, getting them interested, then giving them a stake in its success before they fully realized what they had gotten into. The list of individuals and organizations who signed on to the Manhattan Bail Project before it started is a testament to that. He had used his skills on me too, stoking my indignation about the plight of individuals who couldn't make bail, then drawing me into accepting the job at Vera in spite of my conviction that a controlled experiment in court was unachievable.

As project routines got established, one of the interviewers took over as the daily manager and Herb and I spent less time in the courthouse. We wouldn't know the outcome of the Manhattan Bail Experiment for a year. Herb was already at work developing and getting support for future justice system reform projects.

Part Three
The Urge Toward 'More'

CHAPTER **12**

Yes, I'll Climb That Cliff

ELI AND I continued our cycle of occasional heavy conversations about how we could get along better, vacations from each other, and passionate reunions. It was always Eli who appeared first to reestablish our connection. I took his complaints seriously and tried to understand what he needed. Each time we got back together we thought we had resolved our issues.

"We finally have it right now," we told each other. And often, for a while, it seemed as if we did.

In the fall, after the Manhattan Bail Project was well along, Eli and I were invited to the suburbs to have dinner with Bert, one of Eli's new advisors, and his wife Jill. Bert met us at the train dressed in jeans, had an easy low-key manner, and didn't seem much older than we were. Jill met us at the door of their New Jersey suburban split-level home, looking a little frazzled. She was pretty, plump, and dressed in young mom casual.

"Don't mind the mess," she urged with a welcoming smile. "It's impossible to keep things tidy with three children under five."

Children's toys filled the corners of every room except the dining room, although no children were in sight.

"We shipped them off to the neighbors," Jill laughed, "so I could cook."

Bert and Eli immediately settled into easy chairs in the living room to talk. Jill and I moved into her modern kitchen, with its green walls, wide counters, and bottom cupboards with toys spilling out onto pink tiles. We connected easily. She treated me like I was an emissary from a foreign country in which she had once lived and missed terribly.

"I used to walk by the married student housing when I was in graduate school and saw all the mothers tending their kids," Jill recounted wistfully, "and I'd think there's no way that will happen to me. No way. And here I am. We kept trying different kinds of birth control. We have a kid for every method."

Three kids under five years old, *three* methods of birth control. One of those methods was surely mine. The statistic made my stomach jump.

"But there is the new pill now. We're trying that… and they'll be out of the baby stage in a few more years. It will be easier."

I wanted to cry as I listened to her. I liked her a lot, yet she personified the woman I was most terrified of becoming, the woman who fell in love and settled down. I could imagine the dreams she had had, dreams like mine. Career, interesting work, making a difference in the world. Maybe she could make them happen someday, but not anytime soon. I wondered how many other women like her were out in the suburbs, yearning for a larger life.

We would soon learn that there were a lot. Less than two years later, in 1963, Betty Friedan would give voice to untold numbers of mothers like Jill in her book, *The Feminine Mystique*. "Who am I?" they screamed through the pages. "I am a mother, a wife, a daughter, but **who am *I?*** "

Our dinner was pleasant and soon after Bert and Jill invited us to their house again, this time for mid-afternoon. A third person, Jason, another researcher at Columbia, was also included. He and Bert mentioned something about going to the Gunks and climbing, although Bert had said nothing about that to us. Jill didn't seem to have much idea about what was going on either, although as adults and kids all piled into two cars there was some talk about a playground.

About 45 minutes later we stopped at the bottom of a sheer cliff that went straight up. To my inexperienced eye it looked solid with no footholds anywhere. Though I had never heard of the Gunks then, I learned later that the name is short for Shawangunks, a long ridge of quartz conglomerate in New York state, solid rock with horizontal rather than vertical cracks. It is described as one of the premier climbing areas in the United States.

Still a little confused about what we were doing, I looked around for a playground as we all climbed out of the car. It didn't look like playground territory. Jason and Bert began pulling their climbing equipment out of the car trunk.

"Who else wants to climb" Jason asked.

Eli shook his head no. He had discovered during his summer in Boulder that he didn't like rock climbing. Jason and Bert looked at me.

"What about you?"

"I've never climbed before."

"That's okay. We'll teach you. We'll all be roped together."

"I'd make it more dangerous for you."

I really wanted to go. I was nimble and loved clambering around on rocks. The summer before in Boulder I had been fascinated with rope climbing but had never had a chance to try it. When would I get another opportunity? How could I pass it up?

"No! It won't be more dangerous. Come on," Jason urged, "You'll like it."

"Okay."

As I look now at pictures of climbers on the Gunks, I am astounded at my audacity that day. I had never been athletic or particularly strong.

The two men tied me in behind them and we started up. I looked down to see Jill and her three small children standing beside Eli looking terrified. The climb wasn't bad at first. We went up a chimney, so I didn't feel especially exposed. As we ascended however, we moved out onto the sheer face of the cliff. Even with the safety of the ropes I felt the challenge. I was alone, trying to find places for my feet where no toeholds were visible. The ground below was straight down and far away. I looked down only once. After that I focused all my attention on the only thing that mattered, the rock in front of me.

Near the top I got stuck. My legs shook with the unaccustomed exertion. I couldn't find a crevice big enough to get a grip. Jason and Bert, out of sight above me, called down encouragement and instructions about where to find the foothold that continued to elude me. I was alone on the side of a cliff and through the power of my body and will I had to scale it. We had started late in the day and the sun began to wane. The rock turned chill and light went flat. I felt a moment of terror. I had felt a little like that when I was eleven and had to jump off a low bridge abutment into a creek to pass my beginning swimming test. After hesitating on the concrete abutment for a few minutes, I made myself jump into the water. It was a life-imprinting event. After that I knew I could *make* myself do anything.

I concentrated on locating the chink in the rock. It had to be there if Jason and Bert had just had their feet on it. At last I felt it. Using all my strength I levered myself up and then up again, until I was standing next to my fellow climbers on a small ledge. My relief was momentary. How much further would my rubbery legs take me? And how would I find the energy to get back down?

"Great work. The rest is easy."

They were right. A few more positions and we all reached the plateau above, and there was a simple, easy path to take us back down. The two men praised me lavishly.

"Here's a souvenir from your first climb. You did well," Jason said as he handed me a karabiner from his pack.

I held it tight, euphoric. I felt I had risen to the challenge, wanted to do it again, and understood, finally, why climbers kept trying to scale mountains. As we rode back to Jill and Bert's house I was exuberant. I could think of nothing except my successful climb. New York was changing me. I was taking risks and rising to challenges in a way I'd never done before.

Eli never once praised me, as the other men had. As soon as we got back to Jill and Bert's house, he made sure I understood that Jill, who had never seen Bert climb before, had cried the whole time we were on the cliff, sure Bert would fall and die and she would be left alone with three preschoolers. Shame pulled me down from my climbing high. Had we been invited so that I could hang out with Jill and help her with the kids while the men climbed? Was my expected role to normalize the situation, distract her from the fact that her husband was hanging off a cliff? Instead I had, with my lack of experience, made the climb more dangerous for him. Caught up in my own desire to try something new, I had abandoned a woman I had come to like and empathize with. I had broken free as a woman at another woman's expense.

CHAPTER **13**

Letting Go

AFTER VERA'S HECTIC summer and early fall, life slowed down to a more normal pace. The bail project was going well, and the day to day results we were seeing suggested that the court was releasing a substantial number of our experimental cases. Herb was laying the groundwork for some possible new projects for Vera, and I was setting up and supervising a study of Manhattan Court records similar to the Federal Court Study we had just finished for Attorney General Kennedy's Allen Committee. In this one, fortunately, I didn't have to do the coding of cases. Our law students coded during afternoons when there were fewer bail setting cases coming into court. Herb and I, with Vera's legal expert Chuck Ares, a New York University Law Professor, were also starting to work together on a *New York Law Review* article about the bail project. Overall my work at Vera was going well.

Eli and I were still seeing each other. He took me to his parents' apartment for Thanksgiving and his parents seemed very pleasant. I liked his mother and thought we got along well. Eli made it clear to me afterwards, however, that she had treated me quite differently than his old girlfriend Sarah. Nevertheless, his parents invited us to several events with them over the winter. I enjoyed their company and took their invitations as a positive sign about our relationship. By then Eli had also introduced me to most of his friends, and we often went out with them. These all seemed like positive developments in our relationship, but nothing between us was getting any better. He was in a crucial phase of his dissertation experiment and was often moody and annoyed. I tried to understand.

I had often fantasized about meeting Eli's old girlfriend Sarah, the beautiful, brilliant, bewitching Sarah, who remained an ever-present part of my relationship with Eli. Our actual encounter in late March, with Sarah and a man she introduced as her fiancé, occurred unexpectedly when Eli and I crowded into the front end of a subway car and suddenly found ourselves facing them as they sat along the side. All I could think to say when Ed introduced us was, "Hello." It didn't really matter. One look and my image of Sarah as a sexy, bohemian beauty with flowing hair fell away.

As the overcrowded train jolted back into motion we all called "great to see you" as Eli and I hastily pulled open the door beside them and walked through the clattering passage into the next car. I sank down weakly in the first empty seat, shaken but mostly astonished. I had just faced the remarkable woman I had been mentally competing with for over a year and a half, and she looked remarkedly ordinary! I wanted to jump up and go back to peep at her again through the train window to confirm my discovery. The encounter freed me. I hoped Eli could also let go of his obsession with her, but as we got off the train and walked on to our destination he had nothing to say.

Meeting Sarah marked a turning point for me. I realized that I, as well as Eli, had allowed the fantasy of the irreplaceable Sarah to shape our relationship. It had always left me feeling second best. Once I met Sarah, the myth lost its power for me. I began to want more from my relationship with Eli. When I told him I had signed up for a class in German so I could begin to work toward the Ph.D. language exams I would have to take if I went back to graduate school, I expected encouragement. He was dismissive.

One night I got so angry at him for squelching my ideas that I threw pillows at him. When he threw a Kleenex box at me in his lab a couple days later because I disagreed with something he'd said about nuclear disarmament, I left in a huff, sure this was the end. He came over the next day and we made up yet again. The ongoing rapid alteration of feelings was exhausting. The length of our separations stretched longer. I began to go adventuring around New York on my own. At last, I faced the reality I had been avoiding for months. Nothing changed between us no matter what we did or how much we talked. Nothing was going to change unless I took action. And there was only one action I could take--a final, absolute ending of the relationship.

The end came with little drama on a Sunday in April. We'd been to a play and had had a pleasant enough time, although Eli was quiet. I tried to make conversation but could feel Eli's distance. Suddenly I had had enough.

"I can't go on this way."

"What's bothering you?" I sensed annoyance in his voice, sudden tension in his body.

"Nothing changes. Our relationship isn't going anywhere."

"You know how busy I am with my dissertation and the Disarmament Committee!" His voice took on a note of 'poor me' pleading as well as rising anger.

This was our usual conversation. I refused to go there this time

"Do you think you could ever love or marry me?" I asked.

"I can't conceive of myself getting married to you. Some people are attuned to each other and some aren't. I don't think we are."

I sat stunned by his cool analytical statement and flat certainty. We were in the same place we'd been a year and a half ago on my first visit to him in New York, when he told me he could never love me. Then he'd called me within 24 hours to say he wanted to get to know me better. We'd been rerunning that same script ever since.

"How do you feel when you think about life without me?" I asked

"Scared. I'm very dependent on you," he said slowly, his voice low.

"Why did you call me up the last time we stopped seeing each other?" I persisted. I felt like a prosecutor, but I had to get answers to these questions.

"I loved you very much that night. Sometimes I love you, but it doesn't seem to sustain itself."

That was the answer I had to live with.

It was the answer that explained all the ups and downs, the break-ups and reunions, the answer we kept trying to skitter around in all our discussions. I let go, or at least began the process of letting go. I had come to New York to see what would happen in my relationship with Eli. Now I knew.

"Then there is really nothing more to say, I'll get my things and go."

"Wait till morning to leave. It's safer."

He was right. The West Side of Manhattan in 1962 was many neighborhoods in one area. Each had its own population and its own time. The darkest part of the night was not the time I wanted to be walking alone with a big purse along dim sidestreets, and I was un-likely to see a cab. Maybe I could get a little sleep if I stayed. And perhaps, somewhere deep inside, in spite of my certainty that this was the end, I held on to the hope that a few more hours might pro-duce a miracle.

We lay back to back, each hugging our edge of the bed trying to sleep and not touch. I ran my fingers up and down the ridge on the side of the mattress and wept a little, quietly. No hysterical wailing this time. I felt too empty inside, devoid of hope and energy. As soon as the sky was light I got up and dressed quickly, twisted the key to his apartment off my ring, and laid it on the table. My legs quivered as I walked down the four flights of stairs. The sun shone on the street and the fresh clear morning smelled of spring. As I walked up West 122nd Street toward the subway, I knew absolutely this would be the last time. There would be no going back, but I didn't know how I could ever fill the void inside.

My boss Herb and I sat in our Vera office talking about ideas for a future project. I wanted to tell him that I had just broken up with Eli and kept trying to figure out a way, but the conversation never went the right direction. Unable to hold in the news any longer, I blurted it out.

"I'm not sure whether I'll be here for the new project. I just broke up with Eli and am not sure what I'll do next."

He focused totally on me and listened as I spilled out my story, my decision. He and his wife Elizabeth had invited Eli and me to their home several times so they knew us both. After I'd wound down my explanation, he finally spoke. I expected him to console me, give the usual platitudes, but he didn't.

"Elizabeth and I felt rather sad to see you with Eli," he said, "He never let you blossom as a human being."

I looked up at him in surprise.

"You went into a shell when you were with him. He never gave you anything, never referred to you, tried to build you up, or bring you into a conversation!"

Elizabeth and Herb had assessed my relationship with Eli exactly. Herb articulated simply what I had been feeling, the truth that I had resisted so long. But it didn't make the emptiness and pain go away.

"I think of you as a good friend," Herb continued. "I hope you consider Elizabeth and me good friends too. We are there for you any time you need us."

I nodded my thanks. I knew them well enough to know that they would indeed be there, anytime, day or night, if I needed them. Their support was like an embrace. They couldn't work through my grief for me. But if it got overwhelming, they offered a safe haven. After work I walked Herb across town to Penn Station to catch his train to Princeton, as I often did, to have a little extra time to talk about projects.

"How about a drink?" he asked as we neared the station.

"But you'll miss your train," I demurred, knowing that was something he usually tried to avoid.

"That's okay. I'll call Elizabeth. I told her about Eli. She'll understand."

We settled into a booth at a bar filled with commuters, ordered beers, and talked mostly about what we thought was important in life. The conversation let me fly a little, took me beyond the moment, my immediate situation. When we parted an hour later and I turned toward my subway stop, the cold empty space inside had a little warm spot in one corner.

I got off the subway at West 96th Street so I could walk home along Riverside Drive to my apartment on West 106th Street. Tears streamed down my cheeks. It felt good to cry and I wanted to do it here, alone, without drama, before I got home and told my roommate Lois and other friends. I sat on a bench overlooking the river. A long barge train glided upstream behind a large green ship. The warm April wind ruffled my hair. I felt free, relieved, a whole person. Dusk settled among the trees and the sky reflected pink on the river. I had come through wiser, deeper, even though three months ago I had been terrified of a world without Eli. Up until now my life in New York had been entwined with his. Now I saw the world, the river, the park, as if for the first time, new, fresh, through *my* eyes. I was alive again. I was me.

Even if Eli called in a few weeks, as he probably would, I knew my decision was complete. Final. I had desperately wanted our relationship to work. We had experienced a companionship and intellectual camaraderie in Colorado and during my trips to New York that were new to me. I still wanted that kind of connection, but Eli could not give it to me in an ongoing relationship. I couldn't imagine him in the work/family partnership I envisioned for my life.

Over the next few weeks, even though my resolve that the relationship was over remained firm, I caught myself looking for Eli everywhere. Habit had held us together in a web of invisible connections to almost every place I'd been in the city and most of the people I knew. Nearly all my New York life, except for Vera, had involved Eli. Without him, everyday life was full of holes. I wondered how many people stayed together because it seemed easier than breaking the habit, destroying the web. How often did habit stand in for love and result in marriage? That was not the kind of marriage I wanted. In order to free myself from my dependence on Eli I was going to have to let go of a lot of old habits. A friend had once told me that it took 21 days to lay down a habit. I hoped the process went the other way as quickly.

Spring helped ease my sadness. The weather for my first Easter in New York was perfect. I wandered the city, drifting like a spirit with no point in time or space, simply letting in beauty, replenishing my spirit with a Rodin sculpture and two cerulean blue vases at the museum, two dark-haired little girls dancing in matching red lace dresses in Riverside park, warm cheese pastry in a Turkish bakery.

CHAPTER **14**

Moving On

IN A FEW months I would be 25 years old. In the United States at that time, the average age of marriage for women was around twenty. The age for men was twenty-two. The pool of eligible men for women my age was shrinking. Worse, there probably wasn't even a *pool* of eligible men for career-oriented women like me. Having experienced love and intimacy, even though the relationship had not worked out as I had hoped, I understood that they were essential for my life. I still wanted both work and love. And I was not about to just sit around and wait demurely for the love.

My apartment-mate Lois had stopped seeing someone about the same time that I had broken up with Eli. For the first time since we'd moved in together we were both spending a lot of time in our apartment and began to deepen an already good friendship. What could we do, we wondered, to improve our defunct social life?

"Maybe it's time for a party," suggested Lois who had gone to college in the partying city of New Orleans.

We decided to invite everyone we knew who was in our general age group and sat down excitedly in our living room to make a list. After we had wracked our brains for every possible appropriate party candidate, we stared at it in dismay. It was pitifully short.

"We hardly know anybody," wailed Lois, "Maybe we can ask everyone to invite all their friends."

So our "bring your own bottle and all your friends" party came into being and became a tradition. It opened two avenues to an expanded social life--new friends of friends who came to our party and return invitations from our guests to parties they gave. It became our stock solution whenever life got dull. Our first party was rather small, but it was big enough to give us a lift because we had a good time ourselves and realized how easy it was to give parties. Our New York world began to expand.

I decided I needed to go even further than that. I started a campaign to meet a new man every week. Anxious to get outside into the natural world, I joined the American Youth Hosteling Association, which organized hikes every Saturday. I also began hanging out regularly on a rock in Riverside Park on Sundays. The park was the Upper West Side's backyard and drew lots of people from the area including many associated with Columbia.

On my first hike in May I met Sam, a biology doctoral student who thought I was wonderful. We started to date, but after an initial glow I found it hard to maintain enthusiasm. He was full of platitudes.

"All people have to do to succeed is work hard," he announced.

"But what about poor people who have everything stacked against them?" I asked.

"They can do it if they really want to."

He was the first person I had dated since I'd stopped seeing Eli, and I worried that I might be overly critical of him because of that. I tried to stay open. When he invited me to go folk singing one Saturday night on the Staten Island Ferry, one of the most romantic pastimes I could imagine, I accepted. The excursion would surely stir my desire.

The night was clear and warm enough to sit outside. We and two of his friends, one of whom brought a guitar, rode back and forth singing from 9 to 11 p.m. We stopped occasionally to listen to the river's music against the dull roar of the engine, the shush of the ferry cutting through the black water, and a ship's full-throated moan somewhere in the darkness. The lights were like music too, the city big and flashy at first, then smaller and twinkling as we moved toward Staten Island.

Halfway across the river stars filled the sky, then faded, overcome by the glow from the approaching shore.

The Statue of Liberty stood luminous. I moved to the railing to view her every time we passed. In that era, she represented to me much that I thought was good about America--compassion, hope, acceptance, freedom, and a commitment to the ideal of diversity. I tried to explain all that to Sam. He didn't seem to get it. Nor did he argue, as many of us probably would today, that in reality, those wonderful ideals were not then, and still are not now universally available to everyone in our country. He just didn't seem especially interested one way or another. Instead of firing up my passion, our potentially romantic date confirmed my suspicion that Sam and I had very little in common.

My park adventures weren't going much better. The person I had had my eye on for a couple weeks was a tall, thin fellow in a yellow sweater with blond hair and a pipe, which was usually upside down in his mouth. He settled regularly on a blanket near my rock with his New York Times and a book. Sometimes he looked my way. Was he watching me as much as I was watching him? When he didn't make any overtures, I decided to approach him.

"Could I borrow your *Times* for a few minutes."

"Sure."

"Live around here?" I asked when I returned the paper.

He did, exactly one block from me. My new friend Devon was a Ph.D. student in physics. Coincidently his advisor was Jason, the professor I'd climbed with in the Gunks.

After we had chatted for a while he asked me if I would like to go to the beach on Saturday. I accepted with alacrity. I hadn't yet been to a New York beach in the summer. On Monday I raced to Macy's to buy a new bathing suit. On Wednesday I lay out on my tiny balcony to get the start of a tan so I wouldn't burn on Saturday, overdid it, and burned on Wednesday.

Jones Beach was mobbed by the time Devon parked his two-seat sports car in the back row of the biggest parking lot I'd ever seen. After we had traipsed through lines of parked vehicles we emerged onto a quarter mile stretch of beach covered with thousands of nearly nude bodies crammed blanket to blanket. We found a sliver of sand for our towels, then clambered toward the water through umbrellas, coolers, and loud music.

Gyrating bathers shrieked and guffawed as waves slapped their thighs and they tried to splash and dunk each other. After wading in the crowd for a while Devon and I retreated to our spot. Conversation started and stalled. We walked down the beach to where the crowd thinned out and we could see a swath of sand. After standing awkwardly for a few minutes gazing at the sea, we turned and waded back through the throng of sunbathers. I was physically attracted to him, as I had been in the park, and detected the glimmer of a laconic sense of humor. I suspected if we could get beyond his shyness he would be good company, but there seemed to be no way to get conversation going. At the end of the afternoon we walked in awkward silence from his car back to our street and I guessed we wouldn't see each other again.

The next weekend when I was sitting on my rock in the park reading I looked up to see not Devon, but Eli, coming straight toward me. My stomach dived. Over two months had passed since we'd spoken.

"I've missed you," he said.

"Oh?" I asked, shifting on my towel, wondering how many times I'd heard him say that after we'd been apart for a while.

"I've *really* missed you."

"I'm sorry," I replied. I didn't know what else to say.

And somehow, I don't know how--he intimated that he wanted to get married.

Damn. He couldn't even *ask* me or say it straight out. It was so oblique I couldn't quite figure out how it had happened, what exactly he'd said.

"I don't think I want to marry you," I said slowly.

I didn't want him to go away. I couldn't imagine our getting back together either. I felt like I was standing on the edge of a cold sea. I wanted to *want* to dive in, but all I could think about was how cold the water had been the last time I did.

We talked mostly about what he was doing, as usual, until the sun slanted long across the grass and my bare feet chilled. I shrugged on my sandals, stood up, gathered up my things and let him take my hand as we walked slowly up to the steps that led to my street. Then I dropped his hand and we went our separate ways.

As I climbed the steps to my apartment I basked in the pleasure of again being with someone I'd been close to. I missed that feeling of shared intimacy. Maybe we could make it together after all, I mused. Maybe I'd give him a call. But back in my apartment, when I sat down beside the phone, I could not bring myself to lift the receiver.

We kept in touch. Occasionally I got a letter or postcard about what he was doing. Six months later he sent me a hand-written announcement of his marriage. Eli and his bride had been married in the home of her parents in a Jewish ceremony. I was glad it wasn't me.

CHAPTER 15

Sociologists Just Wade In

IN EARLY SUMMER 1962, around my one-year anniversary of starting work at Vera, I began to feel stagnant. The excitement of getting
the Manhattan Bail Project underway was over. Although the project
had a few more months to run, we could already see that our experiment was proving what we had hoped it would. I still had lots to do,
analysis of a new set of bail data from the Manhattan Criminal Court,
as well as the results from the bail study itself, and talking with Herb
about new projects. Why, with so much interesting work, did I feel
no forward movement in my life? Much as I liked working at Vera, I
couldn't see myself settling in long term. Something was missing.

My life outside of Vera felt empty too. After hanging around poetry readings in cafes in Greenwich Village for several months trying
to be a hippie, I'd come to realize that, although I *wanted* to be a
hippie, I wasn't one. I was too logical, had too much drive, and too
little patience with poetry I didn't understand. I loved the modern
dance classes I took at the New Dance Studio in Times Square and
my writing classes at the New School, but neither met the vague need
I couldn't name.

One day, as I browsed in a Columbia University bookstore near
my apartment, I picked up a flyer advertising Columbia summer
classes open to the public. One, a class in questionnaire development offered by the sociology department, sent a shot of adrenalin
through my system. It was scheduled for Friday afternoons from three

to five in August and could be useful for my work at Vera. I broached the idea of taking the class to Herb, who not only agreed to give me the time off to attend, but also said Vera could pay for it.

The class, held at Columbia's Bureau of Applied Social Research in an old brownstone a few steps off Broadway, was just up the street from my apartment. I approached my first class with keen anticipation but was severely disappointed when the instructor announced that we were going to develop and test a questionnaire about New Yorkers' preparation for nuclear attack. The topic was of major concern at that time. The cold war was raging and both Russia and the United States had a variety of hardware loaded with nuclear weapons aimed at each other's cities. The popular press was full of discussions about how to increase survival during nuclear war and New York apartment buildings stocked large containers of water and other supplies in their basements in case of attack. Eli and I had even toured a backyard bomb shelter model, an especially popular attraction at the 1961 Danbury Fair in Connecticut.

I had had my fill of talking about nuclear attacks. Eli had been an active member of the Nuclear Disarmament Committee, and when we were seeing each other he had plied me with more casualty statistics and vivid descriptions of nuclear devastation than I had ever wanted to see. it was a relief after we split up not to have to read, talk, or think about nuclear annihilation all the time. Perhaps it wasn't politically correct, but I wanted to focus on living, not on a disaster over which I had no control. Now in the place I had hoped to find something to give my life a new spark, I had to confront the possibility of nuclear war again.

Once the class got underway, however, the topic of our survey became irrelevant to me. I was ecstatic to be back in a sociology class and soaked up everything--reading, expanding my skill in creating good questions, and discussions about the ethics and social relevance of research. I hadn't realized how much I had missed school. Our instructor was a recent Columbia Sociology Ph.D. graduate who ran an informal class. We eight students got to know each other quickly. I was especially fascinated by two lively, young Italian priests, who described their weekend trips to Jones Beach with great animation.

"What do you do there?" I asked.

"Swim," they replied smiling.

"But what do you wear?" I asked, as I remembered my trip to Jones Beach with Devon and visualized them cavorting through the waves with the scantily clothed multitudes in some kind of old-fashioned bathing suits topped with clerical collars.

"Bathing suits, regular bathing suits, they explained laughing.

In late August after we had finalized our questionnaire, our instructor announced that our final paper would be the write-up of our individual experience of pretesting the questionnaire in the field. He gave each of us a list of randomly selected building numbers in Greenwich Village and told us to go knock on doors and conduct interviews.

I had knocked on doors before. When I was twelve I peddled *Readers' Digest* subscriptions in the veterans' temporary housing units about a mile from my house. When my friend Norma thought her hamster was pregnant I went with her to the same housing units in an unsuccessful attempt to get orders for the future baby hamsters. But knocking on doors in New York City to talk about a nuclear attack? My entrepreneurial childhood gave me no experience for that.

The day was gray as I set out to conduct my interviews, and I got a later start than planned. On a map I located my assigned addresses, which appeared to be along the fringes of the Village, rather than in the Village, a big difference at that time in terms of who might answer the door. I suspected, as I looked at my assigned numbers, that our instructor did not have as good a working knowledge of the Village as he thought he had. As I walked from the subway toward my interview area, the street grew increasingly shabby. Sociologists were supposed to be able to wade into any new situation and do their work. I really wanted to be a good sociologist, but also knew to be cautious about where I walked alone. On the corner around which my numbers were clustered I stopped and took stock.

In the year I had been in New York I had learned to assess an unknown neighborhood. If it felt creepy I tried not to go there at night or alone. I definitely didn't knock on doors. This neighborhood was marginal. The street was wide, which was good, but was also almost empty except for a few men. Although I had learned to feel safer around people, a group of men could signal danger to a woman alone. There were several empty lots with construction trash, usually a bad sign, but there was an apartment complex about a block south that looked fairly middle class.

My creepy-block meter jiggled a little but didn't go wild. I decided to go to work. The first number on my list should have been on a building beside The White Horse Tavern, where Dylan Thomas supposedly drank himself to death. The Tavern looked closed and there were only a few scattered bricks left on the vacant lot beside it. The spot where the second number should have been also appeared to have been demolished. My third number existed above a door with peeling paint and I knocked with some trepidation. The man who opened the door spoke no English, but his tone of voice and body language communicated an adamant 'go away.' I retreated quickly.

My list of numbers had not been long to begin with and was getting uncomfortably short. Would it be possible to get *any* interviews? I cheered up a little when I saw that my fourth number designated the apartment house that I had spotted down the street. I walked rapidly toward it, hoping my initial evaluation of it as more inviting was accurate. It was. I decided to do the rest of my research right there. After trying three doors I connected with a man who spoke to me through the crack provided when he kept his chain lock on.

"Yes, I do worry about nuclear bombs," he told me, "But I haven't made any plans."

I wondered how the two priests were doing and hoped they'd worn their civvies. I could imagine the terror they might strike in the hearts of New Yorkers who opened the door to face a priest who wanted to quiz them about their preparation for a nuclear bomb.

After two more no-answers, I found a couple eager to talk. They invited me in and offered me tea. I pulled out my questionnaire and we all sat down cozily in comfortable chairs to discuss a nuclear war. The couple talked at length.

"We have spent a lot of time talking about what we would do if the bomb came," the woman Grace said.

"We've decided we want to be together, if possible," her partner James joined in.

"We both work at home so we should be close, but what if we happen to be in different places when we hear the alert?" Grace continued. "Then, we've agreed we'll try to get to each other."

"Of course, if there isn't any alert, if it just comes...." James' voice trailed off.

We all sat quietly, contemplating the possibility of nuclear attack, with or without advance warning. I wished I had someone to run to. It seemed such a human thing to want to be with someone you loved when your world ended.

After that, our interview quickly wound down. It was starting to get dark outside and I decided it was time to get back to the subway. I had gotten one rich interview and decided that was enough. The more I thought about the mission we students had been sent on, the more amazed I was that I got even one interview. There couldn't be many people in New York City in any neighborhood who would open their door to an unknown person who wanted to interview them about their preparation for nuclear war.

It was just a few months later in October 1962, that the questions we had matter-of-factly developed and asked in our interviews took on a terrifying and immediate reality. As President John F. Kennedy and Soviet President Nikita Khrushchev faced off in the Cuban missile crisis we all sat glued to our televisions and radios confronting, in real time, the possibility of imminent nuclear annihilation.

CHAPTER **16**

Self-Promise

EXHAUSTED, I HALF dragged and half carried my heavy suitcase up the four flights of stairs to my apartment. In early September, shortly after my sociology class ended, I had taken a week's vacation to visit my cross-country, camping partner Penny, who now lived in San Francisco. On my last night we took a camping trip 'for old time's sake' to Mount Shasta without enough warm clothes, and I had slept very little. All I could think about was collapsing in bed.

With a sigh of relief, I flung open the door. Then stood nonplussed. Four sets of eyes peered at me. Four persons, one of them my current apartment mate Lois, rose to greet me.

"Meet your visitors," Lois announced.

I stared at them in confusion. They didn't look like *my* visitors. I didn't know them.

Then I vaguely recognized one. Her name was Cindy, I thought. A friend of my Northwestern colleague Shig. I'd never seen the other two before.

The three of them had just come from the annual sociology convention, Lois explained. Cindy and her friend Louise needed a place to stay for the night, and she had just offered them space on our living room rug.

As I was trying to process all this, Cindy turned to introduce me to the third visitor, her friend Hugh, who had been waiting quietly during the bustle of first greetings. He was a sociology professor, she explained, and lived just three blocks up Riverside Drive.

"So I thought you two should meet each other."

I focused on him with interest. He was a few years older than I, with rumpled brown hair, warm greenish brown eyes, and tiny lines around his mouth that crinkled when he smiled. I forgot I was tired. When he left we exchanged phone numbers.

Hugh called a few days later. We began seeing each other almost every day and quickly moved into an intimate relationship. Although I had briefly dated several men since I had broken up with Eli, Hugh was the first man I had spent much time with or to whom I felt any sense of emotional attachment. As I sat in my apartment reading sociological theory for the second class I had decided to take at Columbia, I often envisioned the way his face brightened all over when he smiled and longed for the next time I would see him. Hugh was a quiet, gentle man, whose values were similar to my own. Although quick to expound on his ideas and perspectives, he was willing to listen to mine too. Hugh's priorities were clearly academic. His office/bedroom was mostly office. It had an oversize desk in the middle, packed bookcases lining every inch of wall space, and a double mattress on the floor squished between two file cabinets.

We often spent time working together in his apartment. He worked in his office. I spread out my Vera work or sociological theory books on his dining table, where I paused more often than I should have, to stare at the room's sweeping view of the Hudson river. We broke occasionally to visit for a few minutes and talk about what we were doing, or ran out to a movie, then dinner at the Hungarian cafeteria just a few blocks down Broadway. I enjoyed the companionship of being together while we each did our own work. It was a piece of the work/family partnership that I envisioned for my future. Life with Hugh was easy and interesting. Sometimes he took me to explore small neighborhoods in New York that I had never visited. I began to realize that a relationship didn't have to be as fraught as the one I'd had with Eli.

Hugh had a wide circle of friends that included well known social activists and liberals in New York city. It was pleasant to be associated with him. At parties in spacious, well-appointed West Side apartments his friends sought me out to ask what I was doing and made me feel that I too was engaged in important work. It was as if I had leaped ten years ahead of myself, bypassing the noisy BYOB parties in funky graduate student pads. Still, I sensed that I was less well read and informed on local and national issues than Hugh and his friends and sometimes felt the strain of trying to keep up. I didn't want to embarrass him by sounding naïve or offering a lightweight opinion.

I thought that I was falling in love with Hugh, but sometimes worried that I was more attracted to his status than to him. Being connected with a well-established and admired man was very seductive. In the 1950s and '60s women were expected to date up, marry up. They got ahead and improved their social status on the coat tails of men. At that time, the few women in sociology were almost all affiliated with male sociologists.

After a few months together, our relationship began to unravel. I wanted more time together, some elevation of our relationship on his priority scale. Perhaps he wanted someone more mature and experienced. Shortly before he went away for a few days, we agreed to be friends rather than lovers. While he was gone I entered his apartment for the last time to return his key and water his plants, which I had been doing for him when he traveled. His presence and the smell of his pipe tobacco still floated through the rooms. I dropped his key on the dining table where I had so often worked and lingered for a final glimpse of the river. The Hudson's gray mist accentuated my sadness. I opened his door and slipped out.

I had liked the rhythm of our lives together, liked Hugh as a person, and thought I loved him. but as I asked myself what emotional connection held us together I had to admit it was more friendship and affection than love. We remained friends, stayed in touch, and occasionally did things together.

As I thought back over this and other relationships, I realized that dating different men had given me a better sense of what I wanted in a life partner. Social, political, and ethical values similar to my own were essential. Also, much as I hated to admit it, as an only child I expected a fair amount of attention and needed to know I was loved and important to someone. None of the men I'd been attracted to so far had given me much of the latter. Clearly, my choice of men was one part of my problem in maintaining a long-term relationship, but when I was honest with myself I had to admit that I also carried a lot of the responsibility. Was I too needy? Too selfish? Did I ask for too much? Send contradictory messages? Some of my friends were seeing psychologists. Perhaps I needed to consider that too. Maybe talking to someone could help me understand how to go about finding the right man and establishing a strong bond with him.

The idea of seeing a psychologist was scary! Perhaps I should give myself one more chance before taking such a serious step. If I have one more failed relationship, I vowed to myself, I will find a shrink.

CHAPTER 17

Challenge to Standard Practice

THE WINTER SUN shone thinly into Herb Sturz' Vera office in the brownstone on East 39th Street. It momentarily caught the intense blue of the Oriental carpet, which bled out between the three of us: Herb, Chuck Ares, a law professor at NYU Law School and the legal advisor for the bail project, and me, the research associate. I was well into my second year at Vera. We had completed our year-long Manhattan Bail Project and were now preparing the big rollout of the Project's main results in Herb and Chuck's article for *New York University Law Review.*

I sat against one wall at a wooden drop-leaf table, my work area in our tiny one-room office. Computer printout, hand drawn tables, and manuscript pages kept slipping off the table edges into the lap of my skirt and down my nylon-clad legs. As I bent to retrieve them I gazed at the intricate designs sprawling across Herb's blue oriental rug, hoping their beauty would calm my growing anger.

We had documented in the analysis of data I had done on the project that judges were more likely to release defendants without bail if they had verified information about them. We also demonstrated that the freed individuals came back for their court dates without the incentive of financial bail. Nobody had ever obtained that kind of research-based information before.

The three of us labored over different sections of the article. I was responsible for two major pieces. One was a description of the

Manhattan Bail Project's research instruments, procedures, and results. The second was a description of a separate, statistical analysis of 1960 court records that showed how the New York's bail system had been working before we intervened. Together the two required the construction and explanation of twelve tables.

Chuck sat reading in the antique chair near Herb's desk, with one hand thrown loosely over the side. A few wrinkles lined the skin near his eyes; his sandy hair had just a touch of gray. His easy posture communicated who he was, an established law professor. He was working on the structure and legal parts of the article. Unlike Herb and me, he had written law review articles before.

Herb sat writing furiously at his large wooden desk cluttered with the papers of our draft. His thin, angular body hunched forward in concentration as he tried to convey, in a legal format that allowed little room for anything but dry, precise facts, the importance of our results and his passionate caring about the arrested individuals we had kept out of jail. I could hear his intensity in his impatient shift of papers and rapid scratch of pen. We three worked as equals. Good colleagues. We all made suggestions, raised questions, listened, incorporated each other's ideas. We all knew how important this article was. It had to be good.

But outside this room the article was *their* article, Ares and Sturz. No matter how closely we worked here, my name would not appear in the journal's Table of Contents or at the top of the article. I would remain a faceless, nameless, unacknowledged contributor. I didn't know exactly what I wanted, except some indication somewhere that I was present, as involved in the process as they were.

So silly to feel this way, I told myself. In two years of graduate school I had rarely read an article or book with a woman's name on it. Women--secretaries, research assistants, clerks, professionals--did a lot of the work that men presented to the world. That was standard practice, the way it had been for a long time. Women worked for men, often very competently, writing, typing, analyzing, and putting together presentations that men took into the world and received credit for. That was the way things were done. Nobody gave any thought to whether the women behind the scenes should receive recognition too.

Still it rankled. Herb was often lavish in his praise of my contributions to Vera and stressed how important my research analysis and writing had been to our projects. Surely though, if Herb and Chuck thought I should be included as an author on the article they would have mentioned it.

I kept trying to let it go. I wasn't a pushy, demanding person, one of those overbearing women my mother disliked so much. Then suddenly my thoughts just spilled out, broke into the room's silence like a wave.

"I'm wondering…since we're all working on this together," I said, lifting my head from my work. Heat infused my body in what felt like shame. Shame at asking for something inappropriate, that I didn't deserve, that would lower their opinion of me.

"Yes," Chuck and Herb both paused and looked up.

"Since I'm responsible for a big part of the article with the data analysis and tables and all…"

They waited expectantly, eyes fixed on me, Chuck's light brown, puzzled, Herb's dark, supportive, questioning.

"Maybe, well I was wondering if perhaps… my name could be on the article somewhere, not necessarily as an author, but maybe in a footnote or something…?"

There was total silence. Both men stared at me, faces momentarily disorganized, startled. I saw two sensitive, caring men committed to social justice who realized that the idea of including my name on the article had never crossed their minds.

"Absolutely," said Herb who recovered first. "As an author." He smiled broadly. "Yours is the most important part. Of course."

"Of course," echoed Chuck, shifting uneasily in his seat.

Ready to argue my case, explain how it was fair, I sat speechless.

"We'll do it alphabetically. Ares, Rankin, and Sturz," declared Herb. "And the next article, the one about the connection between pretrial detention and conviction that you have been working on, will be yours, single-authored."

That 1963 Ares, Rankin, and Sturz article, "The Manhattan Bail Project: An Interim Report on the Use of Pretrial Parole" is still referenced today.

CHAPTER 18

Momentous Decisions

THE NEWS WOULD be like a bomb to my mother. I could see my parents in their living room in Meadville, my mother in her spot on the tan couch with a cigarette in her hand and my father getting ready to sit down in his tilt-back chair across the room facing her. He would have picked up my letter from the mailbox down the road on his way home from work as an accountant at the nearby Viscose textile plant.

"Looks like a letter from Anne," he'd say smiling, as he slit it open and handed it to my mother to read first. My mother would put on her glasses, pull it out, and start reading with anticipation. Then she would wail to my father.

"Graduate school. She says she wants to go back to graduate school for a Ph.D.! When she's got such a good job. Why isn't she ever satisfied? Why does she always want more? She'll *never* get married."

And my father's response as he shifts his chair with a creak, into its tilted position, "Well, if that's what she wants to do, that's fine."

My mother might have raged about my decision to my father, but she never communicated her angst to me. I didn't then appreciate enough my parents' willingness to roll with the fully formed decisions I kept throwing at them. I just took their support for granted, assumed it would be there no matter what I decided to do. And it always was. Now I look back in amazement at their flexibility and realize how remarkable it was for that era.

My mother and I had different approaches to decisions. She

agonized over all the possible obstacles and got bogged down in the "what-ifs." I tended to focus on the goal, think through if and why it was important to me, and then just jump in and try to swim. I knew if I stopped to think about the obstacles I'd get paralyzed and never do anything. My decision was momentous. Going back to school for a Ph.D. would take at least three to five years, would cost a lot of money, and probably would limit my marriage prospects. But it felt right. The course I had taken at Columbia in August had been the trigger. The class had energized me so much that I had signed up for another one on sociological theory in the fall. Dating Hugh had been a factor too. I had enjoyed talking sociology with him and his friends and liked the kind of life he led as a college teacher and researcher.

I valued my work at Vera but, committed as I was to Vera's work in social justice, it wasn't my place in the world. I was eager to continue on my own journey, learn more about how society worked. I still wanted to be a college teacher.

"If I want to go back, I'll go back," I had told my friend Shig and other colleagues at Northwestern when they warned me that I'd never finish my Ph.D. if I left school without it. Now it would give me pleasure to prove them wrong. I had gained confidence in my ability to do graduate work and in my own professional identity. Now I believed I could finish school, even if I fell in love.

Choosing schools was difficult. I didn't know much more about graduate schools in 1963 than I had known in 1959 when I ended up serendipitously at Northwestern, but I hoped to be more intentional in my choice. I finally decided to apply to three universities I knew. The University of California Berkeley was appealing because it was a hotbed of radicalism and I'd fallen in love with the campus when I had toured it on my previous summer's visit to California. It was a long shot. I didn't know a single person there.

Columbia seemed a reasonable choice. I enjoyed my classes there and knew several Columbia professors through my work at Vera. Its close proximity to my apartment was a big plus. I wouldn't have to start my life all over again in another city and find new friends. Columbia also offered a fellowship in Law and Sociology, one of the first in the emerging new field that I had stumbled into when I went to work for Vera. Ironically Herb's idea that there should be a Sociology of Justice, which had seemed naïve in my first phone conversation with him, was actually coming to pass—like his idea for a controlled experiment in criminal court.

After long deliberation I decided to re-apply to Northwestern. My education there had served me well in my Vera work, and I had come to appreciate its excellence. Now that I had gained more self-confidence and work experience, I felt I could function well there, maybe even hold my own. I was willing to try, especially since my old friend Shig and some others I knew would still be in residence.

As soon as I started working on graduate school applications I let Herb know that I would probably be leaving work in August 1963 to go back to school. The break from Vera would be hard, but my sense that it was time to move on ran deep.

"You'll always have a job here Anne," Herb said simply when I told him.

Meanwhile I was busy enough to keep my mind off the vagueness of my future, at least during the day. I was doing statistical analysis for our second planned article for the *New York University Law Review*. My preliminary results suggested that individuals who spent time in jail before trial were more likely to be convicted and sentenced to prison than comparable defendants who were free pending trial. I had to explore further to see if this association between pretrial detention and a prison sentence after conviction was significant or the result of other factors, like a defendant's previous record.

If our initial results held up after further exploration, the study would provide important empirical evidence that an individual's inability to make bail increased his chances of being incarcerated not just before trial, but *after,* as well. The statistical work was tedious. Trying to write explanations in legalese was tortuous. I suspected I might have to take the project with me when I left Vera, no matter where I ended up in September.

Through the late winter and early spring of 1963 my future floated like a balloon, high in the atmosphere, beyond my control. The first response to my three applications was from Berkeley. It was a rejection. The short letter concluded in what I told myself was surely a typo, "...our decision is a reflection on your competence."

After that cheery rejection I heard nothing for several weeks. In early April as I fumbled to balance my dripping umbrella, purse, and small brass mailbox key in the foyer of my apartment building, I pulled out a letter with a Northwestern University return address. Dropping everything in a damp pile I tore it open. There it was in black and white.

"We are happy to offer you a place in our Sociology Ph.D. program and a teaching assistantship with full tuition and a stipend..."

I reread it to make sure there was no negative in the sentence somewhere. Assistantships were highly competitive. I let the victory sink in. The department's expression of confidence in my ability swept away self-doubts and the sense of failure that had plagued me since I'd left my Northwestern thesis advisor's office almost two years ago.

My exuberance lasted just long enough to climb the stairs to my apartment door. The real possibility of moving back to Chicago made me realize how much I wanted to stay in New York and go to Columbia. I opened my door and looked around. This place, the city, my friends, especially my apartment mate Lois, were important to my life. I was a New Yorker. Manhattan was home. I didn't want to leave. I tried not to count the days that passed with no response from Columbia. Then finally, as I swung open the door to our apartment, there was an envelope brought up from the mailbox by Lois, lying on my desk. I walked over, sat down, gingerly picked it up, looked at it, weighed it in my hand, and slowly, fearfully opened it.

"We are happy...offer Law and Sociology Fellowship."

I could stay in New York City and go to Columbia in its new Law and Sociology program on a two-year fellowship. I would spend my first year primarily in law school and would be taking both sociology and law courses throughout my two years.

A few days later, when I was studying in the Columbia library for my sociological theory course I was distracted by a tall, casually dressed man browsing the sociology shelves across the table from me. When he turned around we made eye contact,

"Are you in sociology?" I asked.

Frank was a sociologist who had been trying to finish his Ph.D. thesis at a different university for several years. He was presently working on a two-year appointment at the Bureau of Applied Social Research at Columbia.

"Want to go get coffee?" he asked.

Frank had a high forehead, dark hair, and a smile that promised— what? There was a raw warmth about him, direct, straight from him to me, and depths I could sense, but not understand. I found him intriguing, but he soon began to raise my ongoing anxiety that getting more education would decrease or eliminate my chances of ever getting married.

"I want a woman who acts like a woman," he proclaimed.

Of course, men and women should be equal, he argued, but they are different, and those differences are important. I cringed. In the early 1960s there were few virtues specifically associated with women that I could identify with. The ones mentioned most often were physical weakness, need to be taken care of, emotionality, ir-rationality, inability to make decisions, and being 'natural' caregivers. Even psychologists presented evidence to show that women were less mature than men. As far as I could see, those supposed differences set women up to be treated like second class citizens. I wanted to be a female person with the same capacities and potentials as a male person. Did that desire for equality, that lack of difference, make me less appealing to men, less lovable and less able to love?

"Describe how a woman acts like a woman," I demanded.

Frank expounded unconvincingly on womanliness as he kissed my ear. I shook my head. His explanation, which seemed to focus on the importance of making men feel good, was distressing. Did I need to flatter and play a role to be womanly?

Suddenly I flashed back to my days in graduate school at Northwestern when the graduate students all talked about playing games and taking different roles, and the women dormitory counselors all smiled, no matter what was going on underneath. I had resisted the idea of playing a role then, and I resisted now. I wanted to be genuine, wanted my life to have meaning both inside and outside my family, and beyond my gender. But was there a cost for this choice I was making? If so, was it too high? In my efforts to move beyond the traditional female role had I broken something inside? Was I missing some essential qualities? Was that why I had so much trouble finding the right man?

I tried to be more womanly with Frank, as much as I could figure out what that was without getting into the old stereotypes. I wanted to keep seeing him, even though in my sensible moments I knew nothing could come of our relationship.

A couple weeks after our conversation about women, I was roaming through Riverside Park trying to enjoy an early spring day. The first green leaves laid a thin canopy over my head. Kids were riding their bikes along the path; toddlers crowded around the sand boxes. Two daffodils peeked out of an indentation on the hill. The day and place called for a feeling of exhilaration, but I felt a loneliness I couldn't shake. Frank hadn't been around as much as usual and I missed him.

As I walked I half glanced, with a sigh of envy, at a couple walking half a block away along another path holding hands and laughing, then kissing. Then something about the walk registered, made me look again more closely. Frank. Was he with the English secretary who worked at the Bureau of Applied Research where he also worked? At first I told myself they were just friends walking in the park. But the kiss? How did I explain the kiss?

I knew how to explain the kiss, wasn't really surprised, but the sight, the event, hurt. A lot. I turned away and headed home, no longer registering the gold of the daffodils or the way the leaves curled from their buds. Back in my apartment I sat letting the knowledge wash over me, waiting for it to stick, to soak in. Maybe I'd misinterpreted the scene, I told myself, and he would call tomorrow. Two tomorrows passed and I called him, said I'd seen him in the park.

"Yes," he said. "That's how it is. Something just happened with her."

In spite of my efforts, had I failed to be womanly enough? I had promised myself that if I had another breakup I would seek a therapist. But in spite of my hurt, I backed off. My time with Frank had been short, I argued to myself. It was hardly a relationship. Besides, I had recently picked up an interesting flyer in the Columbia bookstore about a trip to Europe in late summer. It would never do to start therapy and then leave on vacation.

The flyer advertised a cheap, five-week charter flight to Europe from mid-August to mid-September, specifically for Columbia students, designed to get us back two days before fall registration. I'd never slept outside the United States, except for one night on the Canadian side of Niagara Falls, and was eager to explore the world. A European adventure seemed like the perfect transition between work and graduate school. My savings account was fatter now than it would be again for a long time. I asked everyone I knew if they wanted to come with me, but no one else had both time and money. So I decided to go alone. Americans were just beginning to visit Europe in large numbers in 1963, less than twenty years after the end of World War II. My only qualification for traveling alone to Europe was my conviction that if I could survive in New York City I could survive anywhere, a dangerously naïve, but typically New York, attitude.

I applied for a passport, bought French records, drank Italian wine, and studied Arthur Frommer's guidebook, *Europe on Five Dollars a Day*. I tried not to dwell on the realities that I had almost failed French, had no travel experience, and had had serious asthma since early childhood. Since I planned to move around a lot to visit different countries, it would have been wise to pack lightly. I didn't. In addition to my oversize backpack, I filled my largest, heaviest piece of luggage with, among other things, an oversize pair of hiking boots I thought I might wear once to trek in Switzerland.

The airline gave passengers the option of getting off at either London or Rome on our trip over and returned from Paris. Deplaning at London would have made good sense for an inexperienced monolingual traveler like me, but I chose Rome. I made no advance reservations, just assumed I would find a place when I arrived.

CHAPTER **19**

On My Own in Italy

ONLY A HANDFUL of us on the charter flight to Europe chose to fly on to Rome. At the London layover we were restricted to a corner of a drafty hanger where we sat around a table that tipped slightly to the right in front of two half-empty snack machines. I struck up conversation with the only other passenger close to my age. Barbara and I quickly learned that we lived within a block of each other, were both Columbia graduate students, and would be visiting Italy for the first time. We decided to explore Italy together for a few days.

Barbara and her family had come to the U.S. from Czechoslovakia when she was a teenager after they had fled their country in the middle of the night to escape the Communists. She had traveled widely in Western Europe and was now on her way to get married at her parents' home in Munich, Germany, where her father worked for Radio Free Europe. Her American fiancé, also a Columbia graduate student, would arrive in three weeks.

In the few days we were together Barbara taught me how to travel. She was savvy and bold. Her zest for life and openness to new experiences led us into adventures I never would have attempted on my own. When we exited Rome's air terminal the surge of Italians clamoring to rent us a room overwhelmed me, but Barbara quickly negotiated a price with a young boy. He led us through winding streets into a dark building and up in an ancient elevator to his family's apartment. There we were greeted warmly in Italian and shown into a small, clean bedroom. Barbara taught me that a continental breakfast with cappuccino was more substantial than one with a tiny cup of espresso. She explained that price-fixed meals were the best value, bottled water was essential, and that the bowl provided with our meal was to wash our fruit.

When we missed the last bus back from the catacombs to Rome, Barbara suggested we hitchhike. Our thumbs yielded an instant ride from an older man and a young woman about our age, who he referred to as "his niece Serena, who was visiting him for a few days." We called our driver "Uncle" and managed an animated conversation although they spoke little English and we had little Italian. They took us all the way back to our lodging, and when they dropped us off they told us they would pick us up at 9:00 the next morning for a picnic. We assumed we had misunderstood. Why would they take us on a picnic? But at 9:00 a.m. promptly they appeared at the door of our residence, ready to take us sightseeing and to a winery outside the city for a picnic. It was a delightful day. We always wondered who Uncle was. Barbara was sure from the places he took us that he must be a person of some importance.

From Rome Barbara and I moved together to Florence, where after a few days she prepared to go to her parents' home in Munich, Germany and I planned to travel toward Switzerland by way of Italy.

"Would you like to come to our wedding?" Barbara asked as we prepared to say good-by.

"Sure," I said, "I'd be honored." Germany had not been on my initial itinerary, but I was happy to go anywhere I hadn't been, especially for a wedding.

"Would you be willing to be my Maid of Honor if I need one?" she asked. "We have to have U.S. citizens sign our marriage license. Someone who works for my father has agreed to sign for my husband, but my parents haven't found anyone for me yet."

"Of course," I replied. "I'll definitely come, and if you need me, I'm happy to be your Maid of Honor."

"I'll be at your wedding," I promised as we waved goodbye.

Suddenly I was traveling on my own. I stood alone on the Track 2 platform of the Florence train station, still panting from carrying my backpack and heavy suitcase up the steep steps. My plan was to travel by train to Milan, then to Tirano on the Swiss border, where I wanted to stay a night or two to experience a small Italian town. From there I would go to Pontresina, Switzerland. In Switzerland I wanted to do some trekking and experience the mountains by traveling on post buses and narrow-gauge railroads. From Switzerland I planned to come back into Italy to Venice to attend the Venice Film Festival, where a film I was interested in was being screened.

The express train to Milan, for which I had a ticket, was due imminently. Suddenly the loudspeaker, the only indicator of which trains were going where, crackled into rapid, incomprehensible Italian. Travelers around me suddenly picked up their bags and hastened toward the stairs. I realized with a jolt how much I had depended on Barbara. She knew about European trains and had a rudimentary sense for Italian, even though she had never studied it. She would have known what to do. I had no clue. My suitcase sat like a heavy boulder beside me. There was no way I could carry it down and up another flight of stairs to a different platform in time to catch a train, even if I knew where to go. I stood paralyzed beside Track 2 as several trains clanged in and out.

Fear replaced anxiety as I realized that if I didn't get started to Milan soon, I would arrive in darkness and would miss my train to Tirano. That concern spurred me to action as the next train arrived. I pushed toward the conductor.

"Milano?" I asked.

"Si," he said, followed by a rush of Italian and a facial expression that looked like a warning.

But he let me on. I clambered up the steps, hoisting my case in front of me, and lurched with increasing alarm through two long second-class coaches full of men and no empty seats. I felt utterly alone. I had opted for second class because I wanted to travel with Europeans rather than rich Americans. But not on their laps. Out of breath from carrying my suitcase and desperate for a place to sit, I stopped, braced myself against the inside door of the next coach, and raised my eyes to see a car full of dark eyed men, all focused on me. Startled I slid my eyes to a corner of the dingy ceiling, remembering my recent days in Rome where Barbara and I had been the object of exhausting male interest. This narrow, grubby coach had no chic stores to duck into when the attention got too intense.

Suddenly a young man leaped up from a front seat and gestured for me to sit.

"Grazie," I breathed as I sank down, trying unsuccessfully to adjust my knees so they wouldn't bump the four male knees across from me. Calloused hands made space for my suitcase, the men crooning "Bella, Bella," as they caressed it and turned over its name tag for hints about me.

"Parla italiano? Parla inglese? Parla francese, Parla tedesco?" they asked.

I shrank. That's what all the men in Rome asked. I studied my traveling companions from under lowered lids. Their clothes were worn and patched. One man held up his pants with a strand of rope. They all seemed to know each other.

With a roar the car entered a tunnel. We were in total blackness, conversation overwhelmed by the train's hurtling noise. I sat rigidly coiled, waiting for the first hand on my thigh, my breast, or worse, every muscle tensed in anticipation of the first violation. Would anyone hear my scream in this obliterating roar? The tunnel seemed to cover the width of Italy while I waited with taut, cramping muscles. Then with a whoosh we were out, blinded by sunlight. Nothing had happened. We all blinked and smiled at each other.

My companions renewed efforts to communicate. First they brought me a match cover with an unintelligible note that resembled English. Their faces fell when I shook my head. They conferred briefly in rapid Italian. One disappeared down the car, then returned with a tall man in a blue plaid shirt. He approached me with confidence. "Parla inglese," the men exclaimed excitedly, pointing at him. When he spoke, the whole car grew silent, listening, looking at us expectantly. A breath of disappointment passed through the car when I shook my head again and he retreated.

After a couple more tries, an interpreter appeared who spoke a touch of both French and English and finally we began to talk. The whole car focused on us. Passengers gathered around, clutching the seat backs and each other for balance as the train jounced along the track. They fired questions in Italian to the interpreter. Little by little I came to understand that I was in the middle of a group of villagers from Sicily who were migrating to Milano to seek work. Pointing at their watches they showed me that they had been traveling two times around, a full day. I had become their guest, a stranger they wanted to make welcome.

When they found out I was from Manhattan a plump, short woman with a broad, open face and dark lively eyes struggled to her feet and careened down the aisle. She swayed in her neat print dress, one hand clutching my seat back, the other gesticulating wildly. She spoke excitedly as she held up two fingers. She had two sisters in Brooklyn, the translator explained. Did I know them? From memory she recited their names and spelled out their addresses, then waited, looking at me expectantly. I shook my head sadly, trying to figure out how to explain about Brooklyn and Manhattan.

The villagers whiled away the hours of our trip, on what turned out to be the most local of local trains, teaching me Italian. The teenage boy and girl traveling with their parents across the aisle, the only kids I saw in the group, gave me chewing gum and at lunchtime offered me vino. After getting animated instructions from their mother, they poured some from a special bottle into a cup, swished around some of the wine first to clean it, then with solemn smiles, presented it to me as if it were a sacred object. I took a sip while the whole car watched in one held breath.

"Buono," I exclaimed.

"Ah," they sighed and beamed.

In Milan, after learning there were no more trains to Tirano until the next morning, I deposited my large suitcase in a long-term luggage check, where it would stay until I returned to Milan from Switzerland and Venice, Italy. Buoyed by my lightened load and the Italian hospitality of my friends on the train, I set off with confidence to the hostelle e studenta at a nearby university. There I found a good dormitory room, a meal, and a pleasant group of international companions for the evening.

My Swiss excursion, which I had expected to be a highlight of my trip, had been disappointing. Although the scenery was impressive, and I enjoyed riding the narrow-gauge trains and postbuses through the mountains, the weather had been too rainy to walk much. That was just as well. I found myself panting for breath with the least exertion at the high altitude. With my asthma I never could have managed the Swiss version of trekking. Most disappointing, the Swiss chilly politeness left me feeling like a barely tolerated commodity. There were no student hostels permitted in Switzerland so there was no chance to meet other young travelers. The Swiss were known for their comfortable hotels, but they always seemed to put me, as a woman traveling alone, in some out of the way space, comfortable but isolated. I looked forward eagerly to the warmth and vibrancy of Italy as I boarded a train to Venice to attend the Venice Film Festival.

Hugh, with whom I still kept in touch, had invited me several months earlier to go with him to watch the filming of a segment of *The Cool World,* a film about street gangs based on a book of the same name by Warren Miller. It was filmed in an abandoned building in New York with actual street kids as actors. Hugh and I were both excited about the film. I thought it was a stunning way to do sociology. We had both invested in it, although I could only afford $100. The film had been accepted in the Venice Film Festival and I had been invited to its showing. Hugh had been invited too but had been unable to get to Venice. I promised I would tell him all about it.

It was almost dark as I walked from the train toward the vaporetti, the water taxi that would take me to Piazza San Marco. Venice did not immediately oblige my expectations of warmth and vibrancy. The sky hung low and dark. My sense of foreboding intensified as I sat in the vaporetti and watched the canal water lap at the steps of buildings along the canal and seep under the doors on lower floors of homes. Venice, built on a swamp, had been sinking for centuries. Even the floor of the restroom I used in Piazza San Marco was covered with water.

My student hostel guide listed only one place to stay in Venice and I had no idea how to find it. Its address was not on my map. In fact, nothing in the apparently random scrambling of narrow streets and maze of lanes, piazzas, and dead-end alleys seemed to be on my map. As I stood in Piazza San Marco under a dim light in the darkening street, I felt panic start to rise. How would I ever find my way to anywhere? I stopped the first person who came by and showed him the address. He looked at it, nodded, spoke in rapid Italian, and motioned me to follow him. When I hesitated, he motioned again insistently and took off rapidly through a warren of narrow dark passageways. I followed, stumbling in my effort to keep up, glad that my suitcase was still in left luggage in Milan. My trepidation rose. Where was he taking me? What were his intentions? By now we had wound through so many dimly lit byways I was sure I could never find my way back. He stopped in a small deserted piazza in front of a square gray stone structure that looked like a school or convent.

"Hostelle e studenta," he said motioning to the austere, closed-looking building.

My heart sank. This couldn't be it. There weren't any lights on.

"Hostelle e studenta?" I asked dubiously, pointing, hoping this was a mistake.

"Si, Si," he said and disappeared back into the black labyrinth of Venice.

I climbed the steep steps and rang the bell. After a long pause a tall stern woman opened the door and invited me in. No one else was in sight. Student hostels were usually teaming with life.

"Hostelle e studenta?" I asked fearing it was, afraid it wasn't.

"Si, si." The austere proprietor took my passport and required payment for a minimum of three nights. She made a special point, repeated several times, that I had to be in the hostel by 10:00 p.m. when it was closed and locked. She led me up a wide flight of worn stone stairs to a dimly lit large room with eight beds lined up against one wall and high windows on the other. No one else was there.

I went out for food, taking care not to get lost. I could feel my asthma, always with me but usually manageable, intensifying. My worst allergies were to molds. I could sense them, almost feel them on my skin, rising from the myriad waterways, dripping walls, and dank stones. My chest tightened, I gasped for breath. I had had serious asthma since I was a year old. It was a source of both disability and embarrassment. I tried to ignore it as much as possible, vowed I would not let it limit my life. When it got bad and I needed to cough to get the gunk out of my lungs, I tried to go off where I wouldn't bother people. In my college dorm I used to hide in the furnace room.

There were three other women in my room when I returned from dinner, but unlike most student houses, the atmosphere was subdued, with little conversation. I settled into my narrow bed early and tossed restlessly through the night. As I tried to smother my coughing in my hard, thin pillow I thought about Thomas Mann's *Death in Venice*.

When daylight finally filtered through the windows I pulled out the small supply of steroid pills my doctor had given me to use only when my asthma was very bad. I popped one hopefully, not caring at that moment about the long-term consequences of steroids. I counted the remaining pills carefully, worrying--there were so few and I had so many days of my trip left. After breakfast when I went out to explore, I discovered that in the morning sunlight Venice was beautiful and fascinating. I also learned that the Venice Film Festival, my reason for coming, was not actually in Venice, but in The Lido, a beach resort area reached by boat. My official letter of invitation said that *The Cool World* was showing at 6:00 p.m. and my ticket would be at the box office shortly before screening.

In late afternoon I sat exhausted on the edge of my cot in the austere student residence and pulled my best outfit from my backpack, a wash and wear blue skirt and sleeveless blouse. I tried to smooth out the wrinkles, but it was a hopeless proposition. Breathing was difficult. Why was I even trying to do this? They would probably forget to leave the ticket, and I wouldn't get to see the film's festival debut anyway.

But I went, extra early because I wasn't sure how long the boat would take. Breathing was easier as my water taxi drew closer to the Lido. The air felt fresher and drier. I picked up my ticket along with an invitation to a celebration dinner. I hadn't expected the dinner invitation. The film was powerful. It turned out to be the precursor of over 40 social documentaries made by Frederick Wiseman, all devoted to exploring American institutions. It was the beginning of his career as one of America's most illustrious film makers.

Fred Wiseman's wife, Zipporah, with the instincts of a true Jewish mother, took me under her wing as soon as she met me after the screening.

"Which hotel are you staying in?" she asked.

"A student hostel in Venice."

"Oh," she said looking slightly taken aback, "stay here with us. "We have an extra bed in the room where our son and au pair sleep. It's a shame to let it go to waste. It would be so much better."

I thanked her no and lied that the hostel was fine. I always hesitated to accept invitations. Like my mother I worried that people didn't really want me, that I'd be too much trouble, or that I couldn't pay my host back properly.

Our *Cool World* party gathered after the showing for cocktails in a luxurious lounge area. The crowd that flowed around us glittered with flowing chiffon strapless gowns, sparkling necklaces, tuxedos, and bee-hive hairdos. It was a world I'd never seen before, except in movies. I smoothed my travel-worn blue skirt and tried to hide my backpack under my chair. The Wisemans introduced me to everyone as one of their investors. The word investor garnered attention. It implied I had money and knew something about film. I suspected some of the men I talked with were well-known directors whom I should recognize. I tried not to say anything that would betray my ignorance. A gentleman in a tuxedo asked me several times if I would like to join him in the casino. I thanked him no and felt like an imposter.

The cocktail hour dragged on without signs of dinner preparation at the table set up beside us. Fred's wife kept insisting I stay the night with them. As the hands on my watch moved past nine o'clock without the appearance of food, I realized I could never make it back to the hostel before the doors were locked at ten. The next time she asked me to stay with them, I accepted her offer. She lit up with pleasure and told me to go get my things the next morning, come back to enjoy the beach, and stay the next night too.

That night, after a very late and lengthy dinner, I sank into the soft mattress, sniffed the sweet-smelling, clean sheets, and pulled up the air-light white comforter. My asthma began to recede a little. I felt safe and cared for and actually slept. The next day I accepted the Wisemans invitation to go get my things and stay a second night. The rest and clear sea air markedly improved my asthma. I doubt that the Wiseman's had any idea how much I needed and appreciated the haven they offered.

CHAPTER **20**

On Both Sides of the Berlin Wall

I RETURNED TO Milan, retrieved my big suitcase, and flew to London. There I again stowed it in long term storage and set off with my backpack to explore England by train. I stayed in student hostels in tiny towns, conversed with my English hosts about coal mining and race in the U.S., marveled at ancient houses by the sea built of slate, and drank strong tea for breakfast because there was no coffee. In London I went to plays, visited the British Museum, and stood staring at city blocks still filled with the rubble of war.

My travel became addictive. At group tables in small inexpensive restaurants papered with travel posters, in lines at American Express waiting for my mail, I listened to individuals who had been to places I hadn't yet seen.

"You have to go!" they insisted, describing quaint towns, strange rock formations, long white beaches, or the starkness of life in Eastern Europe behind the Iron Curtain.

The more I saw the more I wanted to see. The craving started somewhere around the solar plexus and moved up, infusing my body, my brain. I yearned for the places my fellow travelers described, began plotting to see if I could fit some of them into my rapidly shrinking number of touring days.

Still I kept open Barbara's wedding date. When I arrived in Munich I learned that I was indeed the Maid of Honor. Barbara's parents welcomed me as if I were a member of the family and took me shopping for an appropriate wedding outfit: a blue dress just the color of my eyes and high heeled, pointy toed, white satin shoes. It was wonderful to feel so elegant after wearing the same two outfits for a month.

In my brief exploration of Munich, I stumbled across a German memorial to its World War II soldiers. It was partially below ground, and I stood inside it for a long time. This was my first visit to a monument honoring the soldiers of the 'other side.' I thought at first how much harder it must be to lose a loved one in defeat rather than victory, then reconsidered. The pain was overwhelming regardless. We all lost in war.

Russell, the Best Man, was tall, handsome, and single. He worked for Radio Free Europe in Munich but was expecting to move to New York in a few months. Since neither of us knew many of the wedding guests, we spent a lot of time together during the reception and went out afterwards. He told me he'd get in touch when he moved to Manhattan. I hoped he would.

The morning after the wedding I caught a plane to West Berlin. When I'd been in the American Express office two days earlier, I'd met a traveler who had just returned from there and described his experience walking behind the Berlin wall in East Berlin. He said it had been a fascinating trip. I had just enough time left to go and bought my plane ticket on the spot. Going by train was not recommended because much of the trip was through East Germany, and there was some danger and often long delays.

Berlin, administered in four zones by the Soviet Union, Britain, France, and the U.S., was totally surrounded by Soviet-controlled East Germany. Berlin had been a flash point in the cold war for much of my life. In 1948-1949 the Russians stopped allowing the other three countries to access their sectors of Berlin by land through Eastern Germany. The West countered the move by starting the Berlin Airlift to keep supplies flowing into Berlin's Western zones. In 1958 Soviet President Khruschev demanded the complete termination of the British, French, and US occupation rights in Berlin which, of course, the Western powers would not allow. Tensions eventually rose so high that in July 1961 President Kennedy called 250,000 Army reservists to active duty. A month later, just two years before my visit, the communists began construction of the Berlin Wall. I wanted to get a sense of what it was like behind the wall, although I couldn't really experience or understand it because I was free to leave as residents were not.

Finding a place to stay in West Berlin took a while. The hotel clerks there were even more suspicious of me, as a woman traveling alone, than the clerks in the other countries I had visited in Europe. Once settled, I stowed my overlarge luggage and quickly located a tour bus that regularly took tourists through the Eastern sector of Berlin. I wanted to get my bearings before I walked through Checkpoint Charlie and entered East Berlin on my own. On the tour they, of course, visited the show spots of the city. There were many new buildings, rows of prefab apartment buildings, all identical. Some balconies had flowers. The guide pointed out numerous museums and theaters. But what I saw as I looked out the windows were the faces of the people on the street. I had the odd sense that there was just one face—closed, tense, drawn, watchful.

The next day, my first passage into Soviet controlled East Berlin alone and on foot, went easily enough. The entrance was through Checkpoint Charlie, a small white wooden building in the middle of a street, the only place at which foreigners visiting Berlin could cross from West to East and back again. My first view as I exited into the Soviet side was a wasteland of blocks of huge, war damaged museum-style buildings, barbed wire, and streets devoid of human life. The functioning city was several blocks in from this area.

When I explore a new city or village I try to get a sense of the pulse of the place by taking in the sights, sounds, and smells. In the West, even in small towns, there is usually a colorful bustle of people going about their business, laughing, chatting, buying and selling, complaining. It was hard to get the pulse of East Berlin, even though I walked for miles. There was a silence about it that was unnerving. The city felt stifled. Stores had some samples of goods like those you would find in the west, but there were few customers, who seemed to be just looking. Traffic was minimal. One of my most vivid images was of many men, all carrying what looked like identical briefcases, walking down a main avenue quickly, silently, and alone. I thought of the contrast with the buzz of Fifth Avenue in New York City.

I returned to East Berlin again the next day. On my second visit, as on my first, I had to resist the strong urge to turn back as I stepped into the Soviet sector and faced the blocks of barbed wire wasteland. I kept going forward because I wanted to see areas I had not visited to confirm or reshape my first impressions. What I saw on my second visit was much the same. Away from the tour bus route there was still a lot of war damage that had not been repaired. East Berlin looked like no city I had ever seen. The contrast between it and the busy, vibrant city on the other side of the wall was stark.

On my attempt to cross back across the border through Checkpoint Charlie into the West, the East German guards stopped me. The guard at the desk stood glaring and yelling at me in German with my passport held tight in his oversized fists. I had no idea what he was saying, what I had done wrong. My naïve and dangerous assumption that my American passport would protect me anywhere collapsed.

"They want you to show them your money," a person on a decrepit chair in the waiting room translated.

I pulled out and showed them the small amount of West German currency I had in my wallet, trying to act calm and not think about the other money I had on my person, what I believed to be East German black market cash, that I had picked up in West Berlin. Luckily I had not had the nerve to try to use it, but if the guards searched me they would probably find it. Could I be detained for carrying illegal currency across the border? I suspected the answer was yes. A little late, I comprehended the riskiness of what I had been doing. No one I knew had any idea I was even in Berlin, much less on the wrong side of the border.

There was a brief exchange between the two officers behind the desk. Then the one with my passport shouted at me again and slowly, reluctantly pushed my passport back across the table with a gesture of disgust and waved me through to the West. I stepped out onto the West Berlin Street a few minutes later shaken, wiser, and buoyed by its noise, activity, and freedom.

As I flew from Berlin toward Paris and the plane that would take me home to New York, I began to comprehend how many boundaries I had crossed, both national and personal. My European trip had changed me. I was less afraid to trust and to risk, though hopefully wiser about what risks I took. I was also more confident in my ability to cope, and more open to new ideas and experiences. I had passed through the Berlin Wall and seen the stark differences that repressive political systems could make in lives. Moving to New York had expanded my world; traveling in Europe had blown it wide open.

Part Four
Managing Challenges

CHAPTER 21

Law and Sociology Program

HEAD IN HAND, back just ten hours from Europe, I sat at the small kitchen table in my New York City apartment lethargically pushing raisin bran around in a blue bowl. This was my one-day hiatus between my former life of European travel and work at Vera and my new life as a Ph.D. student in Sociology and Law.

At exactly 9:00 a.m. the phone on my desk began to ring sharply, insistently. I considered not answering it. The energy it would take to walk the few steps from kitchen to living room to pick it up seemed more than I could muster. But it kept ringing, way beyond the time when a polite person would hang up. Desperate to stop it, I roused myself to answer.

"Is this Anne Rankin?" The annoyed, imperative male voice was unfamiliar.

"Yes," I answered tentatively.

"This is Professor Rahmer, Director of the Law and Sociology Fellowship at the law school. We've been trying to reach you for over a week. Where have you been?"

"Europe," I answered, trying to bring my voice to full volume, to sound as in charge as the caller did.

"You should have been back to register and start classes last week."

"I checked about registration before I left," I answered indignantly, now fully awake. "I was told registration started tomorrow."

"Not for first year students in the Law School," he spat out, saying all the words in capital letters. I wondered if he actually left drops of spittle on his receiver. "You need to be in the Freshman Legal Methods class. Now it's too late. It started. You have caused a big problem."

Nothing he said made any sense. I had received no word from the fellowship about coming back a week early for freshman law orientation, even though I had taken the initiative to try to get information. Yet clearly he was blaming me. I felt his ire deep in my solar plexus. Professor Rahmer continued to detail the problems I had created. I tried to resist the guilt he was laying on me, but try as I might, I felt it in my core, that twisting, vibrating pain of having done wrong, even when I knew in my head I hadn't.

"But we may have a solution," he said finally. "Maybe we can get you in the American Legal System seminar, our master's degree program for foreign lawyers."

"That sounds like a wonderful solution," I replied, trying to sound appropriately contrite and appreciative. A master's degree class beat freshman orientation any day.

"But you have to get a waiver," he continued in an ominous tone. "That may be difficult. You need to go right away to talk to the Chairman of the Rules Committee."

I hung up and started searching for clean clothes. An hour later I was sitting in the spacious, well-decorated office of the Chairman, a tall man with a head of white hair and a patrician nose, who was cordial, chivalrous even, until he heard my request for a waiver to take the foreign lawyer course.

"Impossible," he said sharply. "It has never been done. It is beyond my power. I'll have to talk to all the other Rules Committee members. I can't imagine they will agree."

"Why is it such a problem?"

"Unprecedented. Unprecedented," he repeated, "and it will be hard to get everyone together for a meeting anytime soon."

"But I can't make out the rest of my schedule until I know," I argued.

"Come back tomorrow," he said as he turned away and started to shuffle through papers on his desk.

Trying to stuff my annoyance, I headed to Professor Rahmer's office to give him the news. Professor Rahmer had a downturned mouth and piercing eyes. He invited me to sit down and go over the schedule he had worked out for me for my first fellowship year.

"You will take Civil Procedure both semesters, the Law and Society Seminar, the one-hour credit Freshman Writing Course, and hopefully we can get you into the foreign lawyer course. I don't know what we will do if we can't." He sighed, and I could feel his exasperation settling around me like toxic dust.

"I thought we and the sociology advisors would discuss together about what I'd take," I demurred. "Civil Procedure doesn't really connect with my interests as a sociologist. What about Criminal Law? And if I audit all these law courses how will I have room for sociology courses?"

"You need Civil Procedure. It's the basis of all law. You have to take it. And, of course, you'll be taking the law courses for credit," he said in a tone that breached no further discussion.

Taking the law courses for a grade could be a disaster. In sociology graduate school we were expected to keep our grades at B or better. Only the very best law students managed a B average, especially in first year classes. Besides, I had *never* liked anyone telling me what to do, had always, since my first year of high school, planned my own schedule. I had assumed the faculty would treat me as a professional, want to work with my interests and strengths. I pushed down an angry retort. This fellowship made it possible for me to go to school. Without it my life would be a big void. For the second time in just a couple hours I could feel my stomach clench.

After seeing Professor Rahmer, I headed to the Bureau of Applied Social Research to talk to one of my two sociology fellowship advisors. I had known them in my work at Vera and they had encouraged me to apply. Surely they were my allies and could mediate with Professor Rahmer.

I was wrong.

"Yes, we thought total immersion would be the best way to give you a feel for law school."

"It is embarrassing to give you credit for that American Legal Studies Seminar," the Chairman of the Rules Committee announced gruffly the next morning. "You are not foreign, not a lawyer. We've never done it before,"

"But what harm can it do?" I asked. "I'm in a new program that's also unprecedented."

"We'll see what the Rules Committee says," he said, turning back to his work.

Trying to tamp down my exasperation I walked to the elevator and pushed six to go check out the fellowship office to which Professor Rahmer had given me the key. It was probably a broom closet.

I opened the door to a palatial office similar to that of the Chairman of the Rules Committee, except less well furnished. The other Law and Sociology Fellow sat at one of the two facing mahogany desks looking a little bemused. The impressive nature of the office seemed in sharp contrast to the treatment I had received so far as a Fellow. My fellow-fellow Ken, a recent Columbia Law School graduate (who would be studying sociology) and I quickly ascertained that neither of us had received any information about what the fellowship entailed. We bonded in our ignorance and I sensed that he would be easy to work with. He was married so there would be no romantic complications, had a good sense of humor, and was eager to help orient me to law school.

"That freshman orientation is simple minded. Waste of time. You're lucky you missed it," Ken commented after he had given me a 20-minute summary of basic information about what I needed to know and do as I started my first class, including a strong admonition to read ahead so I wouldn't get behind.

For my first Civil Procedure Class on Saturday I rose quietly to avoid waking Lois, opened the small closet we shared and pulled out one of my two suits. The *Law Student's Guide* stressed appropriate dress. A suit on Saturday morning! Shit!

I drank my cup of instant espresso too fast and burned my mouth. My bagel was stale, there was less cream cheese left than I'd expected, and I didn't have time to stop at Chock full o'Nuts for a real breakfast. I slapped on red lipstick, tried to get my short page-boy hair style to turn under, and headed up Broadway at a fast walk. The classroom was a mahogany paneled, semi-circular lecture hall seating about 200 students. Soft black leather seats with wooden desks sloped down to a raised platform with a desk and a blackboard, surrounded by a railing that carried the same aura of hierarchy and power as a courtroom. I noticed a large seating chart on the wall and studied it carefully. It did not include my name.

"What if my name's not on the chart?" I asked a nearby student.

"Shouldn't happen. Everyone has a seat."

My stomach knotted. I'd hardly had a moment in all my dealings with the law school when it hadn't.

"But you can always sit in the back row if you're unprepared and don't want to be called on," he added. I slipped into the back row, wondering how I could get credit, much less a grade, if the professor didn't know I was there. All the seats on the chart had names on them. I suspected I would be sitting in the back row all semester. I wondered if I should ask but decided against it. I didn't have the courage to risk challenging another precedent. I looked around as the seats filled. There were only three other women in the crowd. Everyone was dressed more casually than I. That, at least, was good news. No more suits on Saturdays.

The professor appeared at exactly 9:00, settled into his seat on the dais, consulted his seating chart, and looked out over the classroom. There was a collective intake of breath in the second before he called out a name and began peppering a man in the fourth row with questions about the case we had been assigned. As the process of call and reply continued, it seemed to me the student responses were unnervingly good. I looked at the slightly underlined case in my own book and my blank notebook. I couldn't believe this was the first class. The students acted like they had been there for weeks, with books, notebooks, and cards full of scrawled handwriting. How could I do this? I had been afraid to speak up in my small graduate sociology classes. This was like a rolling freight train. Maybe being in the back row wouldn't be so bad after all.

I quickly realized as I began to study law that it was different from sociology. Sociologists were always looking for the bigger picture, how social context impacted a situation. In law we looked at the facts of a particular case and precedent, what previous decisions said about cases with similar, but slightly different facts. After a few days of reading cases I began to appreciate the legal perspective. Being forced to look only at facts, procedural rules, and previous decisions taught me the discipline of focus and attention to detail. In spite of myself I started to get interested in Civil Procedure.

A week after classes started, the Chairman of the Rules Committee told me, with great reluctance, that I could take the foreign lawyers' seminar. He reiterated sternly that this permission would never be granted again. I had already missed the first session when I walked into the seminar room. The eighteen men and two women gathered around the gleaming wooden table looked like a mini-United Nations. I sat down tentatively in an empty chair near the door. Professor Frankel at the head of the table appeared humorless and a little fierce.

"I am an American and a sociologist, an unprecedented member of this class, but I will never happen again," I announced, hoping to sound humorous.

Professor Frankel laughed, his face transformed into a welcoming smile, "You didn't need all that advocacy to get in," he said. "We're always glad to have another pretty woman." It was still the early 1960s and I accepted his intended compliment gratefully. It was the first nice thing anyone in the law school had said to me.

For five weeks in Europe I had been making the effort to understand and be understood by individuals who spoke languages other than English. The class felt like a continuation of my trip. I immediately felt at home. A few years after the class I took with him, Professor Frankel became a leading Federal judge and, after leaving the bench, he was a strong advocate for human rights. In our class, he argued that the law's dependence on precedent made it conservative. That was positive in promoting order, he said, but individual judges sometimes felt themselves bound by previous decisions that seemed inappropriate in a changing world. His commentary on the role of law in social change, as well as on the history of American law, was exactly what I wanted and needed as a context for my own study of law and sociology. I found myself actually speaking up and expressing opinions in his class, something I had never done freely in my previous graduate work.

"You have a good legal mind," Professor Frankel commented once with an approving nod after I'd made a point. I treasured his comment. It helped me through dark days in other parts of my legal studies, especially our fellowship seminar in Law and Sociology.

I'd been in law school about a month when I ran into Devon, whom I'd met a year and a half earlier in Riverside Park where I watched him reading the *New York Times* with his pipe upside down. We'd gone to the beach together then but hadn't found much to talk about and hadn't seen each other since, even though we lived only a block apart. Standing in the middle of the sidewalk on West End Avenue between West 107th and 108th Streets, however, we found lots to talk about. He was finishing his physics Ph.D. in June and busy on the final aspects of his thesis.

"It's supposed to be nice this weekend, would you like to go for a ride to see the leaves?" he asked as we were about to go our separate ways.

Our excursion went well. After a couple more dates I invited him to dinner one night when Lois was out. We'd finished dinner and Devon leaned against the refrigerator in my small, peach colored kitchen. I'd been physically attracted to him since I first saw him in the park, something about his blond hair, tall lanky body, lean sculpted face, and the way his side teeth protruded just a bit when he smiled. He had on that delightful grin when I took a step toward him and somehow we just melted together in a long kiss.

Soon Devon and I were spending most of our weekends together. We both liked theater and concerts and began to get together with our friends. We fell into a comfortable routine. I thought perhaps I had found the man for me. I didn't really notice that our conversation never went very deep. He didn't talk much about his family or friends and didn't express much emotion, except about dings on his sports car. I had little time to focus on anything outside of school and the security of having a steady relationship helped alleviate the ongoing distress I experienced in the law and sociology fellowship.

Neither my fellow-fellow Ken nor I could figure out what was expected of us in the seminar, but it was clear that whatever it was, we were doing it wrong. We were the only two students in the class. The other participants included our two law advisors and two sociology advisors, plus several others whose connection to the program we never quite figured out. Ken and I had thought the goal of the seminar, in fact our entire program, was to help lawyers and sociologists engage together teaching and doing research in the new law and society specialty. We expected we would be learning how to talk each other's professional language and explore ways in which our different perspectives would enrich our collaboration in shared research. Yet there was no attempt in the seminar to actively engage us, a lawyer and a sociologist, in that process. We were expected to listen to the others talk. Ken and I were never asked our opinion. No one seemed interested in hearing us discuss our respective experiences of being a sociologist in law classes or a lawyer in sociology classes.

Even halfway through the first semester Ken and I were still puzzled about what we were supposed to do beyond providing detailed minutes of each seminar session. We both took notes, spent hours together searching for main themes, then alternated the final write up to be reviewed by one of the seminar advisors and copied for distribution in the next class. Neither of us felt good about the notes. The discussions in the seminar zinged wildly from topic to topic in ways we both found hard to follow. Sometimes members seemed to talk, just for the sake of talking, without logical connection to what had just gone before. If we tried to clarify a statement or line of dialogue, we were usually ignored or lectured. Our feelings of stupidity and incompetence intensified week by week. Faculty grumbling about the inadequacy of our minutes increased too and finally erupted.

"Why these notes are so inaccurate it would take me all morning to correct them," one of the professors announced as he threw them on his desk after glancing at what I had just handed him. "You two obviously don't understand what's going on in the class."

Three days later Professor Rahmer, visibly vibrating with anger, stared at Ken and me as we sat in the middle of the long conference table like two prisoners in an interrogation.

"Look around this table at all the faculty time and talent that is being poured into your education," he raged, "And you are ungrateful, don't appreciate any of it."

The accusation stung. We'd both been working hard and had tried our best. I felt stupid, humiliated, but angry too. Why was the onus all put on us? Did they, as teachers, bear any responsibility for helping us understand? The stomach pains I'd started having soon after I entered law school grew more frequent. They were hard to describe, sometimes like clenches in my middle, other times like indigestion. I worried that something was wrong, that I needed to see a doctor, but there was never time.

I drifted around the school, feeling like an outsider everywhere I went except, ironically, in the foreign lawyer seminar, where I technically *was* an outsider. My Vera identity, as a person valued for my skills and insights, was stripped away bit by bit. I had no new identity except outsider. In my desperate attempt to be somebody I occasionally caught myself telling an individual I had just met that I had been engaged in a groundbreaking legal research project in my former job.

I hated myself for trying to trade on who I'd been, rather than adjusting to who I now was. Even if I remained invisible on the back bench, I worked hard to be a good law student,.

Law school left me little time to work on the law review article I was still trying to finish for Vera about the impact of pretrial detention on the final outcome of a defendant's case. The analysis was complicated, more difficult than any I had done before, and its intricacies were hard to explain in language that made sense to lawyers. The law review's final deadline was in the middle of January, just before my Civil Procedure exam. In early December when I handed my latest version to Herb it didn't feel good enough. Herb agreed and returned it promptly for more work. I couldn't imagine how I could finish the article and take all my final exams in the same week. In the midst of this angst, Rahmer suddenly decided that Ken and I should do a major seminar paper for the fall semester, which would end in just a few weeks. For the first time my sociology advisor, who knew about my Vera article, took a strong stand on my behalf.

"Anne should finish her article for the *New York University Law Review* on the impact of failure to make bail on final case disposition as one of her major papers for the seminar," he announced in a no-nonsense tone of voice. "It's an important piece of work and the Fellowship is best served by giving her the time and the help she needs to make it as professional as possible."

Professor Rahmer agreed. My sociology advisor put me in contact with a person at the Bureau of Applied Social Research who could help with the analysis so I could get the article right, and Herb finagled a deadline extension at the law review. Herb also realized that we needed a well-known lawyer to explain and give legal significance to the statistical analysis I was doing. Patricia Wald, a distinguished lawyer and member of Vera's Board, agreed to write a Foreword to the article explaining its legal implications. The two pieces would appear together but as two separate single-authored pieces. Herb had found a way to keep his promise of single authorship for me, while also assuring, through Patricia Wald's Foreword, that the article would get the legal legitimacy and attention we wanted it to have.

Second semester started off well. My fellow-fellow Ken assured me that the grade I got in my first semester Civil Procedure exam, which I was sure I had flunked, was acceptable, and I actually earned a B plus in the foreign lawyer seminar. The law review article I was doing with Vera was finally moving toward completion. Professor Rahmer had relented on the second semester schedule he had originally laid out for me and said I could take Criminal Law, instead of the second Civil Procedure course, as well as two sociology courses. Criminal Law was exciting. I got so involved in doing a law memorandum in the first two weeks that I momentarily wanted to be a lawyer. Then I remembered all the other courses I would have to take, like civil procedure, taxation, and trusts and estates. It seemed wise to stick with sociology.

My two sociology courses in second semester should have mitigated the stress of the law and sociology seminar, but they didn't. Ken and I continued to feel like vassals in a fiefdom. Our sense that we were incompetent ingrates was reinforced in almost every meeting of the seminar. The feeling that we couldn't do anything right was hard to shake off, even when we were in other environments. My stomach pains persisted. There seemed to be no way to deal with the seminar problem. No recourse. No avenues for expression of our suggestions or concerns. No way out except exit. I'd never been in a situation like that before, although I understood that many individuals lived within such circumstances all their lives. In that respect it was a lesson in empathy.

Could I manage the fellowship's second year? Apart from the seminar, my law school classes had been invaluable both intellectually and for my education in law and sociology. I enjoyed them. But would a second year be worth the physical and psychological cost? Given my desire for a Ph.D. did I have a choice? I had counted on the two-year fellowship for support through most of my Ph.D. coursework and one of my required language exams. What other job could provide that level of income and leave enough free time for school? Bad memories of rejections in my job search before coming to New York weighed heavily. I had been lucky in the end, but that kind of luck didn't happen often.

I never said the word "quit" out loud. I was not a quitter, was willing to work hard for goals that mattered. I tried to convince myself that I could not afford to even entertain the idea of quitting. Still, it hovered in the back of my mind.

Then suddenly one day, without warning, it landed.

"You know I'm about ready to quit," I told Ken in exasperation as we sat across from each other agonizing over how to handle the most recent fellowship seminar furor.

"I've been feeling that way too. Let's do it," Ken responded without a second of hesitation.

And we did.

On March 6, 1964, in an era when men in gray flannel suits, and almost everybody else, were expected to do what their bosses told them, Ken and I defied that precedent. We each wrote a resignation letter informing the program that we would leave in May, at the end of the first year, and not continue into the second year. To our amazement, after all the complaints they had made about our work, the faculty members expressed surprise and dismay at our desire to leave and asked us to reconsider.

It was too late. I was already giddy with the prospect of freedom. Even if the cost was taking longer to finish school.

CHAPTER 22

Summer of Changes

MR. FARMER, OWNER of the brownstone in which Lois and I lived, arrived home one early April day just in time to see Lois' piano swing out through our large fifth-floor window and balance precariously over the balcony. Normally a quiet, pleasant man, Mr. Farmer went apoplectic, gesticulating wildly.

"Stop. Stop. You cause structural damage."

His pleas did not deter the movers, although his agitated commentary in an Eastern European language that nobody seemed to recognize, accompanied the piano in a rumble as it inched down the front of the building, swaying slightly. With a final sigh of pulleys, the piano reached the street and was hoisted into the truck emblazoned in large gold letters 'We Move Pianos'.

After two and a half years of sharing an apartment Lois and I had decided that, although we remained close friends, we each wanted our own space. The doubling of my rent, just a month after I'd resigned from my fellowship and given up the income I'd been counting on for the next year, was scary and a little like the piano going over the balcony edge.

I spent a couple weeks half-heartedly looking for a cheaper place, but everything I saw was more expensive and not as nice as the apartment I loved. Having my own place seemed like the next step in becoming fully adult, especially since my parents had sold our house in Pennsylvania where I'd grown up and were building a new home in

Florida. The last time I had been in Meadville they were getting ready to move and had asked me to go through everything I had in the attic.

"Sort out what you want to save," Dad said, "and we'll send it with our things to Florida. Just remember that long distance moving is expensive. Be sure you want to keep it."

I settled cross-legged on the unfinished attic floor under a bare light bulb, surrounded by boxes. 'Sure I want to keep it'? How could I gauge the future value of high school annuals, diaries, photo albums, old clothes, and other connections to my past? If I tossed some memento that seemed insignificant now would I be sorry later? In a moment of radical decision, I committed to throwing out possessions aggressively in a ritual of leave taking, of putting childhood and my parental home behind me. Now I would be *visiting* my parents but going *home* to 303 West 106 Street in New York, where I'd lived for nearly three years. Home. A constant in my life. Somehow I would find a way to cover the rent.

With Lois's piano out, the narrow living room seemed enormous. I planted yellow and gold marigolds and red petunias on the half circle front balcony. In the bedroom I tied together the legs of the two narrow single beds to make one wide one, then made it up with double sheets. As I rearranged furniture, searched for just the right fabric for new drapes, and put up different pictures, I nestled in to create a space that expressed who I was, that supported me as I moved through the activities of my day. Crazy as it seemed, I held on to the idea that I might get married there someday in front of the fireplace.

Having my own space softened my life, gave me more freedom. I started studying more at home. Tucking into my overstuffed chair to read an assignment seemed less like work than sitting surrounded by driven students in the law school library. At home I felt like a free, competent person, an antidote against the ongoing sense of oppression in the law and sociology fellowship, which would remain a part of life until the end of spring semester when our resignations took effect. I tried not to think about what would happen when the fellowship money ran out then too. Herb had offered me a summer job at Vera, so I was okay until September, but what then?

In keeping with our old party tradition, Lois organized a new-apartment-painting party shortly after she moved into her new studio apartment and invited everyone she knew and all their friends. I was assigned to paint a tall front window frame with Al, an engineer who maintained hospital equipment, whom Lois had just met and invited on the spur of the moment.

We crouched together companionably in the oversized window, trying not to kick over the paint can or drop splashes of linen white paint on each other as he took the high parts and I took the low ones. We worked carefully, watching the rain outside and occasionally swapping bits of information about ourselves. After we'd finished, we exchanged phone numbers in the usual New York singles ritual. It was one of those simple acts, insignificant in itself, like the flap of a butterfly's wing, a chance moment in a chain of apparently unconnected events that would eventually shape my life.

When I first settled into my own apartment, I hoped that Devon, who I had been seeing since the previous October, would spend more time with me there. That didn't seem to be happening. Devon was working hard to finish a long list of Ph.D. degree requirements before he graduated in June. He was also looking for jobs. There were none available in New York, but he was considering one in Boston. We never talked about the fact that he would be moving somewhere else and what impact that might have on our relationship. The total lack of communication on this topic seemed odd to me, especially since we had spent so much time together over the past year. Did Devon even think about this? It was on my mind all the time. Would he want to try to keep our relationship going?

I caught myself putting my future life on hold in case he might want me to move somewhere with him. Two times before I had let the direction of my life be influenced by my interest in a man: when I changed plans to stay in Chicago and enrolled in Northwestern, and when I'd decided to move to New York because of Eli. Now I found myself considering doing it again. I hardly dared articulate this idea, even to myself. It was inconsistent with my declared independence and commitment to a career, especially now when my career was solidly based in New York City. What was I thinking? I knew what I was thinking. I was 26, and I thought Devon and I had developed a good relationship over the past several months. I had hoped we might have a future together.

Our time with each other became increasingly unsatisfactory and less frequent. We spent most of it rehashing old, well-chewed arguments. "We're both stubborn," he had always said when we disagreed, but stubborn didn't seem like the right word to me. I was beginning to see that we had different approaches to life. As far as I could see, Devon had never evidenced any deep abiding centers of passionate concern, even about physics, that drove his life or were intrinsic to who he was. I couldn't conceive of just going along, living from day to day without getting excited about something that mattered. Maybe he didn't feel strongly about anything, including me. It was time for me to start looking for jobs in New York.

I quickly discovered Columbia's Employment Center and signed up. This was a resource I had not had when I had been job hunting before moving to New York. I also realized as I filled out the registration form that I now had two years of work and a year more of graduate school since my last job search. Maybe I could actually get a job. Almost immediately a job teaching criminology and first year social science at Brooklyn College was advertised. I met the qualifications, applied, and got the job, sealing my commitment to stay in New York.

Devon took the job offer in Boston and it became clear that our relationship was going nowhere. He brought back a few possessions I'd left in his apartment, the most final of final actions in an ending relationship. Our parting was awkward and impersonal, almost a denial that we had ever been together. Afterwards, deeply hurt, I threw myself on my recently constructed double bed and sobbed. Once again I was back to zero in my search for a partner. Would I ever find a home and family? Was a feeling of warmth and companionship impossible to sustain between two people? Did I really want too much?

I had promised myself after I had stopped dating Hugh that if I had one more love affair that ended unhappily, I would find a therapist. I had failed to honor that promise the previous spring when Frank had ended our relationship because I wanted to travel to Europe. There were no excuses now. I wasn't going anywhere. I had a full-time job for fall so should be able to pay rent and take a class or two at Columbia and still have some money for a psychologist. One of my friends had just started seeing one and had gone through a family service agency that had a sliding fee scale.

Even after I got the phone number of the agency from my friend, I didn't call right away. All my carefully protected self-reliance screamed no. I didn't need help. I was doing fine. But I wasn't. I was stalled. Everyone I knew from school was married. I didn't get wedding invitations anymore. Just baby announcements. I'd made a pact with myself and prided myself on keeping my promises. It took two attempts for my trembling fingers to correctly dial the number of the family service agency my friend had given me.

On a bright day in June, a week after I'd spent a morning taking personality tests and talking to an intake officer about why I wanted to see a therapist, I walked from my apartment to my new psychologist's office in one of the elegant old buildings that lined Riverside Drive. With trepidation I entered the door with a brass nameplate labeled 'Dr. Bryan, Please Come In', and sat down in the foyer-size waiting room. A few minutes later a man of slight build, with a lined pleasant face opened the door.

"Hello," he said. "You must be Anne Rankin. I'm Dr. Bryan. Please come in."

He led me into a high-ceilinged room with a multitude of plants and windows looking out toward Riverside Park and the Hudson River and motioned me to a comfortable chair across from his desk. So far so good. Behind me was a couch, which I eyed with concern.

I didn't want to be a caricature, down on a couch, like in all the *New Yorker* cartoons. I wanted to be upright, person-to-person, like equals. That must be for other patients, I thought, who need serious analysis.

What would happen to me here, I wondered. Could talking make any difference? I gazed at Dr. Bryan as he began to ask questions, clarify what we would be doing.

"What do you want to get out of our time together," he asked.

"I'm pretty healthy," I told him. "Just need help in finding someone to marry."

How could I trivialize it like that I wondered as I heard the words coming out of my mouth. 'Just,' I'd said, as if it were nothing, when in fact it was the biggest problem in my life. Would he discount my concern the way I had just done? I looked over at Dr. Bryan. He seemed attentive, interested. His voice was calm. I felt comfortable with him. Until. Until he said that when I came next time he'd like me to lie on the couch and talk from there. I did not want to lie down on that couch. It was too unequal. Left me out of control.

"I'm not here for psychoanalysis," I said, shaking my head. "Just for therapy. I shouldn't need a couch."

It seemed very important to me to make that distinction. I wasn't a couch-type of patient. Wasn't that bad off.

"Most of my clients find it's much better," he said in his quiet voice. "It's more comfortable, allows them to think back and remember more easily. Let's just try it next time, see how it works."

"Okay," I agreed reluctantly. "I'll try."

I wanted to be a good patient. And I did pride myself on being willing to try things. Two days later, at my second visit, I approached the maroon couch slowly, eyed it nervously, ran my hand over the smooth cover. Great couch for a therapist, I thought, easy to wipe up tears. I sat down gingerly, pulled one foot up first, then the other, leaned back, felt its support, and settled in. By the end of the hour I discovered that I liked not having to look at someone when I talked.

The therapy process, coupled with my recent breakup with Devon and the difficult year I'd just completed in law school, left me

emotionally hypersensitive. Even though Dr. Bryan was very supportive, the remembering, thinking, and talking under his gentle questioning brought up issues, insecurities, and fears that I generally tried
to ignore. I had held on tight, maintained control for a long time.
When I allowed myself to let down, as I lay on that couch, emotions
and fears tumbled out in a deluge.

"It would be nice," I said, "if I could stop worrying about getting married. Just quit. Stop trying. Never go to any parties again.
But I can't." Dr. Bryan listened without speaking, but I could feel his
attentiveness.

"Have you had a happy childhood, Anne?" I remembered my
mother asking me once out of the blue as we sat chatting. "Mine
wasn't and I tried so hard to make yours different. Has yours been
happy?" There was a pleading in her blue eyes that I didn't want to
see. How could she ask such a question? How could I answer? I
remembered good times, had always been loved and cared for. But
I also remembered the loneliness, the imaginary playmate Dodo I
created for company, how hard I tried to cheer up my mother when
she was feeling down and my ongoing failure to do so. What was a
happy childhood? I wasn't sure but knew there was only one answer
I could give.

"Yes," I said, "a happy childhood."

Now I was giving full attention to that childhood.

The summer of 1964 was unusually hot and humid and my top
floor apartment sweltered. I spent most of my free hours during June
and July lying in my shorty pajamas on my blue couch, curtains
drawn in a futile attempt to keep out the stifling heat, reading poetry,
listening to tragic operas, and sobbing over myriad long-buried hurts
and losses. The release felt good. One day I suddenly realized that I
had had no stomach pains since – well, actually, since I'd left the law
school. I'd done the right thing when I resigned. The nagging guilt I'd
felt about bailing out of the fellowship program fell away.

Through everything I wrote my usual cheery letters home to my parents, a skate across the surface of my life, to assure them I was happy and counter my mother's expressed fears that my therapist would think she wrote too many letters to me. We both wrote every couple of weeks, which seemed about right to me, but I knew my mother worried that Dr. Bryan would conclude that whatever problems I had were her fault. She personalized everything.

Most therapists in Manhattan went on vacation in August and we who spent hours pouring out our lives to them suddenly had extra money and time to think about something besides our psyches. I'd been trying to understand myself for six weeks and was ready for a break. It was the perfect time for a new man to appear, in the good-looking form of Russell. Russell had been Best Man when I was Maid of Honor at my traveling friend Barbara's wedding in Munich the previous summer. We had spent time together in Munich and he had told me then that he would be moving to New York to take a new position. He had arrived. I was delighted to hear from him. He was as tall and handsome as I remembered, with a classic Marlboro Man look relieved by a wide, goofy grin. He liked to do simple things like I did. Initially I was smitten and we seemed to enjoy each other's company.

"He's over 40 and a confirmed bachelor," my friend Barbara warned me, "don't get your hopes up."

One night he invited me to go down to the docks on the Hudson River to watch the S.S. France sail. Commissioned in 1962, just two years earlier, the S.S. France was then the longest passenger ship ever built. It sailed at midnight with several other large liners following at five-minute intervals behind it. The docks bustled with excitement as baggage carts, liner employees, and well-dressed voyagers and friends all jostled together on the long dock made brighter than day by a thousand lights twinkling and re-twinkling in the water. The famous ship and Manhattan each rose radiant against the sky. The longest and the biggest. Tugboats scuttled back and forth whistling insistently. The horns of the great ships moaned till the sound vibrated in the bottom of my stomach.

As soon as The S. S. France set sail, we jumped into Russell's red sports car and drove down to the Battery to watch it come slowly down the Hudson River toward us. It was breathtaking with lights flashing and giant red and black smokestacks emitting wafts of white steam that floated against the dark night sky.

The night had the potential for romance and I hated to admit to myself that the spark wasn't there. Although Russell and I had initially enjoyed each other's company, over time we had found ourselves struggling to find topics for conversation. Seeing the big ships sail had been a special experience, but there was little zest or excitement between us. By early fall, we had drifted apart, although we remained friends.

The best part of the summer actually came at the beginning of September when I started my new job teaching sociology at Brooklyn College. I set the clock for 5:00 a.m. to make sure I had enough time to get organized and take the hour and a half subway ride to the last station in Brooklyn for my 8:00 a.m. class. After a quick breakfast I took out the hair rollers I'd slept on all night, put on my favorite suit, the blue, red, and pink tweed one with the straight skirt, pulled on my panty hose, and slipped my feet into low-heeled black pumps. Into my oversized purse I stuffed my packed lunch, books, and notes. A brief case might have worked better, but it seemed too masculine.

An early fall drizzle coated the streets as I walked toward the subway station. The smell of rain rising in a mist from the pavement reminded me of earlier fall days as a kid, when I'd bounded across the field between my house and school at the first peal of the school bell. Fall had always been the time of new beginnings for me. Going to school as a teacher instead of a student was a huge new beginning, almost like starting first grade.

As soon as I faced the room of twenty students and started class I knew that I loved teaching and that I could do it. It was more stimulating and satisfying than any other work I'd ever done. The students looked interested when I talked. They asked good questions.

My undergraduate career counselor had been right. College teaching was the career for me. I had been afraid to give up my fellowship and take a job that might slow down my graduate work, but teaching had just the opposite effect. The knowledge that it was absolutely what I wanted to do with my life motivated me to finish my Ph.D. like nothing else had. It would keep me going through foreign language exams and all the other hurdles I had to jump over. My early morning teaching schedule helped too. It gave me afternoons free for classes at Columbia and time to study French for my first language exam.

Once I got comfortable with my job and my new Columbia classes, all sociology now, I started a new 'meet men' campaign.

CHAPTER **23**

Bursts of Understanding

I STARTED MY new social campaign in mid-October at the 4:00 p.m. Friday tea provided by the Faculty Wives' Club in the old high-windowed, graduate student lounge in Columbia's Philosophy Hall. Two well-dressed ladies in white gloves, presumably wives of faculty members, poured hot tea into china cups as we stood in line beside the carved table covered with an embroidered cloth. While we waited our turn, we tried to scarf up as many little cookies as we could without being too noticeable. There were usually more women than men taking tea, but that Friday I met an attractive male Ph.D. student in philosophy who didn't stay long but took my phone number before he left.

The next evening, Saturday, I went to a party given by Al, with whom I had exchanged phone numbers after we had painted my ex-roommate Lois's front window frame together at her recent apartment-warming event. At Al's party I slipped from room to room hoping to see at least one familiar face. Parties where I didn't know anyone were especially hard. I got tired of trying to be vivacious and charming, trying to meet men. No not just men. The right man.

Someone put on a Beatles record. The Beatles had recently taken America by storm. Their strong rock and roll beat replaced Dean Martin's crooning of "Everybody Loves Somebody," a song that intensified my feeling of loneliness.

"Where's the bathroom," a man in a striped shirt asked me.

I shrugged.

"You in the group ski house with Al?" he asked.

"No. Is that where everyone's from?"

"Yeah, and some from Fire Island."

As we drifted apart I contemplated the idea of a group house in a ski area or on the beach. Sounded interesting.

The party was like most parties I'd been to, dark, loud, crowded. The Greenwich Village apartment was cool, but it still held just another party. My mind drifted to what it would feel like to not have to attend these parties anymore. I'd be at home with someone I loved, reading or working side-by-side, or snuggling and making love. Or even going together to a party, where I could drift off to talk to friends, secure in the knowledge that my love was there, to whom I could always return to share a squeezed hand or an appreciative glance. But I couldn't let myself think ahead to a successful future. I had to make my future, start over again, keep starting over. I moved away from the pounding sound of the Beatles, spotted a man by himself, leaning against the wall as if he had a backache. I liked the way he looked, big dark-rimmed glasses, thick dark hair, bushy eyebrows, and a bit of a cleft chin.

"Hi, I'm Anne Rankin," I said, sticking out my hand. "Who are you?"

"Barry Mahoney," he said with a wide grin, taking my hand in his warm, firm grasp.

"How do you know Al?"

"From Fire Island."

"So what's a group house?"

"A group of people who get together and rent a house for the season. They divide the rental price by the number of beds. Everyone gets a share and can go every weekend. Some people split their shares so they only go half the weekends."

"Sounds like fun."

"Yeah, it's a good way to ski in the winter and get to the beach in the summer. What do you do?"

I told him about Vera, graduate school, and Brooklyn College. Barry had actually heard of Vera. He was a lawyer and worked for the New York Attorney General's office. He got excited when I told him about our recently published *NYU Law Review* article, the one I had finally finished after so many months, that argued that pretrial detention increased a defendant's chances of conviction and prison after trial.

"Whew. That's important. Can you send me a copy right away," he asked, rummaging in his pockets for a pencil and paper to jot down his work address.

He was the first person I'd talked to outside of Vera who understood how important our findings were. Barry was a good listener and kept asking questions about everything I was doing. His work was interesting. At the moment he was working on a U.S. Supreme Court case that he thought was really important. It seemed like he wanted to make a positive difference in the world like I did. As he leaned against the wall, I wondered if he really did have a bad back. I couldn't figure out what it was about the way he stood that made me think that. I didn't want a guy with a bad back.

"I'd like to see you again," he said as he took down my phone number. "I'll call you."

I was interested, but doubtful about him. With a name like Mahoney he was probably Catholic, and I didn't want to marry a Catholic. I might marry someone Jewish or Black, but not Catholic. I didn't want anyone telling me I couldn't use birth control or how to raise my kids. Besides he was a lawyer. I didn't want to marry a lawyer. They worked all the time. I wanted someone who could balance work and life. Not a good prospect I decided.

Barry called two days later, asked me out to dinner, and came upstairs to my apartment afterwards. We talked all evening and discovered that neither of us wanted to live in the suburbs, we were both Democrats from strongly Democratic families, and wanted interesting work more than a lot of money. I told him about my Dad's heart attack right after I'd graduated from college, that he'd retired a year ago and my parents had moved to Florida where they owned an orange grove with my dad's brother and seemed happier than I'd ever seen them. He told me he was a New Yorker from Queens, had gone to Bryant High School, which he loved, then on to Dartmouth and Harvard Law School. His parents had moved too since he'd left home, from Jackson Heights where he'd grown up, to the suburbs. Like me he'd never really felt at home in the new place.

"You're great. I've never met a woman like you before," he said and kissed me enthusiastically.

I'd had a pattern of choosing men who held back emotionally, barely gave me compliments, and always left me feeling like I didn't measure up to what they wanted in a woman. Barry's open and enthusiastic appreciation scared me. The only way I could think of describing him was boring, but I couldn't put my finger on why.

Two days later the philosopher I'd met at the graduate student tea invited me to dinner and we ended up in my kitchen in a laughter-filled evening making ratatouille, which I'd never tasted before. He seemed dashing and exciting.

Barry called the next weekend to ask if I wanted to go to the Penn-Dartmouth football game and a related gala event with a reception in the Philadelphia Art Museum. I'd had no experience with the Ivy League social life that revolved around football games long after college was over and said I was busy. The next time Barry called, the philosopher had just asked me out for a second time, so I told Barry I'd started seeing someone else.

"I'm disappointed. I really like you as a person. If we can't date I'd like to be friends. Maybe we can have dinner once in a while, some evening when I'm at the Columbia law library doing research on one of my cases."

Friends! I'd been single in Manhattan for three and a half years and no man had ever expressed interest in me as a friend after I'd rejected him for a date. How could I possibly say no to that? I said okay, but still felt uncomfortable about his liking me and hoped he would never actually call. At my next therapy appointment, as I was running through my man-meeting program of the past several weeks, I summarized my experience with Barry quickly.

"He's a person I should like, but he's Catholic and a lawyer and boring. I've told him I won't see him again."

"What does he do that makes you think he's boring?" asked Dr. Bryan.

"He really likes me a lot, but he's not very interesting."

"What makes you think he is uninteresting?"

"I don't know. My mother always doted on me and I don't want that feeling of obligation. He's just not my type.

The probing questions kept coming in Dr. Bryan's calm voice. My annoyance mounted as I realized that my hour, *my hour, the hour I paid for,* was being given over to a discussion of a man I had already eliminated from consideration. Maybe I should get a different therapist.

"For some people there are many possible mates and finding the right person isn't so difficult," Dr. Bryan commented toward the end of the hour. "For others whose interests are more unusual, like you, the pool is smaller. You have to look harder and further. It takes longer."

"What do you mean 'unusual'? Hopeless?" I asked defensively.

"Oh no, just that there are fewer men you would consider good possibilities. You're independent and career oriented and you want a man who supports that. You don't just want a marriage you want a deep partnership."

"Yeah, that's it."

"Your search may take a little longer, and it's important to stay open minded. Don't be too quick to dismiss a man based on external characteristics. Give him a chance, take a little time to get to know him."

Annoyed as I was at his focus on Barry, I felt overwhelming relief at his final observations. My search was taking longer because I was looking for someone unusual. Because I was a bit unusual. I didn't need to settle like my mother intimated I should. I just had to keep looking. It was *okay* for me to want more.

My romance with the philosopher fizzled out on the next date. I surmised that he was married and lost all interest. Two prospects found, considered, and rejected. It was time to start over again. How many more times could I do this?

Dr. Bryan and I talked week after week, month after month. The light coming in through his big windows shifted its pale patterns across the wall as winter came and receded. Twice a week I plopped down eagerly on the once-dreaded couch. I never left tears on its smooth easy-wipe surface, but memories spilled out in a continuous flow. I regaled him especially with stories about my life in my yellow frame house in Linesville, Pennsylvania where I lived until I was twelve.

Both my mother and father thought outside the box in that age of conformity and small-town conservatism. They each gave me a legacy of freedom. The Rankins prided themselves on being independent thinkers. My father helped me understand that it was good to be a little different, that I didn't have to feel guilty about thinking in ways people around me did not. My mother minimized feelings of guilt about my body. In an era when most kids were told that babies came in the doctor's black bag, she gave me the real story about where babies came from, with a chance to ask questions. The time she found me in the living room in front of the fireplace on my back with my legs up in the air and my hand between my legs demonstrating to my six-year-old friend Sally about the 'good feeling spot,' she didn't lose her cool or get angry. "That's something we do in private," she'd said matter-of-factly, "and let others discover on their own." She must have worried about what Sally would tell her mother, whom even I could see was uptight, but she didn't show it. I brought my legs down, turned over, and Sally and I moved on to other activities. I didn't think Sally got what I was talking about anyway.

Though I felt close to both parents I appreciated, and eventually emulated, my father's worldview and independent spirit. Though he was quiet, I counted on him for solid, caring, unwavering support. I rarely talked about him to my friends or Dr. Bryan. The relationship seemed unproblematic, constant. Simply there.

It was my mother I railed against in life and in therapy. In spite of her modernity, her many strengths, I realized early that she and I took different stances toward the world. She fumed for days over imagined insults or small incidents that I thought were nothing. She had no self-confidence, was always worried that she had said or done the wrong thing. I kept trying to help her see the reality I saw, but she never did. As a child I desperately wanted her to be happy.

The exchanges Dr. Bryan and I had over several weeks seemed to merge into one long conversation in which I tried to unravel, among other things, the contradictory feelings I had about my mother. I admired her difference from other women but didn't want to be like her. I fought against her efforts to keep me close. I knew with absolute certainty deep inside that I had to distance myself psychologically from her for my own survival.

"I feel responsible for her," I told Dr. Bryan, "like when she told me there wasn't any Santa Claus when I was six because she thought I knew. She felt bad when she realized I hadn't known until she told me. I understood I had to tell her it was okay, so it wouldn't spoil her Christmas."

"What about *your* Christmas?" Dr. Bryan asked softly.

"I could handle it better than she could. I understood that if there wasn't a Santa Claus then there wasn't, and I might as well know. That's the way it was. I could accept that. But she wouldn't be able to get over spoiling my Christmas. She wasn't good at letting things go. And I was the most important thing in the world to her. A big responsibility for me. She always told me I was wonderful. Like I'd give her a poem I'd written, and she'd say 'That's wonderful, Anne. Wonderful.' But she didn't really register it. Take it in. Her praise was meaningless."

"What did you want her to do?"

"Say something about the poem, like 'you've described the coming of the storm so well, Anne, I can see it.' Anything. Anything that let me know that it spoke to her, that *I'd* spoken to her, even if it was a suggestion to make it better or a question. Anything…"

I trailed off, realizing that I was close to tears, surprised at how desperately I had craved that kind of recognition from my mother, amazed that in the midst of so much verbal approval I'd felt such a lack of genuine content, such dearth of appreciation of who I was. I wanted her to respond to *me*, not some image of me, some paper doll figure.

"She never challenged me to go further," I went on, feeling a sense of surprise. I'd never thought about that before, that part of what I missed was an invitation to go on. Her response of 'wonderful' invited me to stop, to explore no more, relax. She always wanted everyone around her to relax. It was like a mantra. Relax. Relax. She kept pulling me back, especially as I got older. She quelled my headlong rush into activities. 'Don't do too much.' 'Take it easy.'

Yet as I grew up my dreams rolled out in an unstoppable, noisy, uncontrollable torrent. Did they challenge her efforts to muffle her own life force? Was she pleading, 'don't go where I can't go, because then I can't live through you anymore'?

"Maybe that's why I get uncomfortable when someone says they like me," I mused, as much to myself as to Dr. Bryan. "I discount it. I associate it with someone not knowing me, not wanting to know me, someone who doesn't get it, who wants me to stop being who I am. I respond to that person the way I came to respond to my mother. I try to distance myself as fast as I can."

"What do you think your mother wanted?"

"She wanted me in her realm, inside a world she could understand. Yet I rejected her world, a world based on trying to relax, avoidance of unpleasant or new things, the unreal world of her own imaginings, where someone was always trying to make her unhappy. I was cruel sometimes in pushing her away, rejecting her interest and care, her worlds. I could have been more kind. My grandmother told me once her hair turned white when my mother, ten years old, was hit by a car as she jumped off Aunt Lizzie's hay wagon into the road. My mother was unconscious for ten days. She recovered fully Grandma said, but I always wondered if the accident caused some minor brain damage that made her difficult to relate to sometimes."

Then one day as I lay on the smooth maroon couch, while the sun slipped almost imperceptibly across the wall and Dr. Bryan and I talked back and forth in a sort of call and response of questions and reflections, I experienced a burst of understanding way inside.

I was *not* responsible for my mother. It wasn't my job to convince her that my view of the world was more real than hers. She had to live her own life in her own way. My Christmas was important *too*. She would never understand who I was, why I always wanted more. Suddenly that was all okay. Something deep inside let go. A burden I didn't know I had lifted. I didn't have to feel responsible for my mother or guilty that I wanted my own life. I could never fix my mother's. Not everyone who complimented me or liked me was like my mother. A sense of well-being flooded over me.

"That's all the time we have today," said Dr. Bryan.

It was all the time I needed. I walked out the door, down the hall, in and out of the elevator, moving light as a sunbeam, a dream, a thought, a hope. I had no words for what had happened. I only knew it was momentous.

My therapy moved quickly after that day, although I still couldn't articulate just what had changed. Summer was coming, and I decided that expanding my social network by spending money on a half share in a summer house on Fire Island would better further my goal of finding the right man than continuing therapy. Dr. Bryan agreed and we said a cordial goodbye.

My need to explore was also exerting itself. Europe was calling. Herb Sturz had asked me to work at Vera again that summer, and I could carve out a five-week break between that and the part-time job as a research assistant I had just accepted for fall at a social science research organization. I had hated to give up teaching at Brooklyn. It had been deeply satisfying, but the 8:00 a.m. classes and the long commute were wearing me down. The job had enabled me to finish my course work for the Ph.D. and pass my French language exam, as I had hoped. The coming year I needed extra time to study for an advanced mathematics class that could fulfill my second language requirement and start preparing for my oral comprehensive exams. Orals would take a year or more of intensive study. The European trip would be my last fling before I settled into a long stretch of serious work and anxiety. On this trip to Europe I wouldn't have to travel alone. My good friend Becky, who had replaced me in the second year of the Law and Sociology Fellowship, wanted to go to Europe too. Her experience in the program as the *only* fellow, had been even more stressful than mine. She was eager for a break from school.

In the midst of developing the plans for Europe, I got a call from Barry Mahoney, who I hadn't seen for a few months, but remembered my interest in Fire Island group houses. He wondered if I was interested in buying half his share in a summer house in Kismet since he would be away several summer weekends. The house was a good one, he said, well-run by a core group of people who had been together for several years. One person served as manager and another organized the food and cooking. Everyone at the house for a weekend split the food cost and helped with cooking and cleaning up.

It sounded ideal. But did I want to be in a house with Barry? I could tell by his tone of voice that he still liked me. In spite of my therapy I remained wary of him. I stalled, said my friend Becky and I were thinking of looking for a house together.

"Oh, I think there might be another half share," Barry said. "Let me get back to you."

While Becky and I waited to hear back from Barry, I managed to convince myself that if Barry and I shared a share we would never be at the house at the same time. When he called to say there was a space for Becky too, I said yes to both. I could already hear the waves on the beach.

Part Five
Something Electric

CHAPTER **24**

Kismet

THE COMMUTER TRAIN rattled along early Friday afternoon of Memorial Day weekend releasing workers from the city stop by stop. I'd just finished teaching at Brooklyn College and hadn't started my summer job at Vera yet. Becky and I were on our way to Fire Island, a sandbar 32 miles long off Southern Long Island, to share a beach house in the community of Kismet with a group of people we didn't know.

The train wheezed to a stop in Bay Shore, about fifty miles east of Manhattan. We bumped our bags down the steps and stood momentarily confused in the midst of two diverging streams of humanity, unsure which led to the ferry. We followed the throng with the most baggage and soon spied it, belching smoke and straining at cables like a horse at its starting gate. We pushed through the crowd, worried that there wouldn't be room for us or that the boat would leave before we could get on. We stumbled up the gangplank, pulled on jackets against the sharp wind, found seats, and sat listening to the flapping ropes and slap slap of water against the hull.

The ferry sounded its deep final call. A gaggle of late passengers clambered aboard just ahead of the crew, who pulled the gangplank up behind them with a clang. Engines roared and waves smacked the boat harder as we churned out of the ferry slip.

Next stop Kismet.

Half an hour later Becky and I stood uncertainly on the Kismet dock in front of a weather-beaten building labeled 'General Store.'

The few passengers who got off were busily organizing boxes of supplies they unloaded onto small red wagons. The breeze was cool but
the sun shone brilliantly in a sky more clear and vivid blue than any
I had seen since I had visited my parents in Florida at Christmas. By
process of elimination we quickly located our housemates loading
toilet paper and fresh vegetables on one of the wagons. We followed
as they led the way along the boardwalk toward our house.

The house was smaller and more ordinary than I'd expected, with
no view of the sea unless we climbed a rickety ladder to a makeshift-
looking sundeck on the roof. It had three small bedrooms, each furnished with 2 or 3 single beds and a small dresser. A tiny kitchen
opened into a dining/living room with a big table, comfortable chairs,
and a fireplace. One of the shareholders, who doubled as house manager, had the privilege of a private room behind the kitchen, just big
enough for a double bed. We all shared a bathroom. Becky and I settled into one of the rooms and stowed our stuff in the limited space,
realizing with embarrassment that we'd brought way too much. Then
we headed down the short path toward the beach. My disappointment that the house didn't look out over the beach fell away as I
stopped at the bottom of a large dune and stared in awe at the wide
swath of soft sand that spread in both directions as far as I could see.
We didn't need to see the beach from the house. We could get to it in
two minutes any time we wanted.

"Wanna come gather mussels with us for dinner?" called the
group's main cook.

"Sure," I said with no idea of where one harvested mussels, what
they looked like, or how they tasted. We donned shorts, grabbed buck-
ets, and headed to a rocky area on the bay side of the island where
we took off our sandals and waded in. The water was icy, though in
our protected spot the sun felt warm on the backs of our legs. The
mussels glistened just above the waterline, shiny black curved cylin-
ders nestled in against the rocks, splashed regularly by gentle waves.
I liked the feel of their wet ridged shells but felt a pang of regret as I
picked off each mussel, separating it from its shimmering community.

The mussels were plentiful, and we worked longer than we had expected. I felt exuberant in the clear air as I worked companionably with women I had already come to like. As we headed back to the house, our cook counted off on her fingers,

"Now how many are we having for dinner? "We've already got six here with four more coming on the 6:30 boat, Barry…."

"Barry?" I asked, "How can he be coming? He and I are sharing a share, we shouldn't be here at the same time."

"No problem, we're flexible. One of our other members is on a trip now so can't come, and Barry's going to Europe later in the summer."

I kept walking with my pail of mussels, my calm pleasure in the expedition suddenly gone. Now I'd have to worry that Barry liked me. What if he hung around me all the time?

Soon after the ferry tooted its arrival, Barry came trooping into the house with three other housemates. He greeted me warmly, introduced me to the others, but certainly didn't hang around. He was too busy responding to the enthusiastic greetings of everyone in the house, as well as friends from other houses who stopped by. They all lit up when they saw Barry, clapped him on the back, asked how his winter had been, made plans to get a beach volleyball game going first thing in the morning. He responded to them with pleasure, laughing a wonderfully infectious laugh I'd not heard. This social, easy camaraderie was a side of Barry I hadn't seen in my brief encounters with him in the fall.

Our first dinner, starting with the mussels, which I relished from my first slurp from the shell, was full of wine, good food, and laughter. Barry had a distinctive laugh when something really tickled his sense of humor. He crossed his hands over his chest and held his shoulders as if trying to contain himself while his whole upper body shook with mirth. He ate enthusiastically with appreciative comments to the cooks and was quick to help clear the table, drying dishes diligently until the last one was done.

The next morning Barry was ready early for volleyball on the beach. I noticed he looked really good in shorts, athletic, lean, and strong. But there was no game that day. Although the weatherman had promised sun, Fire Island was socked in with rain. We all sat around the fireplace in our cozy living room reading and engaging in a spirited game of poker for pennies and nickels. Because Barry was the only person I knew who was familiar with the island I found myself hanging out with him, asking questions. *I was hanging out with him!*

We got our first volleyball game of the season the next morning as the sun burned off the mist. Barry played enthusiastically, well, and fairly, quick to give the other side the benefit of a doubt on a close ball. Clearly he had no back problems! How could I have been so far off last November?

"Want to take a walk?" Barry asked after the game and our do-it-yourself lunch of cheese sandwiches. "I'll show you a little of the island."

I hesitated, still guarded.

"Okay. Just a short one."

Across from our house we picked up the trail through the dunes that connected the seven towns on the western end of Fire Island. The intense blue sky seemed to pulse above our heads. A slight breeze, just warm enough, tickled our ears. The Atlantic Ocean appeared and disappeared through breaks in the dunes. Our conversation soon moved into the easy exchange of friends. It was pleasant just talking and walking, discovering how much we had in common. Sometimes we just paced quietly side by side, no tension. We both reveled in the beauty of the early summer day, glimpses of wildlife, the whisper of grasses, the dull primal roll of waves in the distance. Maybe we should go back we said, but we kept walking and talking until clouds started rolling in.

Barry and I were at the beach house together every weekend in June. We walked often and watched the houses that dotted the shore wake up one by one as the owners cleaned and repaired them for the summer. We danced together at the only bar in Kismet and hung out with each other at parties in other houses nearby. No one in our house seemed to notice how we gravitated toward each other and we didn't either. One Sunday night later in the month I was struck, as I got off the train from Kismet in Manhattan, how happy I felt after a weekend on Fire Island. Odd, I thought, Kismet is nice, but not *that* great. I mostly hang out with Barry. Barry! No, he couldn't be the reason. We were just friends.

Two weeks later Barry and I took a long stroll along the beach after dinner. It was shortly after the longest day of the year and the sun hovered low over the waves as we talked about oceans and mountains. Barry said he had always loved the sea. I told him I'd fallen in love with mountains on my western camping trip a few years earlier. As we reached the path to our house we sank down, side by side in the dunes, not yet willing to join the others. The air was summer balmy. Day had faded without much of a sunset, but light still lingered at the edge of the sky.

Barry was leaving in a few days for his two-week Army National Guard summer camp, and this would be his last time on the Island for several weekends. I realized I'd miss him. I couldn't believe I'd thought him boring and uninteresting when we'd first met. That night he was worried about the possibility that his Guard training might turn into full military activation. It was the end of June 1965, and the Vietnam War was heating up. All reports said that President Johnson was going to call up more troops in a few days. No one was sure what he would do. Barry probably would be in uniform, on active duty when the decision was announced.

"Johnson can increase the draft or call up the Reserves, including the National Guard," he said quietly. "Kennedy called up the Reserves for the Berlin Crisis in August 1961. Truman called them up for Korea. This may be the last time we see each other for a long time."

Although he kept his voice matter of fact, I sensed the tension in his body. His immediate future, maybe his life, hung on a decision by someone in Washington who didn't know he existed. I felt a cold shiver. Barry was now a good friend, someone I cared about.

Suddenly the war seemed uncomfortably near. It was hard to contemplate in this place of peace as the last light faded, and the ocean brushed the shore in a calming lap-lap-sigh rhythm. Laughter and voices floated from down the beach and houses behind us. There wasn't anything we could say. Or do. The possibility of Barry's going to Vietnam hung in the air around us. We tried to slap it away like a cloud of mosquitoes. We moved a little closer, talked of other things. Somehow we got on the topic of love.

"Someone told me that you know you are in love when you get more pleasure from watching the other person eat a perfect peach than if you ate it yourself," I said.

"I like that," Barry said as we leaned toward each other. The talk of love awakened something electric between us that didn't fit with being just friends. The sand was cool under my shorts as the beach turned dark. We should head back to the house, we told each other. But we stayed on, watching the moon rise. I liked sitting quietly with him, comfortable in our silence.

On July 28, 1965 I stood on the southwest corner of Broadway and W.116th Street outside Chock full o'Nuts, a popular chain lunch counter across from the entrance to Columbia University. Someone had strung up a speaker to broadcast President Johnson's news conference about Viet Nam and a small group, mostly young men of draft age, gathered around. I stood on the edge of the crowd. All I could think about was Barry in summer training. I wasn't exactly sure when he had left for summer camp, or if he had returned yet, but as near as I could calculate he would probably still be there.

The day was cloudy. Newspapers and trash blew along Broadway. Passersby stared curiously at our small tense huddled group. How could anyone pass by, I wondered. Didn't they know the import of this speech? The announcers made small talk about the pros and cons of calling up the Reserves or expanding the draft. I shifted anxiously from foot to foot thinking about Barry. I realized suddenly how much I wanted to see him again. Then the President came on. He said we didn't want an expanding struggle, but there are great stakes in the balance. Then it came.

We must send more troops by raising the monthly draft calls from 17,000 to 35,000. There was an audible intake of breath in the crowd. It was not essential, the President continued, to order Reserve National Guard units into service at this time.

We stood in silence. The young men standing around me looked shaken. Then everyone talked at once. But none of us understood then just how great the repercussions of Johnson's decision that day would be, how it would rip the fabric of American society and lay waste, perhaps for generations, to the sense of patriotism and trust in government that I had grown up with during the Second World War.

I stood immobile. The Guard hadn't been called up. I'd see Barry again on Fire Island. I felt light with personal relief, but heavy with the crush of what President Johnson had just said in his Texas twang. He was enormously expanding the war. It probably wouldn't take my friend. But it would take someone else's friend. Thousands of friends.

One day in early August I suddenly felt ready to get married, not frantic about ever getting married as I had been so many times before, but ready. My friends would laugh if I told them. But this felt different. It was less a panic than a sense of rightness. I sat back and asked myself, who among the men I knew would I like to get to know better? The answer was surprisingly immediate and clear. Barry Mahoney.

My timing for this revelation was not the best. Becky and I were leaving in two weeks for Europe and Barry was leaving almost immediately. The three of us had talked briefly about our trips to Europe while we sunbathed on the Kismet beach and discussed the possibility of trying to meet in Denmark during our first week and his last week, but we hadn't made any definite plans.

Not one to wait around once I'd made a decision and needing to tell somebody even though I knew she would probably laugh, I called Becky.

"I think I'm ready to get married now. I've decided I'll start by getting to know Barry better."

She didn't even take time to laugh.

"Well you better hurry up. He's leaving for Europe right about now."

I called him immediately. He answered on the second ring.

"Just thought I'd call and wish you a good trip," I said, "and make sure you have the address of our pension in Copenhagen, in case you decide to visit Denmark."

"You got me just in time. I'm just finishing my packing, have to leave in a half hour. Let me get a pencil."

I could hear him rummaging around, then "Okay, give it to me."

He took down our date of arrival and address and then repeated it back to make sure he had it right.

"I'll see you in Copenhagen," he said.

But I doubted if he would remember as he got caught up in the time warp of travel.

CHAPTER **25**

Tulips in August

"MANASKYOU," THE MANAGER announced glaring suspicious-
ly when Becky and I arrived at 6:00 p.m. at the austere Mission
Hotellet Ansgar in Copenhagen where we had made a reservation.
It was run by the local Temperance Societies to provide low-cost,
alcohol-free accommodation, was very inexpensive, and had been
highly recommended in Arthur Frommer's *Europe on 5 Dollars a
Day.* She hesitated before showing us to our room, as if she were
considering whether to honor our reservation and let us stay. Becky
and I looked at each other blankly. We felt like we had done something wrong but were too jetlagged and exhausted to decipher the
meaning of her words.

Then with a flip in my stomach I thought I understood. Barry. I
hadn't really expected him to meet us in Copenhagen, sure he'd get
sidetracked in his travels and forget. But an hour later there he was,
standing on the front steps of our hotel, smiling widely at us and the
manager, who seemed somewhat reassured when she saw that we all
seemed happy to see each other.

The three of us were good traveling companions, cheerful in
rain, eager to try new foods, and considerate of each other's interests
and needs. Late in the afternoon of our second day of sightseeing
we walked out of the royal reception rooms of Christiansborg Palace
unable to face another grand chandelier or elaborate, gold-framed
portrait of a Danish royal.

"What I really want now," I exclaimed, "is to sit down with a beer."

We'd seen cafes and restaurants everywhere, or so it seemed, but now frantic with thirst we saw nothing. As we turned a corner we spied a canal, identified on our map as the Nyhavn, with a long string of café-like buildings on the far side. We moved toward them with the intensity of desert travelers who had just spotted an oasis. I could already taste the beer and feel the relief of getting off my feet. Upon closer inspection the bars looked rather seedy and seemed surprisingly quiet for early evening.

"Is this where we want to go?"

"It's good to get off the tourist trail."

"Oh, look, there's a Texas Bar."

"How can we resist the Texas Bar in Copenhagen?"

In we trooped. We choose a table in the middle and sank into the seats thankfully. No waiter appeared immediately, surprising since the place wasn't busy, just a few tables of couples, scattered around the edges of the room. When one did approach, he acted almost reluctant to take our order.

As we waited for what seemed an inordinately long time for three beers, we became aware that the dim bar was strangely quiet except for our own chatter. When we glanced around we were startled to notice that we were in the middle, literally surrounded by tables, each occupied by one man and two heavily made-up women. We fit right in. Except that we didn't. We were interlopers, competition, and all eyes were on us. I could feel the tension of the room in my stomach.

Just as our beers arrived one of the men got up and approached us slowly. There was something menacing about his manner, as if he were weighing options about what to do about us. I could feel the eyes of all the others silently observing. Even the waiter stood to one side, on alert. The man did not smile, spoke in a language we did not understand, and waved a cigarette, apparently asking for a light. The three of us felt a sense of urgency, a need to accommodate his request, a sense that our inability to do so might negatively dictate future events. But we were all nonsmokers.

Barry rummaged in his pockets. The man waited, holding the cigarette, staring at us appraisingly. As Becky and I watched Barry search with the same absorption as everyone else, I wondered why he was even bothering. Barry wasn't going to have a match.

Then, like a magician, Barry pulled a book of matches from some deep recess of one of his pockets. He handed it to the man, who took his eyes off us long enough to flip it over and examine it impassively. He returned his gaze to us as he took a match, struck it, lit his cigarette, and handed the matchbook back. There was no a sound in the room. He uttered something we didn't understand, then returned to his table.

"We need to get out of here," Barry said quietly, urgently, as he put the money for our beers on the table. I chugged most of mine, unwilling to leave behind what I had coveted so much. We gathered our belongings as casually as we could and headed toward the door, avoiding all eye contact, but feeling the heat of being watched.

Once we got down the steps we walked as fast as we could until we got back on what we happily recognized as the 'tourist trail,' for which we now had a new appreciation. We found out later that Nyhavn at that time was the sailors' quarter, a "rough area full of 'nasty' bars."

"Listen to this," I read from Frommer guidebook the next afternoon, "If you come to Copenhagen and miss Tivoli Gardens, Copenhagen's world-famous amusement park, you are simply off your rocker."

Not wanting to appear off our rockers, we headed to Tivoli. It captured us with all the magic we thought we'd left behind in childhood. Memories of the long summer days I'd spent as a kid with my friends in Conneaut Lake Park near my hometown flooded back. I remembered laughing with the fat lady in the house of fun, screaming at scary objects that jumped from walls in the tunnel of love, playing, ever-hopeful, for prizes in ring toss and ball throw booths, agonizing over which ride to take with my final two tickets. In Tivoli Gardens I slipped back, we all slipped back, into a world where the tawdry glittered and the worn was enchanted.

Hungry, we stopped at an open-air, white-framed restaurant with immaculate linen tablecloths. There were no diners, but a few waiters stood around with arms crossed over long white aprons. We asked if it was too late to eat, never suspecting it might be too *early*. In answer a waiter led us to a table and handed us menus. When we opened them, we looked at each other in consternation. The simplest meal would deplete at least a week's budget.

"Let's just get soup," Becky said, "That looks reasonable."

The soup of the day was asparagus. None of us had ever tasted it; in 1965 American tastes were still limited. Two waiters arrived with a large silver terrine from which one meticulously, lovingly, ladled a light green liquid into elegant china bowls. The other set forth a large plate of bread and two dishes of butter patties. The soup was cold, refreshing, and delicious; the terrine seemed bottomless. The Tivoli evening wove its magic around us. Lights twined and twinkled along edges of buildings and branches. Carousel music floated on the breeze. With reluctance we pulled ourselves away from Tivoli to move on to our last Copenhagen event, music at one of Europe's best jazz scenes, Jazzhus Monmartre. There Barry, Becky, and I huddled around a tiny table in a small space with a big sound and walls covered with plaster masks created by artist Mogens Gylling.

After the first set Barry slipped his hand into mine under the table, tentatively at first, then more confidently, clasping tightly. I responded,. Whatever had been holding me back when we had first met a year earlier was gone. I liked everything I had seen about him since our first day together on Fire Island and in our travels as a three-some. With his free hand he poured a fresh Torberg beer and smiled as he pushed it over to me. I drank, pushed it back and squeezed his hand in reply. I knew we were both remembering our Kismet talk about love and sharing a peach. I felt the same charge between us I'd felt the night we sat on the beach on Fire Island, now intensified by touch and the rising abandon of the music.

Later that night, as Becky and I packed to leave early the next morning on a train to Amsterdam, where we would again meet Barry who was traveling by air, I straightened up suddenly.

"I think Barry and I are going to get married," I announced.

Becky looked at me with amusement.

"Yeah, sure. I've heard that before."

"No, seriously, I think we'll be married before Christmas."

"Umm," she said and went back to organizing her clothes.

Immediately after Becky and I checked into the Anne Frank Youth Hostel, where we were staying in Amsterdam, we went next door to tour the hidden rooms where Anne and her family had lived for two years during the Nazi occupation of Holland. *The Diary of Anne Frank* had affected me profoundly when I first discovered it in 1953, shortly after it had been translated into English. I kept a diary too. My name was spelled the same way as hers, and I was then around the age she had been when she described her life there. When her diary ended abruptly on August 4, 1944 with a brief postscript by the editor explaining that the Gestapo had found her family and sent them to concentration camps at Auschwitz and Bergen-Belsen, I sat stunned, unbelieving for a moment, before I held the book close to my chest and cried.

My own memories of World War II in a small interior Western Pennsylvanian town, with its nightly blackouts, daily rationing, and the fear that each air raid drill might be real, remained vivid for me. I remembered watching news reports of children in England returning from air raid shelters to find their homes reduced to piles of smoking rubble. I felt their desolation and understood that it could happen in my town too.

Barry appeared at our hostel shortly after Becky and I returned from our Anne Frank tour and the three of us diligently followed Frommer's touring suggestions in his *Surprising Amsterdam* guide-book. We roamed the city's streets and canals, sampled broodjes-winkels and herring for lunch, tried the 'Dutchman's favorite aperitif, genever, and consumed an East Indian Rijsttafel with its unbeliev-able number of courses. Barry never made any attempt to be with me alone or in any way exclude Becky, even though he and I both sensed the energy flow between us. For me this sensitivity to others and to situations was an essential characteristic in a partner. Barry's responses to the inevitable ups and downs of travel also revealed a lot about his character.

An article in the New York Times travel section about tulips in Haarlem, a short train ride from Amsterdam, had caught my eye in the spring just after I'd decided to go to Europe. It described miles of blooming fields of red, yellow and orange tulips in all their varied shades, as well as the city's old church and a Frans Hals art museum. It seemed like the kind of off-the-beaten-track excursion I loved and was high on my Holland must-see list. Barry and Becky both looked at the article and agreed it would be a good exploration. Our last day, our last chance to travel to Haarlem, dawned cloudy and damp, but we decided to go anyway.

The three of us settled into a well-cushioned compartment on the nearly empty train. The lights glowed warmly as the weather moved from damp to wet. Barry had picked up the *International Herald Tribune* at the station. We divided it between the three of us, ex-changing tidbits from our sections as we nestled into our cozy shelter, soothed by the rain and the hum of wheels along the tracks. I sat on the seat beside Barry, watching him as he read. I liked his face, his quiet chuckle as he read something amusing. This is what I want in a marriage, I thought. This sense of companionship, being liked for who I am, a willingness to explore, even in the rain. It was an or-dinary experience, riding on the train, but something shifted in me that morning. I felt sure about Barry. Our relationship felt right, the kind of rightness that could last a long time. There was more than electricity between us. My sense of ease and simplicity in our being together was different from anything I had experienced in previous relationships.

In Haarlem the rain beat so hard on the terminal roof we could barely hear the rumble of baggage carts along the platform. We waited patiently in the station entrance for a let-up. When none came we decided to put up our umbrellas and make a dash for a café part way down the block. Dripping and cold we ducked into a large room in which every table was covered with a rug, each different, but all full of the rich reds, blues and oranges of Dutch master paintings. We dropped into the comfortable armchairs and ordered ham and cheese sandwiches with large steins of Dutch beer. I would have been happy to settle in for the day, but we came to see the tulips. When we asked about them, the waiters, who spoke little English, shook their heads in puzzlement.

"Tulips? How you say?" One waiter waved his hand backward. "No now."

"Sprang." Another volunteered.

"Spring?" we asked.

"Ya Ya."

Spring. Of course! What had I been thinking? Tulips bloomed in the *spring*. I had dragged Barry and Becky in the rain in *August* to view tulip fields in bloom. How could have I been so stupid? I felt ridiculous, but neither of them said a word, never made a disparaging comment, didn't even tease me, just accepted the fact that there were no tulips in August and moved on.

"Well let's check out the church and head toward the museum then," Barry suggested, as enthusiastic as ever.

The rain continued all day as we visited the town's Grote Kerk (cathedral) and the Franz Hals Museum. Umbrellas didn't help. We dodged from doorway to doorway, soaking our shoes in the rivulets of water running through the cobbled streets. But I didn't care. For me the day felt glorious.

After dinner back in Amsterdam Becky went back to our hostel, giving Barry and me our first time alone since we'd been traveling. The rain had stopped and the night was warm and washed clean. We walked together along the twinkling, humming canals, stopped under a tree and kissed. We had kissed before on our first date, but I hadn't had the same feelings then. From my point of view, I counted this as our first *real* kiss. Amsterdam lent its magic to that kiss and those that followed. The water sparkled with colored reflections, a small boat glided by with a whish, whish, the air smelled of the sea. We let go of time as we walked, holding close to each other, letting the sounds, and sights of the canal district merge with kisses, a kaleidoscope of feelings and senses. The click of heels on cobblestones, frequent at first, ceased. Light in windows along the canal blinked out. Barry left me at the door of the Anne Frank student hostel with a forever kind of hug that said everything, or so it seemed.

The next day he picked me up in a cab so I could see him off at the airport bus station. We rode quietly, speaking once again through our entwined fingers. The bus to the airport was already there when we arrived. I stood nestled tight against Barry until the driver reached to close the door.

"I'll write."

"I will too."

That was all we promised each other out loud. I felt we were saying more through our tightly held hands and long embrace, but perhaps that was my fantasy. We were going to be separated for four weeks, while Barry went back home to New York City and Barbara and I continued on our tour. Anything could happen in four weeks.

CHAPTER **26**

Courting by Mail Across Europe

I STOOD LOST, shivering in pouring rain and staring at the map of Amsterdam while trying to keep my red umbrella upright by holding the handle under my armpit. After leaving Barry I'd been wandering in a residential neighborhood trying to find the tram station. The longer I walked, the more despondent I became. Barry and I had spent a week in Europe and taken a few long walks together on Fire Island, all vacation time. We hardly knew each other. How could I possibly be thinking about love or marriage at this stage of our relationship? I remembered what a good time I had had with Eli in the Rocky Mountains and on my first trips to New York City and how bad that relationship had been for me in the end. My sense that Barry and I had an unspoken agreement that we would marry soon was preposterous. In my agitation I loosened my grip on the umbrella and caught it just before it dropped, spattering more rain on the already deteriorating map.

"Can I help you with something?" asked a diminutive woman who suddenly appeared beside me.

"I'm lost and my boyfriend just went back to the U.S.," I wailed, realizing as I spoke that I wasn't even sure Barry was my boyfriend.

She clucked sympathetically, asked where I wanted to go, pointed the way to the tram, then asked if I would like a cup of hot tea in her flat. I looked at her, thought I spotted laugh lines in the wrinkled face that peered from beneath a large black umbrella, and said yes. She led me along a cobbled street, into one of the narrow 17th century

193

houses that lined the canals of Amsterdam and up steep stairs to a tiny second floor apartment.

Her name was Tine Joosten. She was 69, she told me as she put on the tea, and had worked for 46 years in social services. She spoke excellent English, with just a slight accent. Her place was cozy, with warm colors, copies of Dutch paintings, and books everywhere. Tine Joosten immediately made me feel like a friend. She asked what museums we'd seen. I told her we had visited the Franz Hals museum in Haarlem and loved it.

"Ah yes. His portraits show so much character, so much life, don't you think?"

I nodded wordlessly as she walked over to a shelf, searched for a moment, and then pulled out and handed me a book that included black and white plates of all Halls' paintings.

"Take it," she said, "It is a gift. You will remember me by the book."

Tine Joosten's kindness and friendship were precious that bleak day. I sensed wisdom, a life well lived, deep and abiding kindness. She seemed like a blessing, a good omen who appeared, as if by magic, out of the rain.

Back in the Anne Frank hostel, with rain still beating against the window, I settled in to write letters. The first was to Barry. I had given myself such a strong reality check about what had *not* been said between Barry and me that my letter to him was restrained. I started out, "I miss you. The sun has gone from Amsterdam in many ways since you left," but then proceeded in a less romantic tone, mostly about my encounter with Tine Joosten.

The second letter I wrote was to my parents, to whom I had promised travel updates. Probably unwisely, I allowed myself to write a rave review about Barry. They had received several enthusiastic letters about men I was dating over the years, who I had subsequently stopped dating, but this was about someone they had never even heard of. Just two weeks short of being 28 years old, I gushed like a teenager.

...I feel that Barry is absolutely right for me – that I couldn't find anyone better. I've never felt about anyone else the way I feel about Barry...

Ten days later in Nice, France, the first place I could expect to get a letter from Barry, I joined the horde of scruffy young Americans with oversize back packs, long-worn clothes, and stringy hair who milled around the American Express mail window. The neatly dressed employees looked at all of us with a hint of distaste, but as long as we claimed we bought American Express traveler's checks we were customers and there wasn't much they could do.

"Rankin," I said when I finally reached the counter, "RA, Anne."

I waited without breathing while the clerk pulled a stack of mail from the R box and began to sort methodically. She stopped, her fingers poised at the edges of a long fat envelope, which she pulled out and plopped in front of me.

"That you?"

"Yes," I said as I glanced at the New York postmark.

At least Barry had written. I pushed through the crowd, got outside and sat down on an empty bench. I needed to open the letter sitting down.

"Halfway across the Atlantic already...."

He hadn't wasted much time writing. But the news was mundane. He'd visited his aunts in London, the airplane food was fairly good, he was starting to think about work. Clearly I had totally misread our time together. I stopped reading, a knot growing in my stomach.

I picked the letter up again and suddenly the tone changed.

I've been trying to put together my thoughts and feelings just now...a great jumble of pictures and you in every one of them. Anne, Anne, Anne--what can I say to you? Only the one thing I didn't say during the past week (at least not verbally) – I love you... It's a wonderful feeling....the very real feeling that I want to be with you always.

I sat holding tight to the folded sheets of legal-size yellow pad, covered with writing, partly in pen, partly in pencil. I hadn't been wrong, had not imagined love because I wanted it so much. I hurried back to my hotel to reply.

Your letter made me very happy...I almost told you that I loved you. It seemed such a natural thing to say and feel. But I didn't, probably because I was wary of something that came so fast and in such glamorous surroundings as a European vacation....

Our letters grew more romantic and intimate as my month of travel wore on. I tried to share with him Becky's and my adventures as we laughed, looked, ate, and drank our way through Europe. In Nice we discovered rose wine and mussels. We ate in the same restaurant three nights in a row and ordered the same thing, except each night we got a larger carafe of wine. We decided we better move on before we became alcoholics. Becky and I celebrated my 28th birthday in Austria. We discovered that Austrian pastries were the most amazing we had ever seen or tasted, and I announced that since it was my birthday I was going to eat as many as I wanted. My main memory of Austria was a pastry shop.

In Austria Becky and I separated for a few days. Becky went on to London where I would meet her, and we would catch our plane back to the U.S. Still curious about what lay behind the iron curtain with its concrete walls and barbed wire, I had obtained a visa to visit Prague in Czechoslovakia. My train from Vienna to Prague stopped for several hours at the Austrian-Czechoslovakian border. It was a desolate area, crisscrossed with barbed wire and cement watchtowers. After a long wait the Border police entered our car. They expressed no interest in my luggage but demanded that the Czech couple in my compartment pull out and open every suitcase they had. The police went through them all, pulling out seemingly innocuous items with grunts of disapproval. They departed and quickly returned to ask the couple to accompany them and bring their luggage. The couple never returned.

When I arrived around nightfall at the Prague hotel, where a pre-paid reservation had been made for me by the Czech travel agency in New York, there was no record of me and no vacancy. After some discussion and several phone calls, the two clerks sent me to a nearby hotel. There the hotel clerk surreptitiously hugged me in the elevator and whispered that the Czech people loved Americans. Loved or not, I was convinced that my bleak, bare room with the single dim light bulb was bugged. It didn't really matter; I had no one to talk to.

Prague was intrinsically beautiful but, like East Berlin, it was run-down and depressing. Almost none of the city's considerable war damage had been repaired. The stores were poorly stocked. There were a couple of places to get take-out food and some kind of drink made from dried milk that was popular with the dinner-shoppers, but there were very few restaurants. Although the atmosphere in Prague seemed a little lighter than in East Berlin, citizens still moved purposefully about their business. I roamed the streets during the day and attended rather dispirited ballet performances in the evenings in a theater close to my hotel. There were thirty or forty attendees in the large theater both nights, all clustered in the best seats down front. Most of the audience looked like tourists. Like Berlin, Prague pulled down my spirits. It was as if there wasn't enough air to breath, as if the oppression I felt everywhere had sucked it out.

Two days was enough. There was one plane a day from Prague to London, alternating a Czech and British airline. I had tickets on the Czech plane, but decided to leave a day early and changed them for the British flight. After a long, unexplained delay at the airport, it was with a deep sense of relief and escape that I felt those British tires leave the ground. In my two cross-border visits to Eastern Europe I'd glimpsed a way of life unlike any I'd seen before. It left me terrified and thoughtful. I could hardly wait to talk to Barry about my experiences.

CHAPTER **27**

Coming Home after a Long Journey

BARRY MET ME at the airport when I landed in New York after my five-week European trip. He found us a cab, lugged my suitcase up my four flights of stairs, then left me on my own, sensitive to my need for sleep. I invited him for dinner the next evening and fell into bed. The next evening after dinner Barry and I sat close on my couch. It was just twilight. The air was still warm, and my floor-to-ceiling window was open all the way. In spite of our amorous letters we were both a little shy, not quite sure how to move our relationship from friends to lovers. We leaned toward each other.

"I've been so eager for you to come back," Barry whispered as he kissed me.

I let myself feel the heat and love in that kiss all the way to my toes and kissed him back with the same intensity. We snuggled together. I liked the way our bodies fit each other, the way his arms felt around me. We sat gazing at the sky, lit now by New York's perpetual glow, feeling our own glow at being together.

"Would you like to stay tonight?" I asked.

"Mmmm," he said.

"Is that yes or no?"

"Yes," he said startled that I hadn't understood him. "Oh, definitely, yes."

"Mumbling will get you nowhere," I laughed.

There was freedom and joy in our lovemaking, without barriers between us--no previous girlfriend or fear of commitment, no more unease about getting close to a man who said he liked me. I felt as if I had come home after a long journey.

Barry pulled me close, suddenly serious. "I really want to be married to you. Would *you* like to be married to me?"

"Yes, very much," I said.

And that simply, after all my years of concern and angst about being lovable and womanly enough to ever get married, we became engaged. We made love again to celebrate, slowly, deliberately, taking time to explore each other's bodies.

What if I'd realized there were no tulips, I mused, and we hadn't gone to Haarlem? There would have been no train ride. Would I have had my epiphany about Barry? The ride, circumstances, feeling of certainty, was a definitive moment in my life. Probably it would have happened some other way, in some other place, but I treasured *that* moment, that extraordinary memory of sitting in a train compartment, with rain pounding against the window, feeling a sense of deep happiness.

In retrospect our sudden decision to marry seems reckless, crazy even. But we had no doubts. I felt I knew Barry better than anyone I had ever dated. We would both be 28 years old when we married. We thought we knew the difference between love and infatuation. To us the decision was straightforward and sensible.

"I'd never met a woman like you before," Barry said as we talked about our first date months earlier, "You were the kind of woman I wanted to marry."

I'd never met anyone like Barry before either, it just took me some time to realize it. He was the partner I'd been searching for, a man who knew how to express love openly and freely, who valued me as a whole person and encouraged and celebrated my efforts to move beyond old boundaries to find both love and work. He made it clear that the completion of my Ph.D. would be a top priority in our marriage.

Barry wanted to get married soon. I did too. We felt sure of each other. The first wedding date that seemed possible was Thanksgiving

Saturday, about two months away. I wanted the wedding in New York, in my apartment, the realization of that crazy hope I'd always had about getting married there. A long weekend might make attendance more likely for my out-of-town family and friends.

We decided to tell both sets of parents first, before we announced our engagement to others. That was simple for me and I called Mom and Dad the next day. Although they had at least heard of Barry because of my Amsterdam letter, my call to announce our engagement two days after I'd returned to New York must have come as a shock. They rose to the occasion gracefully, as they always did when I presented them with an unexpected, fully developed decision.

Barry's situation was more complex. He had been raised Catholic and his family would expect us to be married by a priest. He wanted to think through how best to present our engagement to his parents. We hadn't talked much about religion in our short relationship. Now we both had to give it our full attention.

"I was never enthusiastic about Catholicism even as kid," Barry mused, "but I went along. As an adult I've become increasingly uncomfortable with it."

As a Unitarian I believed that each person had the right to develop his or her own spiritual direction. Barry had to work through his own perspective, and I couldn't help. As we talked about our individual beliefs Barry finally summarized our situation simply.

"You're a Protestant agnostic and I'm a Catholic agnostic. We started in different religions but ended up in the same place."

We were in agreement on our religious beliefs. Our problem was how to get married the way we wanted without alienating Barry's family, especially his father who felt strongly about the Catholic Church. Barry was pensive for a while, then announced.

"I'd like you to meet my parents before we tell them we're engaged, so they can get to know you as a person first. They'll really like you."

He had told his mom and dad about his travels with Becky and me and convinced them to include Amsterdam in their upcoming

European trip, so it seemed natural for him to invite me to their home in Scarsdale to talk about Holland. He set the meeting up immediately. We went out to his parents' home the next afternoon. They may not have understood it was 'Meet the Parents Night,' but I did, and I was scared.

Except once I got there I wasn't. I liked Barry's parents immediately, as well as John, one of his younger twin brothers, who was at the house that evening. Their home, though larger than my parents', was unpretentious and filled with comfortable chairs, books, and pictures. Barry's mother was petite and elegant in a quiet way. She settled herself in what was clearly her chair, at right angles to the couch, where she invited me to sit with Barry beside me. She was an exceptionally good listener and kept asking me about my work at Vera and my interest in sociology and getting a Ph.D. Barry's dad, with a head of thick white hair, a big voice, and a hearty laugh, jumped in and out of his oversize blocky armchair across the room to serve drinks and snacks. The scene felt familiar, like home.

Conversation ranged widely. Barry's mother had worked for years after college in a variety of teaching, business, and advertising positions, in Muncie, Indiana, where she grew up, and in Washington and New York, where she met Barry's father and married in her mid-thirties. Barry's father had grown up in Maine. He had gone to MIT, become a chemical engineer, and started his own company. I could see my parents with the Mahoneys, all staunch Democrats, sitting in the living room having drinks together, discussing politics and the state of the world. I liked Barry even more after seeing him with his family. One reason we got along so well, I suspected, was that, in spite of their different religious backgrounds, our families' basic values were strikingly similar.

Two days later Barry went out to tell his parents that we were engaged, intended to marry in November, and that since I was not Catholic, we probably would not get married by a priest. After he got back that evening, we planned to officially celebrate our engagement at the Rainbow Grill, a famous restaurant at the top of Rockefeller Center on Fifth Avenue.

Barry was subdued after he returned from Scarsdale but didn't give many details. His mother and father each told Barry how much they liked me, that they were delighted, though a little surprised, at our sudden decision to marry. The atmosphere changed explosively with the revelation that we would probably marry outside the church. "You're denying your heritage," his father protested.

I was glad I had had the opportunity to meet Barry's parents before all the tumult started. Without that connection, I might have envisioned them as adversaries, and they might have had a similar image of me. Barry had been right to make sure we all got acquainted before he told them about our marriage plans.

"It's not about you," Barry kept reassuring me, "Pop gets upset and carries on and then gets it out of his system. He'll come around."

Still Barry didn't look much like celebrating. Our potential marriage clearly was not just about us. It affected Barry's family deeply, their standing in a large extended family, in their church, and among their friends. To them it probably felt like a deep failure.

"Shall we wait?" I asked.

"Absolutely not. We've told both sets of parents and are now officially engaged."

We drank champagne, ordered steak, and tried to act celebratory, but there was a pall over the meal. Barry was clearly still shaken by his father's reaction and neither of us had much appetite. When the bill came it was more money than we had, except that Barry managed to fish an emergency ten-dollar bill out of a special compartment in his wallet, much as he had magically produced a book of matches in the sailors' bar in Copenhagen. With that we even had enough money for a good tip, which we both agreed was always important. After a final tour around the glass-enclosed restaurant to view the glorious New York skyline we returned to my apartment, where we'd been living together since we had decided to marry. Our engagement was official, but still felt problematic. I tried not to think about that.

Being engaged was delightful. What could be more special than being in love and about to get married?! My approach to it, however, remained low key. I had been in several large weddings as a bridesmaid and had no desire to have one. My dream was a small casual ceremony in my apartment. When Becky, who I had asked to be my maid of honor because of her travel involvement with both of us, asked if I wanted a bridal shower, I answered with a resounding no. Without any intention on our part, however, we did have two surprise engagement parties. One was put together by Barry's colleagues in the New York Attorney General's office. The other, organized by our Fire Island housemates, was as much of a surprise to us as our decision to marry must have been to them.

Barry wanted to get me an engagement ring, but I was adamant that I didn't want one. It felt too much like a trophy. That wasn't me. I suggested we go instead to get special wedding rings at Tiffany's on Fifth Avenue. We dressed up and tentatively entered Tiffany's imposing doorway.

"Do you want a ring with diamonds," the saleslady asked, looking at me with her hand poised over a case full of rings that glittered like recovered treasure in a Disney movie.

"Oh no. Just plain gold."

So many rings, wide and narrow, white gold and yellow, intricate and plain. Barry, as quick to choose a ring as he had been to ask me to marry him, selected a narrow gold one composed of three thin circles with the middle one raised. After much searching and deliberating and my sense of the growing impatience on the part of the clerk, I finally decided on a band of three connected circles. We each have rings with three circles I told Barry, the three circles represent you, me, and us. Choosing our rings made our approaching marriage feel real as nothing else had.

In between the events in our lives we talked with each other for hours, pouring out our histories, fears, and enthusiasms.

CHAPTER 28

Marriage and Religion

ENGAGEMENT SWEPT ME along in a happy fog. I gave little serious attention to my new job as a research assistant, which was getting off to a slow start through no fault of mine. I'd been attending classes for the advanced mathematics course I was taking as an alternative to the second foreign language required for a Ph.D. but had not yet opened the textbook. It was becoming abundantly clear that just going to class was not going to be enough to yield a passing grade. The instructor assumed that we had all taken calculus. I had never taken calculus, had had no math, in fact, since my junior year in high school. Although I had always done well in math, I was in way over my head.

My search for a wedding dress caused the first hiccup in Barry's and my relationship. I started, in my nontraditional mode, looking in regular dress departments. I found a dress in white satin, modeled after the then popular Nehru jacket style, with a high Mandarin collar and braid on the shoulders. It fell straight to below my knees with no waist. Excitedly I took it home to show Barry.

"How do you like it?" I asked. "Isn't it great!"

Barry hemmed and hawed, looked distressed and finally said, "Ahh...I know you like it, but, well...I'm really sorry, but...I don't think it does a lot for you. You have a really nice figure and it hides that. It looks so, so military."

He looked miserable. I was hurt. How could he not like the dress I thought was so beautiful?

"I didn't feel I should say I liked something I didn't, but I'm sorry to make you so upset."

"Okay," I said in my best martyr tone, "I'll take it back."

As I gazed again at myself in the mirror I could see what he meant. It *was* sort of military. I didn't want to look like I was going into battle when I got married.

"It's okay," I reassured him, "You're right. It's not good. I'm glad you said what you thought, even though I didn't want to hear it."

I returned the dress and decided to look in bridal departments, even though they all seemed to be controlled by stiff, dark-clad older saleswomen who looked like bastions of tradition. I had already discovered that everyone had an opinion about, and was eager to tell prospective brides, what weddings SHOULD be like. Most of the 'shoulds' were aspects I hoped to forego.

On my next lunch hour, I went to the bridal section at Saks on Fifth Avenue. There were no other customers in sight. With dismay I realized that I would have the full attention of not one, but two, sales ladies and steeled myself for saccharine conventionality.

"I'm looking for a simple street length dress for a small wedding at home," I announced firmly.

To my surprise the ladies were pleasant, not at all condescending, and brought out eight lovely and appropriate dresses. One more prejudice fell away. I tried on all but the three strapless ones, with the ladies hovering appraisingly in the background as I twisted and turned in front of the three-way mirrors. I loved clothes and the dresses were all beautiful. After several more try-ons and preening in front of the giant mirrors, I decided on one with a wide scooped neck, elbow-length sleeves and a row of tiny pearl buttons down the back. It fit my small waist perfectly and soft pleats flared out into just the right amount of fullness. I loved it and knew Barry would too. I was so glad he had nixed the other one. This was everything I could ever want in a wedding dress. It was beyond perfect.

"I'll take it."

"You'll need a headpiece also."

"A what? You mean a veil? I don't think so."

I associated veils with the old custom of the groom raising the bride's veil after the vows, which seemed an act of ownership. I wanted to marry into a partnership.

The bridal ladies looked at me in dismay. "But you want to look like a bride," they chorused.

"You could use the bow that came with the dress," the lady with the black lace top under her jacket exclaimed. "It would fit nicely on your head and you could attach a simple veil in the back. See."

She pulled out a square of netting and held it up behind the bow. It did look nice. I decided to get the headpiece made up and decide later about wearing it.

My biggest concern, woven through all the fun of parties, wedding rings, and dresses, was Barry's and my serious attempt to resolve the family conflict about our wedding. Although we both agreed that we would not promise to do something and then not do it, Barry decided he owed it to his parents to see if there was any way we could, in good conscience, be married by a priest. I really wanted to marry Barry, but I knew I had a bottom line. I could not raise my children Catholic. One of the greatest gifts my parents had given me was freedom of thought, including the right to think through the meaning of God and religion for myself. I could do no less for my own children. If it came down to that, I couldn't marry Barry. We'd have to stop everything, tell everyone. I would have to give up the warmth and love we had together, give up having him beside me every night, our laughter together, our animated conversations.

I had to wait, be silent while Barry figured out for himself who he was. Marrying outside the church would be a public statement that he was no longer Catholic. Barry had to be sure for himself that was what he wanted. We agreed we had to get it right now, before we married. In daylight I felt confident that we could work everything out. Nighttime was different. Sometimes when I couldn't sleep, even as I lay nestled beside Barry, the 'what ifs' circled around me. What if Barry suddenly feared going to hell if he stopped being a Catholic? What if, in the end, it came down to a choice between his family and me?

"Do you suppose just *exposing* our kids to Catholicism would be enough," Barry mused.

I said it would work for me. I wanted to expose my kids to many religions so they could choose what worked for them. We both knew it was a fantasy, I think, but it buoyed us for a few days. Barry decided to talk to the campus priest at Columbia, who he thought would be up to date on all the current liberalizing changes set in motion by Pope John Paul XXIII in Vatican II.

Barry came back after his visit to the priest chuckling. "The Monsignor is very understanding and personable, but when I sat down across from him at his desk, it seemed like I was several inches lower than he was. Maybe it was just my imagination."

The church was changing, Barry reported, birth control was less of an issue than it used to be. But there was no easing of the rules about children. The Monsignor took a hard line. A priest would marry us only if we both agreed to raise our children Catholic. Raising them Catholic meant baptism, first communion, and preparation for confirmation. Exposure to Catholicism was definitely not sufficient. We sighed. Barry was thoughtful for a moment.

"I remember disliking the Catechism as a kid, but don't remember much about it. I think I better read it and find out what it says."

A couple days later Barry came home with a copy of the Catholic Baltimore Catechism.

"I'm going off to read this alone, I want to know what kids learn if they are raised Catholic."

I caught my breath. What if?

He appeared from our bedroom awhile later and handed the slim book to me.

"You need to read this. I don't want to be here when you do. I'm going out."

I turned the book over in my hands as he clomped down the stairs. Didn't want to be here when I read it? What did that mean? The neon of the overhead light hummed slightly as I sat down at the kitchen table, catechism in hand. The content was far more fantastical than I had expected, certainly not what I wanted my children to learn or believe without getting other perspectives. What did Barry make of it? I waited anxiously for his return. He was gone a long time. Or so it seemed.

"So, what did you think?" Barry asked when he returned.

I wasn't sure what to say. It was what he thought that mattered. I looked at him trying to gauge his reaction, his mood. I hesitated. Was this the moment of the end of our relationship? Of the wonderful dream we had been living? I tried to hedge.

"It was interesting. I've never read anything like it before. What did you think Barry?"

"I don't want my children required to learn and believe what is in that book," he declared. "No way."

We fell into each other's arms in relief. We were in agreement. No priest. But could we find a way to reconcile Barry's parents? They had already left on a long-planned European trip and Barry wrote a long letter to them at their French hotel explaining the reasons for his decision. Part of his explanation focused on the catechism:

> [even as a kid] I thought that the whole idea of doing something good for the sake of an ultimate reward was contrary to everything we learned at home. That idea—and its converse, that one does not do something bad solely because of fear of hell—permeates the whole catechism. There is little, if anything, in it about the idea of doing something good because it *is* a good thing, or because it will have good effects for someone else…

His parents' response came swiftly in a strong letter written by Barry's mother detailing his father's distress. She also raised her own big concern. We were marrying much too soon. Wouldn't April be better, she asked, or at least February? In retrospect that suggestion seems eminently sensible. Our limited length of acquaintance was certainly not within the range recommended in success-in-marriage books.

Although it never crossed our minds then, we were involved in what in that era was referred to as a 'mixed marriage', one between persons of different races, religions, or ethnic groups. Barry was Irish and Catholic on all four sides and I was Anglo-Saxon Protestant. Mixed marriages were believed to be less happy and stable because of conflicting personal and family beliefs and practices. Barry and I were in agreement about how we wanted to marry, how we wanted to raise our children, and how we wanted to live, but we couldn't deny the family turmoil that was swirling around our wedding plans.

Barry responded to his mother's letter immediately. The decision had not been easy, he explained, but we definitely were getting married on November 27 in a civil ceremony. He emphasized that he loved both his parents very much and did not want to be estranged from them and added:

> I can't imagine it could be any more of a sin to be married outside the church than to be married by a priest when you knew you couldn't honestly say you agreed to the necessary prerequisites….To make such an agreement would, to me, be gravely hypocritical, and I cannot imagine a worse way to start off a marriage…

We'd made our decision but soon ran into new obstacles. Our attempts to arrange a civil service proved unsuccessful. We could find no judges who were interested in coming to my fifth-floor walk-up on the Saturday after Thanksgiving to marry us, and neither of us wanted to marry in the registrar's office in City Hall.

"What about Reverend Bob Smudski?" I asked.

Rev. Smudski had been the minister of the Meadville Unitarian

Church when I was fourteen and my family had discovered Unitarianism. My parents liked him and would be delighted to see him again. He had been an important influence on my growing up. When I was in high school I had always hoped he would be able to marry me someday. Recently, I had reconnected with him when he became the minister of a Unitarian church in Yonkers just north of Manhattan. To my surprise Barry did not rule out the idea.

"I'd consider that, but I would want to meet him first," he said.

A few days later, as we walked up the street from the bus toward the Unitarian church for our appointment with Rev. Bob Smudski, I could tell Barry was nervous.

"I've never had any experience with Protestant ministers. What should I call him?"

"Bob, I think, or Reverend if you feel more comfortable with that. I call him Bob and I'll introduce him to you that way. Just act like you would with a regular person. I'm pretty sure his seat won't be higher than ours."

Barry laughed, remembering his comment about the Monsignor, and relaxed a little. Bob Smudski put us both immediately at ease, and our meeting went well, although he asked us some hard questions in addition to probing the compatibility of our religious beliefs.

"How do you feel about each other's views on money?" he queried. "Have you thought through what kind of lifestyle you want? Do you agree on what that is?"

Barry and I, despite our brief time together, had talked a lot about what mattered to us and had been struck, as we did so, by how closely our views were aligned. I had sensed that same compatibility of family values when I visited Barry's parents, in spite of the difference in religious denomination. After a good conversation, Bob leaned forward in his chair and reached across the table to shake our hands.

"It would be a pleasure to marry the two of you," he announced.

We could put together our own service, he explained, or use and modify one he had designed. We liked his. It was simple, short, expressed our mutual views of marriage, and we could add additional readings if we came across things we wanted. My one request was that he not include "obey" in the vows. He assured me that it was not in his version.

"I like him," Barry commented as we headed back to the bus stop. "I feel good about having him marry us."

My parents would be pleased too. They hadn't met the groom, but at least they knew the minister.

I was particularly eager to have Barry meet my Vera family, especially my boss Herbert Sturz. That opportunity came at a national conference on bail and pretrial projects in New York City in early autumn, sponsored by Vera and the U.S. Justice Department. Everyone from Vera was there, and Barry attended as part of his work at the New York State Attorney General's Office. Barry's meeting with my boss Herb was akin to meeting a parent. Herb would be more critical of a man I planned to marry than anyone else I knew. The morning after I introduced them Herb came up to me with his big smile, face alight with pleasure, to tell me he liked Barry tremendously. I knew Herb well enough to recognize when he was being polite and when he was really pleased. I treasured his approval.

One of my most difficult decisions as I moved toward marriage was my name. In 1965 a woman's marriage usually involved a change of her last name. It was common for women in the 1960s to drop their birth name ('maiden name') and take their husband's last name. Many also subsequently signed their name by simply adding Mrs. to their husband's full name, i.e. Mrs. John Jones. Barry said my name was up to me. The New York law was straightforward. The way I signed my name on my marriage license became my new legal identity.

I wanted to keep my birth name Rankin, but hyphenated names seemed complicated and I wanted the same last name as my children. I had always been called Anne, although Dorothy was my legal first name. Being called by other than the first name on my birth certificate was an ongoing hassle. I decided to drop Dorothy, take

Anne as my first name, Rankin as my middle name, and Mahoney as my last name. It seemed like a great solution. I thought my family would be pleased that I kept Rankin. I never stopped to think then how dropping my first name must have hurt my father and his sister, Aunt Dorothy.

CHAPTER 29

Change in Status

OUR WEDDING PLANS were simple. We planned to marry two days after Thanksgiving on Saturday, November 27th at 3:00 o'clock in my apartment. Becky was my Maid of Honor and one of Barry's friends, Mike McGinnis, was Best Man. Barry bought a new suit, forever after known as his wedding suit. I ordered a tiered cake from Party Cake just a few blocks up Broadway. Mom and Dad were responsible for wine glasses and a case of French Piper-Heidsieck champagne. We planned little sandwiches, one of my mother's specialties, cheese from Zabar's on Broadway, vegetables and dips, and other finger foods that we could prepare the morning of the wedding.

The size of my apartment limited the size of our guest list to close friends and family. My family included Mom and Dad, who planned to arrive by car from Florida a few days before the wedding, and my cousin Bill Fritchman, a pianist who lived in Manhattan, and my former roommate Lois, who I counted as family. She, like me, was at a turning point in her life, and would leave New York City to move back to her hometown Atlanta the day after our wedding. Although most of Barry's large extended family lived in the New York area we could invite only a few—his parents, brothers Bob and John, close cousins Bob Wernet and his wife Nancy, and close aunts and uncles.

We tried to invite Al, at whose party Barry and I met. Al and I got acquainted when we painted a window frame together in Lois' new apartment over a year earlier. He later invited me to his party in

Greenwich Village, to which he also invited Barry, whom he had met when they were both in group houses on Fire Island. We owed Al a lot! If it hadn't been for him, Barry and I probably would never have discovered each other. We were sad that we couldn't track him down and drink a toast of thanks to him.

Barry's parents arrived home just two weeks before the wedding. Emotions heated up immediately. Barry's mother still wanted us to wait until April to marry, oblivious that our planning had gone way too far for that. Barry's father announced that if we went ahead with the wedding he would not attend. Barry's mother tried to mediate, but she finally said she had to support Barry's father and wouldn't come either.

Barry took it all in stride. "It's okay," he explained. "If Pop feels that way it's better he doesn't come. Our wedding will be a lot more fun. My brothers will be there, my cousins, and Aunt Mary and Uncle Edward. Once we get married and Pop has made his point, he'll get over it. He and Mom like you a lot. They'll be fine."

I trusted him.

When my parents arrived from Florida two days before Thanksgiving I took Barry over to their hotel immediately to meet them. Mom and Dad welcomed him warmly as their new son and we all went downstairs to the hotel bar to drink a toast to our approaching marriage. Barry and I decided it would be best if he went out to Scarsdale for Thanksgiving with his family. Mom and Dad and I celebrated in my apartment with my cousin Bill, who was much loved by both my parents, and Lois, who knew my parents and Bill. The five of us laughed a lot as we prepared our turkey in my tiny kitchen and ate it on a bridge table set up in front of the nonworking fireplace in the living room. It was a special time for me, a hug of good wishes from my closest family before I stepped into a new life.

On the morning of the wedding Dad went out with instructions to buy lots of orange, gold, and white chrysanthemums for the apartment and my bouquet at the nearby green grocers on Broadway. An easy, quick assignment we thought, but hours passed. We were just starting to worry when he reappeared, looking triumphant but tired, with an adequate, if not overwhelming, supply of blooms. We had failed to take into account the big run on flowers for Thanksgiving and he had visited every flower shop on the upper West Side.

Mom, Lois, and Becky tried to work around each other in my small kitchen as they prepared food for the reception. I bounced among them nervously supervising and trying to help, but mostly getting in the way. As Mom carefully, painstakingly cut crusts off sandwiches I glanced at my watch, worried that we might not get everything ready in time. 12:45. A jolt like electricity shot through my system.

"The cake! Where's the cake? It was supposed to be here by eleven."

"They're probably just a little behind on deliveries," Mom said. "Let's just give them a little more time."

"We don't have any more time. We're having a wedding in two hours."

I fumbled to find the Party Cake number, managed to locate it under a pile of papers, and dialed, my heart pounding.

"We have no order for a cake for you," the Party Cake order manager announced. "Yes, we made a cake that fits the description you are giving us. We just sent it off for a wedding in Brooklyn."

"Well I ordered one weeks ago, paid for it and have the receipt," I said, panic rising. Brooklyn! The cake I so carefully chose went to Brooklyn!

The order manager put on a supervisor.

"I'm so sorry Ma'am."

"I don't want sorry. I want a cake. My wedding starts at three o'clock."

"We'll get you a cake by two. It may not be exactly what you ordered, but very close. Don't worry."

"What if...? I started.

"Don't worry. You'll have it on time. It will be beautiful."

I worried anyway, but the cake arrived a little before 2:00, beautiful.

I had decided we should adhere to the tradition that it was bad luck for the groom to see the bride the day of the wedding. Odd I should have chosen that custom to honor when we had bypassed so many others. Barry slept in his own apartment the night before the wedding, which left us both very lonely, and I stayed in my bedroom until all the guests had arrived for the wedding. As I paced and primped and re-primped in my narrow bedroom I could hear the animated conversation of arriving guests and realized I was missing half the party.

"Let's get this show on the road," I demanded. "I'm going crazy in here."

As I stepped into the living room to take my father's arm and walk the two steps to the archway where Barry waited beaming beside Rev. Bob Smudski, the minister who had been so important in my adolescence, I felt deeply happy. The people I loved most surrounded us.

"Dearly beloved, out of affection for Barry and Anne we have gathered together to witness their mutual vows which will unite them in marriage..."

Barry and I stood gazing into each other's eyes.

"I, Barry, take you Anne to be my wedded wife....

"I, Anne, take you Barry to be my wedded husband...."

We kissed. Our guests clapped. In a few minutes our legal and social status had changed forever. We were married. We clung to each other for a moment before surfacing to accept congratulations.

Our wedding was the best party I'd ever had in my apartment, an appropriate ending to my four happy years there. I felt beautiful in my dress, set off perfectly by the headpiece with the little veil in the back. The bridal ladies had been right. Dad kept pulling bottles of Piper Heidsieck from our ice-packed bathtub and made the rounds filling glasses. The room was filled with laughter, flowers, and candles. The food was good, and our best pictures were of us cutting the cake we almost didn't have.

Our only hitch was forgetting to pay the minister. Bob and his wife got their coats and hovered around the front door for a few minutes before approaching the Best Man, who customarily takes care of that task.

"We have to leave now."

"Nice to meet you."

There was a moment of silence. "The fee...?" ventured the minister.

The Best Man, bewildered but game, asked how much it was. After rummaging through his pockets, he came up with two fives and sought out Barry, who looked stricken because he had forgotten to make the fee arrangements with him. He didn't have enough cash either and asked another friend who usually was flush. Between the three of them they produced the twenty-five dollars. I learned only later and was embarrassed, but every wedding had to have something go wrong.

We planned to slip away shortly after cutting the cake for our two-night honeymoon to nearby rural Connecticut. We could only take two nights because Barry had his monthly National Guard meeting on Monday, but we promised ourselves a longer trip in the summer. The Best Man had offered us his car for our drive to Connecticut and parked it nearby so we could escape quickly. We got out unobtrusively, but as we reached the bottom of the stairs we heard a sudden commotion above that signaled detection of our departure. We jumped into the dark car, barely noticed the 'Just Married' signs scribbled across the doors and trunk and managed to escape just before our friends spilled out of the brownstone doorway. As we hummed along the highway we sighed contentedly, happy to be married and alone.

"Don't park the car in front of our room," I pleaded, remembering the 'Just Married' signs all over it.

We settled into the dining room in front of a cozy fire, held hands, and gazed at each other in delight. We were married. Even though I wanted to keep a low profile, anyone who looked at us would have known we belonged to that car. In the morning we discovered that the 'Just Married' signs didn't come off as easily with wet wipes as we had expected. We picked up stronger cleaning supplies on our way to breakfast at the local diner that offered 'All you can eat' pancakes.

The pancakes took a while. As we waited we tried to figure out what to do with our newly adorned hands. We couldn't help looking at each other, and our shiny new rings that shouted, 'Just Married.'

"Newly-weds?" the waitress asked a little later as she plopped down Barry's second serving of pancakes. We nodded self-conscious-ly. "Thought so," she laughed, "those new husbands never know when to stop."

The day was golden bright, one of the last of fall. We walked in the woods then went back to the hotel for a nap. That Sunday evening, we decided to celebrate our first full day of marriage with dinner in a cozy candlelit French or Italian restaurant. It was already dark when we started out on our search for a restaurant. We saw few lights as we drove aimlessly around the rural area, except for a pleas-ant looking pizza place that we rejected in favor of something more upscale. The one upscale place we spotted was closed on Sundays. After driving for an hour, we reconsidered and decided a pizza place would be fine. By then we had no idea how to get back to the one we'd seen. The night grew darker. We were starving. We lowered our expectations further. Anyplace would be fine.

"There's a light over there. Let's try that," I exclaimed.

"Oh, it's just a bowling alley. They don't serve food,"

"Sometimes they do. Let's go see."

The bowling alley was nearly deserted except for a man bowling alone on a far lane and a waitress in the worn snack bar watching 'Joan of Arc' on TV.

"Do you serve food?"

"Wadyalooking for? We got hamburgers."

"Great," we chorused.

She pulled out two thin, preformed burgers from the freezer, dropped them on a greasy grill, and plopped a napkin and fork in front of each of us without taking her eyes off the TV screen.

We sat beside each other on the worn, red plastic-covered stools holding hands until she slapped the hamburgers and a bottle of cat-sup in front of us. We ate hungrily to the roll and thwack of bowling balls and falling pins behind us on alley number five and the agonies of Joan of Arc on the TV to our right. We were married and it was a wonderful night.

The next morning, we tried the new cleaning products on the car. They slightly faded, but did not completely remove, the 'Just Married' signs. We considered it a good omen for our marriage, though tough for the Best Man, who had loaned us his car.

Within a few days of the wedding Barry's parents invited us to a celebratory dinner with close Mahoney relatives and pored over our wedding pictures as if they had organized the event themselves.

"Best pictures Barry's ever taken," his mother commented.

I decided to call Barry's Dad 'Pop', as Barry did, and his mother 'Mom.'

Not long after our wedding, one of Barry's cousins got married in a large Catholic wedding at Saint Patrick's Cathedral, complete with mass, and we were all invited. Barry suggested that we arrive just slightly before the ceremony started so we could sit in the back of the church instead of up front in the middle of the family, where our nonparticipation would be noticeable. It was a good idea, but not totally successful. Barry's father arrived even later after dropping off Barry's mother and going off to park the car. He smiled pleasantly as he slipped into the pew beside us. We did not participate in the mass. He did. I worried all through the wedding, wondering what would come next.

Immediately after the ceremony was over, Pop took my arm "I've got some people I want you to meet," he announced as he propelled me through the crowd toward the church foyer. There, and at the reception, he introduced me with obvious delight and pride to every member of the Mahoney family as 'Barry's new bride.' With each introduction he explained to me how each person was related to him. I couldn't have had a warmer welcome to the family!

CHAPTER 30

Love and Work

AT LAST I had the shared emotional relationship I had been stumbling toward, the 'more' I had been yearning for. Now, for the first time I experienced love and work as two legitimate and central aspects of my life. I felt free.

"My relationship with Barry is like the warmth of the sun on the first day of spring," I wrote to my former psychologist, Dr. Bryan, in my letter announcing our marriage.

Dr. Bryan responded with a two-page letter that ended, 'Please give Barry my hearty congratulations. I have good reason to know what a lucky fellow he is.' I felt as if I had received my psychological Good Housekeeping stamp of approval.

A few days after our marriage, we moved half a block across Broadway into a large, two-bedroom apartment on the corner of West 107th Street. As we paused for the last time in the doorway of my old apartment we kissed and gazed at the site of our first love making and wedding, realizing we would never see it again. The apartment represented an important era of my life. It had sustained me from my first weeks in New York through our engagement and marriage. Now I was ready to move on to a different space with room to grow in new ways.

I had found the love part of my life equation, but there was a long way to go to achieve the work portion, especially since I was in real trouble in my mathematics class. Passing this class was my only alternative to learning a new language for the second language exam required for the Ph.D. degree at Columbia. As soon as we moved into our new apartment, I turned my attention to the class and realized that I was much further behind than I had realized. I had been going to class regularly but had not kept up at all with the textbook. The end of the semester was rapidly approaching, and I had no clue what was going on. Failure was not a good start toward my effort to combine love and work! Barry suggested I hire a tutor. I'd never had a tutor before. It hurt my pride to think I needed one, but with Barry's encouragement I called my instructor for a recommendation. He suggested a sociology graduate student with a strong mathematical background whom I knew slightly and liked. We started to work together at once and I quickly understood that the situation was even more dire than I had imagined. Would there be enough time to catch up? The answer was no. I flunked the math class.

I'd never failed a class before. It was an odd, empty feeling. I felt that the sky would surely fall, that no one would like me anymore, that the secret stupidity I had tried to hide for so long would now be obvious to the world. Surely Barry would be ashamed. But nothing happened. Barry and my family still loved me. My friends couldn't have cared less about my math grade. The world kept turning. Failure just created a problem I needed to solve. It was a relief to fail and realize I could survive. It left me more willing to take risks.

All that was fine, but the problem remained. Had I blown my chance to avoid having to study a second language? I went to see my math teacher, and to my relief, he assured me that that was not the case. He usually gave students who failed the test a grade of incomplete. This gave them the opportunity to study more and retake the test before the end of the next semester. If they passed the retake they got the credit for their second language. The research center where I worked was willing to reduce my work hours so I could study, and my tutor agreed to spend more time with me. When we started at the beginning of the textbook and worked our way through, the math began to make sense. In a couple months I retook the test and passed.

As Barry and I began to furnish our new apartment we discovered that our tastes were strikingly similar. Sometimes we toured a furniture gallery separately and ended up standing in front of the same piece as our first choice. When we didn't agree we kept looking until we found something we both liked, a rule we adopted early and retained as a central tenet of our joint decision-making process. Almost always we both liked our final mutual choice better than any of our previous individual favorites.

We laughed a lot, and valued each other's general intelligence, good judgment, and problem-solving skills. Neither of us thought one was smarter than the other, in part because our intelligences were somewhat different. Barry had great rote memory, and spelling, name, and date recall. I was better at remembering conversations and books in great detail and figuring out how things worked.

As we lived together we also began to notice differences of the annoying everyday kind. I stored my papers in folders and file cabinets and thought that throwing things away was next to godliness. Barry kept everything. He piled papers and folders on his small desk, on tops of bookcases, and in the dining room when he was working at his favorite place, the dining room table. Barry was a creature of routine. He liked a similar bedtime every night, a little earlier than I preferred, corn flakes for breakfast every morning, three meals a day, with a substantial dinner at night even if he'd had a big lunch. I needed variety. I was willing to stay up half the night to finish a good novel or work on an interesting project. I could eat any time of day and was perfectly happy with pie, cake or even dinner leftovers for breakfast or snacks for dinner. Little by little we moved into sync, each of us giving a little. A common bedtime was especially important to both of us because we loved the sensuality of cuddling and being physically close. He ended up getting a little less sleep. I got a little more.

Then, unexpectedly, we ran into a serious mismatch. I saw a Barry I had never seen before and I'm sure he felt the same about me. The situation built slowly.

"Those blue blinds have got to go," I said every morning, as I looked up at the venetian blinds left by the previous tenants that hung grubby and a little crooked across our two large bedroom windows and beside the freshly painted white walls.

"I don't think they're so bad," Barry mumbled without looking.

"Not so bad! I feel like I'm living in a tenement. We've got to get them down and put the curtain rods up."

Days dragged into weeks. In February Barry had a day off. "Today." I said. "It won't take long."

"Okay let's get it over with."

Barry scowled and faced the window. We pulled a chair in from the dining room to serve as a ladder. I left him alone so I wouldn't be tempted to make suggestions.

"Done yet?" I asked cheerily, poking in my head after what seemed like a long time.

"No."

The next time I popped back in to check how he was doing, he silently handed me the shades and bent mounts which he had just finished wrestling from the window frame. With a sense of accomplishment, I put them outside the kitchen door for the building superintendent to pick up with the trash. When I returned Barry was standing morosely studying the instructions for the new curtain rod holders.

"How am I supposed to make the holes?"

"Oh, I have a drill."

I produced a small hand drill that required two hands to operate and wobbled. Barry tried it and threw it down in disgust, making noises in his throat. Told me to leave him alone.

"Are you mad?" I asked when he stopped for lunch.

"No," he said, but everything about his body screamed "yes." This was a new Barry I'd never seen before, sullen, silent, withdrawn. I responded the way I used to when my mother had one of her depressed spells. I acted especially, chirpily cheerful.

"How's it coming?" I asked a little later in a lively, lilting voice. "You must be nearly finished by now. Can I help?"

"No."

I thought I heard muttered curses. The afternoon wore on. At last, on one of my frequent trips into the bedroom, I saw that the curtain rods were up. They looked a little wobbly on one side, but I didn't say anything. Barry stood glowering at the window.

"I'm not like your father," He announced emphatically.

I looked at him puzzled. What did that have to do with anything? He said it again louder, with more emphasis.

"I am not handy. I won't ever be handy. I know a man should be handy. But I'm not. I'm sorry if I'm a disappointment to you." He stood with head down in a posture of dejection. "I'm happy to do extra work as a lawyer to make money to pay someone to fix things," he added. "But I never want to spend a day-off like this again."

He was right, of course. I had assumed he would fix things the way my dad always did, had never asked him if he wanted to or knew how, just laid the task on him. I would have been furious if he had taken it for granted that I would handle all the tasks his mother did.

"I'm sorry," I said as I hugged him. "I shouldn't have presumed." We held each other tight, rocked side to side until the tension began to ease. After that I became responsible for fixing or getting things fixed. It was a responsibility that I, for the most part, enjoyed.

I had only two more barriers left on my journey toward a completed Ph.D. They were the biggest hurdles of all--oral comprehensives and a dissertation. I tried not to think about how many graduate students never got past them. In the Columbia sociology department, we took orals in four areas. Social Theory was required for everyone. We could choose the other three from an approved specialty list, which unfortunately did not include the new field of Sociology of Law, my primary specialty. I chose Deviance as the closest match, along with Sociology of Family, and Social Organization. In each area we met, usually just once, with a faculty member who agreed to examine us and directed our development of a two-to-three page reading list of major books and professional journal articles on his area of expertise.

Finding an examiner was not easy. Most of our professors were busy writing books or working on research projects and were not especially interested in spending time with students on their comprehensives. After we had our reading lists we were pretty much on our own. Materials on our lists were often difficult to find or in the reserve section of the library, where we had to use them on site. In 1966, libraries did not have computers, search engines, printers, or copiers. We hand copied the material we needed onto file cards or notebooks, a time-consuming process.

In June 1966 I resigned completely from my research job, effective the beginning of August, to accept a part-time teaching job starting in September at nearby Hunter College. I was eager to get back into the classroom, and teaching Introductory Sociology was supposed to be an ideal review for oral comprehensives.

In August 1966 Barry and I took our belated honeymoon, a five-week camping trip across the United States from New York to Seattle, down the West Coast, and back to New York. Our tent was tiny and the Datsun we borrowed from Barry's brother John was small. Living in such close quarters daily tested and strengthened our relationship. On our way home we stopped in the Denver-Boulder area of Colorado. I especially wanted Barry to see Colorado. When Penny and I spent time there in 1960 I thought Colorado would be a great place to live permanently. Even after the expanded trip Barry and I had just taken, I still felt that way. Barry liked it too.

Studying for my oral comprehensive exams dominated my life for six months, from the time Barry and I got back from our camping trip in early September to the end of February 1967. Our reading lists were the stuff of nightmares, so extensive that we could not possibly read everything. My work was lonely, as my thesis work in Northwestern had been, but my state of mind was totally different. One reason was that I had Barry and his constant support. Another reason was that at Columbia I was part of a substantial cohort of women graduate students. Several of us taking our exams around the same time organized study groups in which we talked about the readings, quizzed each other in mock exams, and shared the angst of the process. We still had no female faculty members and read almost all male authors who used predominately male pronouns, but we women were present, supporting each other, and moving forward in the profession. Most of us had already worked as sociology teachers or researchers. It would be a long time before the Columbia University Sociology Department would give tenure to a woman, and then only after a hard fight. But we women were in the door.

Although I was anxious about the exams, studying for them brought a deep satisfaction. I began to consolidate years of study and felt like I was becoming a professional. The announcement of my orals date, March 1, 1967, typed with a new black ribbon just below my name, came in the mail one snowy winter day. I had only two more weeks to prepare. Most of us women students spent more time than was sensible trying to figure out what to wear for the exams. Did we play down the fact that we were women and wear dark suits like men? Or did we flaunt our femininity in the hope that our attractiveness would add brilliance to our performance? I quickly opted for conservative dress, but then agonized over how conservative and what color.

I don't remember much about my exams, except that the faculty office where the exam was held had a lovely rug, the atmosphere was generally pleasant, my waiting time outside in the hall was short, and I passed. Barry was there afterwards with a big hug. It was an achievement for both of us.

Part Six
New Directions

CHAPTER **31**

Big Decisions

WITH ORAL COMPREHENSIVES successfully behind me, Barry and I took stock of where we were in our lives. It was 1967 and we were approaching age 30. Both of us wanted children. I still had the dissertation to finish. The dissertation was the toughest part of the program and could take years. I sometimes joked that I would be in menopause before I finished my degree. The very thought of that possibility, joke or not, scared me into serious consideration of trying to start a family soon. The older women got, the less likely they were to get pregnant and have healthy babies. I was already well beyond the age when most women of my era had their first, or even their *last* child.

Yet if we had a baby would I ever finish? The messages from the larger world around me were heavily weighted toward "No." I had heard the predictions many times. "As soon as you fall in love and have a family, you'll forget all about school." I had made it through the falling-in-love part. Actually, getting married and gaining the love half of my life had freed me to move forward on my degree. Barry's support had been central. But would I, could I, ever finish if we had kids? A lot of graduate students dropped out at the dissertation stage. There was a term for them, "All But Dissertation," ABD. I did not want to be ABD. It was too much like my mother's position as an almost nurse.

Barry and I talked a lot about what to do. Barry really wanted me to finish my education and assured me that he would help. It was his goal as much as mine. He also noted that we had some good role models for working mothers. Several of his female colleagues in the Attorney General's office were successfully combining family with their work as lawyers. If they did it, we should be able to do it too. We decided that I would start right away on developing a dissertation topic. We also decided we would start trying to get pregnant. In June we found out we were. We knew we wanted to share the raising of our child, but until we asked our friends about recommendations for an obstetrician, we had no idea that we could also share the actual childbirth experience. In the late 1960s, childbirth was still primarily managed by hospitals and physicians, not parents. The father paced anxiously in the waiting room while the mother was either totally knocked out or received 'twilight' drugs that left her awake enough to follow directions, but with no memory of the experience. Babies were kept in nurseries and were brought to their mothers for feeding every three or four hours.

Some hospitals and younger doctors, however, were interested in facilitating a more natural childbirth in which mothers could be awake during delivery and fathers could be with them throughout the labor and delivery experience. They also encouraged "rooming in" i.e. letting babies stay with their mothers all day. Only one hospital in Manhattan, New York Hospital, permitted all these practices. Our friends insisted that having both parents present at birth was a life experience not to be missed. It was a new idea for Barry and me, but our friends' enthusiasm was infectious. We decided to at least keep our options open and chose their obstetrician who delivered in New York Hospital, coincidently the same hospital where Barry and his brothers had been born.

With the possibility of an expanding family, Barry also began talking about leaving the Attorney General's office and looking for a job in private practice. Moving on to private practice was an expected next career-step for a young lawyer who had been in a public sector job for several years. It should ultimately yield a higher income. However, the move to a private law firm usually involved starting at the bottom again with several years of high pressure and late nights at the office. Barry already worked hard, but it was manageable. What I heard about the workload in private practice scared me. How would those hours fit with starting and sharing a family?

Barry liked working at the New York Attorney General's Office. He respected his colleagues, and since 1964 he had been assigned several interesting U.S. Supreme Court cases. He had also recently received a big raise. I sensed he felt real ambivalence about giving up a job he enjoyed. As he began to explore possible private practice jobs, he became pensive and didn't talk much about them. For the first time in our marriage, I felt left out of his thought process.

Barry eventually accepted a job at a small general practice firm in Manhattan, to which a colleague he respected from the Attorney General's office had moved three years earlier. He seemed pleased with his decision and the firm welcomed him warmly. I also started work on a dissertation proposal to study courts. With all these basic details in place, our lives seemed settled and ready for our new baby.

After Barry had been working for a few weeks, I became aware that something wasn't right with him. His new job hadn't changed our lives as much as I'd thought it would, which should have been good, but seemed odd. A spark had gone out. He seemed to be working less, not more, and didn't seem to care much about going to work. He wasn't as much fun, wasn't talking about his cases the way he used to. This was a Barry I had never seen before. One evening in late September he voiced his discontent.

"Private practice may not be for me," he announced. "I don't think I want to spend my life busting my ass to help make rich people richer."

His uncharacteristic behavior over the past several weeks suddenly made sense. I was glad to finally talk about it and loved him even more for his unwillingness to do work he disliked and seemed of little social value. But what kind of law could he practice instead? Barry's Harvard Law School class reunion was coming up in early October and he suggested we attend and find out what his classmates were doing. After talking with several of them, we were both depressed. Barry couldn't see himself in any of the work situations his fellow graduates described.

A week later, about 7:00 a.m. on a Saturday morning, I was aroused by a rustling in our room. I looked up to see Barry staring down at me fully dressed, clearly willing me to wake up.

"What's wrong?" I asked, propping myself up on one arm, trying to get my eyes open enough to focus on him.

Barry was not an early riser, was *never* up and fully dressed at 7:00 am, especially on a Saturday. He was bouncing with excitement.

"I have an IDEA."

"Yes?" I asked, trying to sound animated, puzzled by this totally unprecedented behavior.

"I'd like to go back to school and get a Ph.D."

"You w-what?" I stammered.

Reactions whirled through my head. I was five months pregnant, not working, had not finished my own degree. I had been through two dissertations with former boyfriends. Neither had been a positive experience. One of the things I had liked about Barry was that he was finished with school. The thought of him going back to graduate school had never entered my mind. I tried to get my face in order, my voice under control.

"That's really interesting," I said as enthusiastically as I could while I pulled a pillow up behind me and tried to maneuver myself, with my large belly, into a seated position.

"I woke up early and have been thinking about it for two hours," he exclaimed. "I haven't been so excited about anything or felt it was so right since we decided to get married."

"What would you study?" I asked, beginning to rise to the occasion.

"Public Law and Government at Columbia. Seems like you have really enjoyed graduate school and I think I would too. I'd like to teach, but not in law school."

We discussed Barry's idea all morning. The more he talked about it, the more sense it made. The Ph.D. would give him a wide range of skills and job flexibility, important for our hopefully two-career family. He was right, I had enjoyed graduate school, especially my Ph.D. work. I was sure Barry would too. We both liked to play with ideas and push ourselves intellectually. Money would be a problem, but if he were ever to go back to school, this was the right time, even with the baby coming. We had a large rent-controlled apartment, which we had just finished furnishing, lived within walking distance of Columbia, had some money in the bank, and I was nearly finished with my degree.

He figured out he could get through school in three years if he went full time. Because he had a reputation among other attorneys as a good researcher and legal brief writer, skills always in demand, he believed he could also pick up part-time work, as needed, from legal colleagues.

The next morning, he sent for application forms and information. As he started investigating possible financial aid, he discovered the Herbert H. Lehman Fellowship. It paid $5000 a year for three or four years full-time graduate enrollment in social sciences or political science in a university in New York State. Ninety were given out each fall. They were specifically for candidates with a public service background, for which Barry's work in the Attorney General's office should qualify him. He knew one of the recipients of a Lehman Fellowship at Columbia and talked with him about what candidates had to do to get one.

"To even be considered you need a score over 2100 out of a possible 2400 on the Graduate Record exams (GRE)," his friend told him. "If you don't think you can do that, don't even bother."

That's the end of that, I thought, when Barry told me. Only super brains can do that. I totally underestimated Barry's self-confidence and love of a competitive challenge. He signed up the next day for the relevant tests, came home with a pile of GRE practice test books, and began studying every night and weekend at our dining room table.

"The fellowship is the only way I can afford to go back to school. I think I have a good shot at getting one," he said.

We hadn't yet said anything to Barry's family about his idea. Barry wanted to think it through fully and have time to discuss it with them. As we got ready to go out to Scarsdale one Sunday for dinner, we prepared ourselves for a big blow-up. Pop sometimes got upset when Barry or his brothers deviated too much from the standard career plan of his own era, which was to get on a career path and continue until retirement. We braced ourselves as Barry cleared his throat and started to explain his idea.

"I never thought you were going to like private practice," his dad remarked after Barry finished. "I think your reasoning for going back to school is sound."

We sat stunned and delighted.

"Your father wanted to go to Germany to do graduate work in chemistry after he graduated from MIT and started working," Barry's mother added. "But it wasn't possible because of the depression."

Barry had never known about his father's desire to go to Germany for graduate work. We realized there was a lot we didn't know about how the Great Depression had narrowed the lives of our parents.

I loved Barry for his willingness to take risks to create the kind of life and work we both wanted. Going back to school for a Ph.D. at age 30 was not a conventional career path for a lawyer in the mid-1960s. It took a lot of self-confidence to try to carry it off. The risk of failure was substantial. Still we both wanted to make a difference in the world as well as a living. If Barry could find a way to afford to go to school, we would be in a better position to do both.

CHAPTER 32

Best Laid Plans...

AS WE MOVED through October 1967, Barry and I worked on our respective pre-baby goals. He studied nights and weekends for the GRE exams in early December and tried to work at his private practice job as if he were interested in it. I concentrated on developing a transition plan that would keep my academic momentum up from pre-baby to post-baby life. The only thing I had left to do to complete my Ph.D. was my dissertation. My academic goal before childbirth was to complete and get approval for my dissertation proposal. With that done, I could start working on my dissertation soon after we had the baby.

To that end I had been working on a preliminary draft for an observational study of criminal courts and had signed up for a special seminar at Columbia Law school, taught by Professor Leon Radzinowicz, a well-known criminologist visiting from Cambridge University in England. The seminar looked like fun, and the way the class was organized in three parts should help me re-engage in academia. I had just attended the Fall organizational meeting and had agreed to do a paper on court organization, which I could start researching immediately. We had six months to complete our papers and would reconvene for two weeks in May to present them, when I would be somewhat adjusted to motherhood. My work for the seminar should provide much of the material I needed for my dissertation literature review and also give the professional continuity I was trying to create.

My graduate advisor was Dr. Alan Barton, who had worked with the Law and Sociology Fellowship and had gone to bat for me a couple of times during that year. Alan was Director of the Bureau of Applied Social Research and considered by students I knew to be a good dissertation advisor--helpful, accessible, and generally benign. In November 1967 I dropped off a preliminary dissertation proposal for his review. A few days later I settled into a chair in his office to discuss it. Alan was affable, as usual. His blond cowlick fell over his forehead as he smiled and made small talk in his slow, drawling voice. Finally he got to the point.

"It's hard to evaluate an observational dissertation," he said, "Statistical studies are much easier."

It sounded like he was primarily concerned about how much work he would have supervising my project. I was about to protest when he stopped, looked at his bookcase thoughtfully, and turned to rummage on the bottom shelf. He pulled out a book with a bright blue and white jacket, glanced at it for a minute, then shoved it across his desk to me.

"This just came out. Have you run across this guy in your reading? Seems a lot like what you want to do."

I looked at the cover blurbs. It described a project much like mine by a sociologist/lawyer who had worked in the Manhattan Criminal Court for twenty years. How could I have missed this author, this book? I opened it, stared at the table of contents, and lifted my eyes to Alan's.

"Yeah, this is a lot like what I had in mind."

"Looks like he spent 20 years on it."

I had noticed. What could I possibly add? I was back to zero on my dissertation. Alan slid the pages I had given him back across the desk. The complete shutdown of my proposal without any discussion about possible related topics or other ways of studying courts left me stranded. With mumbled words of goodbye I stumbled out of his office.

Our baby was due in less than three months. The summary dismissal of my proposal shut down all academic interest. I turned all my attention to nesting, starting with the transformation of our office/guest room into a nursery. After painting two chests of drawers barn red, I sewed yellow curtains with ruffles. Barry and I had long conversations about baby names and finally decided on Katherine or Stephen. Barry's mother and I debated what kind of crib to buy. I purchased crib sheets and mooned over cute baby clothes. Some days I wondered if my total baby focus was the beginning of the end of my Ph.D., my slide into permanent domesticity? The messages I was getting from all sides suggested it probably was. Although I didn't feel very pregnant as long as I didn't try to squeeze through little spaces between people on buses the way I used to, others treated me like a walking womb. Hardly anyone talked to me about issues and ideas at social events. All conversations seemed focused on the baby. Women I hardly knew patted my belly, commented on how big I was, asked when I was due, and described their own deliveries.

The one piece of my professional life I kept going, even though it would no longer enhance my dead dissertation, was work on my paper for the Radzinowitz seminar. The library research I did for it was pure pleasure, a lifeline between my past academic self and an uncertain future.

As our pregnancy progressed, Barry and I decided we were interested in the more natural approach to childbirth our friends had recommended so highly. We bought and read Elizabeth Bing's newly published book about the Lamaze method, *Six Lessons for an Easier Childbirth*. We liked it and signed up for a Lamaze class, held a short bus ride down Broadway from our apartment, in the home of Mrs. Bing herself.

When we met her in her apartment the first night, Mrs. Bing didn't act like a "reformer," or "someone who had transformed American women's experience with childbirth," as she was described in her *New York Times* obituary nearly fifty years later. To us she was the kind, unassuming teacher with the welcoming smile who positioned six fidgeting husbands behind their six nervous wives and within

237

minutes got the men rubbing their wives' backs and bellies without embarrassment. In less than half an hour Barry was certain he wanted to be with me in the labor and delivery rooms. Over the next several weeks he made sure we practiced our prescribed breathing exercises every day.

It was late morning, right after Christmas. I was at my desk in our bedroom finishing up some reading for my Radzinowicz seminar when I heard the locks on our apartment door rattle. I jumped up startled, but before I could get to the front hallway to investigate Barry appeared in the bedroom doorway, looking a little disconcerted.

"Why are you here now?" I asked. "What happened?

"I just got politely fired. One of the partners called me in and said the firm and I didn't seem to be a good fit."

"Well you knew that."

"Yeah, but I guess I didn't realize they did."

We were having a baby in less than a month and suddenly faced the prospect of no income and no health insurance!

"He said they would give me as much time as I needed to find a new job."

I stared at him, struggling with my conflicting feelings of fear, because jobs took a long time to find, and relief, because he had been freed from work he disliked. Concerns about his graduate school dream welled up too. Who would hire a person who said he had to leave in a few months to go study for a Ph.D.?

"We'll be all right," Barry said as he gave me a reassuring hug.

Barry was always an optimist. I wasn't sure his optimism was warranted this time, but maybe it was. He was also a doer and immediately compiled a list of colleagues in the field of criminal justice who might know about employment possibilities. He started calling them that afternoon. His first call was to Herb Sturz, my old boss from Vera. Herb asked him to come down the next morning for an interview. Two other calls also yielded possible job leads.

The next morning, even after Barry told him he hoped to go to graduate school in nine months, Herb offered him a job on a new Vera project that involved working to improve juvenile justice in New York's Family Court. Barry explored other options, then decided to accept the Vera job. It was not only more interesting that the one he was leaving, it paid better. The sting of being fired was further salved a few days later by the arrival of Barry's GRE results, high enough to be considered for the fellowship he hoped to win.

Our baby's due date of January 22 came and went. Other dates came and went. Although I had planned to wait until after the baby was born to write up the final version of my paper for the Radzinowitz class, the delay was pushing the seminar deadline uncomfortably close. I decided I better start writing. It was a good distraction. I had no time to sit around trying to create contractions. January passed into February. I was convinced I would be pregnant forever. The doctor said not to worry, we were still in the normal range, but if I went another week without going into labor we might have to do something. I tried to focus all my frustrated energy on finishing my seminar paper, which was taking longer than I had anticipated. At last I pulled the final page out of my portable electric typewriter, separated the original from its carbon copy, stapled it with a loud thwack, and placed it into an envelope addressed to the law school for duplication and distribution to seminar members.

"I can have the baby now," I called to Barry, who was in the kitchen preparing beef stew with beer, one of our favorite meals.

That night, around 3:00 a.m. February 5, 1968, I woke to feel unusual action through my middle. We tried to time the contractions, which turned out to be more difficult than the doctor and childbirth books suggested. The doctor told us to hang out at home as long as possible. We weren't sure where 'possible' ended but decided to catch a cab to the hospital just as the New York skyline was touched with pale winter light. We could have stayed home a lot longer. The day and my labor wore on from early light to mid-afternoon without much action. Barry's enthusiasm never waned as he kept me company and coached my breathing exercises hour after hour. I couldn't imagine going through labor without him.

"We're going to have Katherine or Stephen really soon," Barry exclaimed. "Isn't that exciting!"

"Sure," I said.

The lights were bright as we entered the delivery room. It seemed all silver and white and full of people. Barry stood at my head and a nurse adjusted a mirror above me so I could watch the birth.

'Push' someone commanded. I pushed and panted on cue as I'd been taught. Even this part, which was supposed to be so dramatic, seemed agonizingly slow.

Then suddenly a dark head appeared, followed by a baby.

"It's Katherine," shouted Barry.

Katherine announced herself with a lusty yowl.

"Nine pounds, 4 ounces," reported the nurse as she weighed Katherine, wrapped her in a warm blanket, and laid her in my arms. She had a mop of black hair and stared at Barry and me with intense interest. We smiled back at this new person in the world. We were a family, all finally on the same side of a great mystery. Barry and I were parents.

CHAPTER **33**

High Fever, High Praise, Big Let-Down

THE NEXT AFTERNOON, after Barry's parents had visited to meet and admire Katherine, I lay listening to the three other mothers in our rooming-in unit chatting with each other about their recent deliveries. They seemed very bouncy and full of energy.

"I'm so glad I'm young," one said. "It must be awful for those 30-year old mothers. I feel sorry for them."

Thirty-year-old mother? That was *me*. I was 30. They felt *sorry* for me?

I wanted to holler over to them, "I'm 30 and I feel fine."

Except I didn't.

At temperature-taking time, the nurse took mine twice, and asked me if I was feeling hot. I said yes, although just before that I'd been freezing. My doctor appeared in minutes. "I've ordered some tests," he said. "You've got a pretty high fever." The lab technician arrived as the doctor was hurrying off. When the nurse appeared to check my temperature again, I took a peek when she wasn't looking. The thermometer registered somewhere over 104 degrees.

My doctor reappeared to tell me I had a serious infection, probably from the delivery room, and they had to move me to a private room and start antibiotics. Before I could absorb that information our pediatrician turned up to tell me he had checked Katherine.

"The baby's fine," he said, "just a few bugs on her umbilical cord, nothing serious. We've started her on penicillin and moved her to an isolation nursery."

Before I could fully register that Katherine was sick too, a nurse piled all my belongings on top of my bed and an orderly wheeled me out of the room toward the elevator. The young mothers hardly bothered to turn their eyes to note my removal from new baby paradise. A few minutes later I was in an odd little room about the size of a linen closet with one window that rattled in the wind. A nurse immediately hooked me up to an I.V. and brought in a breast pump "to keep my milk flowing." I didn't understand why I needed it.

The sympathetic nurse tried to explain. I would not be able to see Katherine until we both got better. Not see, not hold Katherine!! How could she learn to nurse?

It was almost dark. New York City was in the grip of an arctic cold wave with record lows. Everyone said the freeze was good because it would stop the stink from the garbage piling up in the streets from the ongoing sanitation workers' strike. My room was dim, just a single light near the head of my bed. I could feel and hear the wind blowing in. I was freezing and burning up with fever at the same time and terrified. Was Katherine all right? Would Barry ever find her or me when he came to visit?

"The wind coming through the window is making my head cold." I told the nurse.

"I make a little tent for you," she said as she started to arrange some towels over the top and side of the bed, "like refugee camp."

Refugee camp? That analogy had never crossed my mind. I looked with new respect at the Asian nurse who had been so kind to me since my sudden arrival and felt ashamed of whining that my room was too small, too dark, too cold.

Barry looked frightened when he finally pushed open the door to my room, but he soon located Katherine and returned to report that she was very cute and getting a lot of attention from the nurses. I relaxed a little.

The next day my doctor told me that every woman who had given birth in the last two days in my delivery room had the same bacteria. I had been the first and was the most seriously ill. In spite of investigations, there were no clues about the source of the infection. It was like a medical mystery novel, except it was me, in bed, getting antibiotics by IV and my fever still wasn't going down. I had read about 'childbirth fever' in novels. The women usually died. Barry tried to act cheerful, but I knew by the tight way he held my hand that he was worried.

The doctor added an additional antibiotic to my IV mix, a rather toxic one I learned later when I looked it up, but its effectiveness was apparent almost immediately. My fever dropped rapidly to normal. My life began to move back toward normal too. The nurses let me take a shower, and when they weren't looking I washed my hair, which enormously improved my sense of wellbeing. An aide took me to view Katherine through the glass of the isolation nursery. Although I was relieved to see that she was thriving, my arms ached to hold her.

After two more days without fever, we were discharged from the hospital. Barry helped me into the taxi, and a nurse laid Katherine, tightly wrapped in warm yellow blankets, in my arms. I cradled her close, feeling the warmth of her little body against my arms and shoulder. As we rode home, Barry and I sat close gazing at and talking to her. She turned her wide-awake eyes on us as if she understood every word.

Our first diaper maneuver at home on Katherine's red changing table started off well. We got the poop filled one off successfully. Then just as Barry picked up her legs to replace it, she pooped again, an exuberant green brown stream that he only partially caught with the clean diaper. We laughed so hard we could hardly wipe her bottom and try again.

"Guess we'll be laughing a lot," I told Barry. "One of our books says breast fed babies can have up to 30 bowel movements a day."

Barry suddenly looked very sober.

We had arranged months earlier for a baby nurse to stay for the two weeks after I got home, but because Katherine was born later than expected, the nurse had had to move on to her next cases. Now because I had been so sick, I *really* needed a baby nurse. Hiring one on the spur of the moment was nearly impossible, yet Barry had somehow managed to locate two highly recommended nurses, one for each of my first two weeks home. My only time alone would be on the first day. The nurse could not get to our place until three hours after Barry had to leave for work.

"No problem," I said. "We'll be fine."

Katherine started fussing as soon as Barry left, and as I rocked her in our brand-new rocking chair and tried to feed and quiet her, I watched the nearby clock. It took an hour for each minute to pass. My arms and back ached. I felt hot. When the doorbell rang I stumbled to the door carrying a crying Katherine. The nurse took one look at us, dropped her bag, and reached out.

"Let me take that sweet baby. You look like you need a break."

Katherine settled down immediately, secure in those experienced, loving arms.

When my parents arrived after the second nurse left two weeks later, I was feeling much better, ready to celebrate with them. We were now referring to Katherine as Katie, the nickname Barry and I decided we liked best. She was a calm baby, and because of her nine-pound-plus birth weight, she started sleeping through the night early. When she was awake she was active, always pushing herself to master a new skill. We all spent a lot of time just gazing at and cuddling her, marveling at her every move. A few days after my parents arrived we had more to celebrate. Barry learned that he had won one of the Herbert H. Lehman Fellowships. His dream of graduate school would become a reality.

By the time my law school seminar started I felt healthy, and Barry and I had settled into parenthood. I reveled in the seminar and felt like a star in the class. It was the best law school experience I'd had. One of the law school professors invited us to a party in his elegant

East Side apartment in honor of Visiting Professor Radzinowitz. It was exhilarating. Several teachers from my former Law and Sociology Fellowship were present and remarkably complimentary to me, in sharp contrast to when I had been on the Fellowship. It made me wonder what the host had put in our drinks. Professor Radzinowicz was also full of praise for my work.

"Your seminar paper was excellent. Have you applied for a fellowship to study at the Institute of Criminology in Cambridge?"

"No."

"That's too bad, because you could have one."

"That's easy to say since I haven't applied," I laughed.

"Well you can have one if you ever apply. Remember that."

I took his offer with a grain of salt but appreciated his apparent admiration of me as a sociologist and a woman, just when I needed it most.

My letdown was intense after the law school seminar and party ended. The seminar had been a nice diversion, but now I had to face reality. I would soon be up against Columbia's time limit for completion of my degree and was still searching for a good dissertation topic. My definition of a feasible dissertation had narrowed considerably since I had become a mother. The ideas I had contemplated over the past year involved extensive field research, and I realized that they would be difficult to do well with a new baby. I needed something I could work on closer to the Columbia campus.

Katie flourished. When Barry and I watched her try to turn over, our own stomach muscles ached, and when she finally succeeded in a new maneuver her look of triumph was so infectious we grinned also. We wanted to spend as much time with her as possible. Perhaps, I thought, I should forget about my degree and stay home with Katie. That's what my neighbor on the top floor of our building did after she had her baby. She put aside her Ph.D. in physics and became a full-time mother.

CHAPTER 34

Facing Boundaries and Picket Lines: 1968

ALL MY LIFE the world had sent me the message that once I became a mother I would no longer *want* a career. I discovered that the world was wrong, at least in my case. I loved Katie more than I thought it was possible to love, but I refused to follow the example of my stay-at-home upstairs neighbor. I wanted to be a good mother and felt I was, and I *still* wanted to finish my Ph.D. and work as a sociologist. In that desire, however, I was now not just ignoring the boundaries my era had created for women, I was also challenging the definition of a good mother, a far more serious transgression. When Americans were asked in public opinion polls if they approved of mothers of young children working, most respondents said no. Good mothers stayed home with their kids. The expectations for mothers decreed by mass media, especially women's magazines, and the casual comments by women themselves, occasionally dropped in my presence, left little room for a woman's own self development.

"No one can take care of a child as well as the child's own *mother.*"

"I couldn't imagine putting my own ambition ahead of my child's well-being. It seems so *selfish.*"

"I've never had a babysitter for my child except my mother. I could never leave him with a *stranger.*"

In 1968, the U.S. Department of Labor Women's Bureau reported that only 17% of mothers with a child under three and a husband present worked outside the home full time. In most of these families, it was believed, the woman worked only because the husband's income was too low to support the family. Childcare centers then were almost nonexistent. They cared for only 6% of the children under six years of age.

Becoming parents was an enormous and ongoing shift for both of us, individually and as a couple, but my transition to parenthood was more complex than Barry's. As a married woman aspiring to work and have someone else care for my children part of the time, I was an anomaly and open to censure. I had no clear right, as men did, to the enjoyment of both love and meaningful work, unless that work was care of my own child.

Nineteen sixty-eight, Katie's birth year, was marked for Barry and me not just by the new experiences and feelings parenthood brought, but also by events that left us and our nation grieving and off-center. The deadly Tet Offensive launched against the U.S. and its allies in the Vietnam War in January and the new draft call for 48,000 men in February sent tremors through all of us. The assassination of Dr. Martin Luther King, Jr. in April triggered major riots in over 100 American cities, and the Poor People's march on Washington a few weeks later drew 500,000 participants, among them, Barry's brother Bob.

Within this context of unrest, Barry was deeply involved in the juvenile court project for the Vera Institute of Justice, happy to be doing work that he felt mattered, while I continued to explore possible ideas for a dissertation topic. We both spent as much time as we could with Katie, whose smiles and constant efforts at self-improvement helped us keep a larger perspective on life. Our efforts to find someone to stay with Katie were initially cushioned by the appearance, a few weeks after Katie's birth, of Genevieve, a Barnard College student who came to babysit for us one evening. She and Katie seemed to enjoy each other, so when she let us know she was looking for a part time job we hired her to take care of Katie three days a week. An early childhood teacher I'd met at Columbia, the wife of a Canadian graduate student, filled in for us for a fourth day. Childcare seemed easy enough to find. We had no idea what lay ahead.

As 1968 wore on, political activism ticked up. Baby boomers had come of age and surged into colleges and universities. They began protesting against the war as well as dormitory rules, racism, and anything else that restricted their and others' freedom. In late April, the political upheaval arrived on our doorstep. With surprising speed and drama in one of the earliest university disruptions in America, students took over or "liberated" five Columbia University buildings, including Columbia's main administration building (known as Low Library), and Fayerweather Hall where Sociology was housed.

On the evening of April 29, after several days of negotiation, chaos and rhetoric, Columbia summoned the police to clear the buildings, by that time occupied by over 1000 students and surrounded by hundreds more supporters. The liberators resisted and police plowed into students, protestors, and bystanders alike, swinging their batons. By the end of the night 711 protestors, mostly students, were arrested and 148, including 20 police officers, were injured. Of the 71 graduate students arrested, 21 were in the sociology department. Our European traveling companion Becky called Barry and me the next morning traumatized. She had been on campus when the violence erupted and got caught up in the terrifying melee of student and police brutality. "I couldn't believe this was happening in America," she said, her voice still unsteady.

Sociology faculty members, many of whom had been active in trying to mediate and calm the university situation, asked for input from the Sociology Graduate Student Society. The Society immediately called us all to a meeting to decide what we would present. I went, eager to be involved. The protesting students raised concerns about the university's collaboration with the defense department and its relationship with the local neighborhood. They also demanded that university faculty members become more responsive to student needs.I agreed with all these concerns and had personally experienced the lack of faculty interest in working with students, as had almost all of us in sociology.

We met in a long narrow room, dimly lit by chandeliers, somewhere in Columbia's main library. Loud exclamations punctuated the buzz of conversation as about forty of us sat on folding chairs studying a mimeographed list of 22 demands the leaders wanted to submit to the administration. The demands looked like they had been put together hastily. Some were redundant. Others were inflammatory. One, amnesty for leaders and students who had occupied the buildings, had already been a major sticking point in earlier negotiations between demonstrators and the university. I was eager to discuss the demands, help decide which ones were most important, and participate in developing a strategy for action. It looked like it would be a long meeting.

The meeting started with a barrage of strident and uncompromising rhetoric from leaders, punctuated by clapping. Someone read off the slate of demands. There was a quick move and second to accept all of them without discussing each individually. The demands were all passed as a block before I could blink. Almost before all hands were down, another motion and second were made to declare all the demands as non-negotiable.

"Yes, yes," participants shouted. "We will not negotiate any of them! The faculty and University must recognize our power." With a final round of cheers the group voted to adjourn the meeting.

I sat stunned by the lack of thoughtful process, sloppiness of stated demands, and decision to refuse to negotiate. My college friends had always teased me about being a radical. Now suddenly I felt that I was on the conservative end of the political spectrum. I hadn't changed, but the world around me had. The baby boomers had arrived with a new radical agenda. My silent generation caution made it difficult, if not impossible, to embrace their tactics. I left the meeting alone, wondering who I was, where I fit in this new non-negotiable world. My self-concept had been seriously rocked.

As student demonstrations spread, Americans all across the country were suddenly becoming aware of this new political and social force. The Columbia protests continued. I retreated from further attempts at political action. Leaders called for a student strike that drew wide support from most students and many faculty members. Protestors again occupied buildings, including sociology's Fayerweather Hall. As unrest continued the administration again called the police to clear occupied buildings. A new riot ensued with more arrests and injuries. School was essentially over for the year, but periodic student protests that closed one or more buildings became a chronic part of the Columbia scene for the rest of my time there.

In June Robert Kennedy was assassinated. Violent riots against the war disrupted the August Democratic Convention in Chicago, as it became clear that 1968 had become the deadliest year yet in the Vietnam War. In spite of wide-ranging demonstrations, or perhaps because of them, our country in November veered politically to the right when Richard Nixon was elected President of the United States. The bright new world that Barry and I thought we had helped set in motion when we cast our first votes for a U.S. president in the election of John F. Kennedy just eight years earlier, seemed a faded, long ago dream.

The world as we knew it was shifting rapidly. The baby boomers were challenging many institutions and prevailing cultural norms, but by no means all. Although they eagerly dismantled the *in loco parentis* phiilosophy in women's dormitories that had frustrated me as a dorm counselor at Northwestern, they did very little to change attitudes about women or women's roles. There were many women in the protest movements, but they rarely moved into leadership positions.

During spring and summer in between the demonstrations, I tried to develop a dissertation topic. Progress was essential. My time limit for degree completion was almost up. Some days the effort to keep trying felt so enormous, so beyond my talent and energy level, I couldn't conceive of ever finishing my degree.

"You can't stop now," Barry exclaimed wherever I expressed my doubts. "We'll do whatever you need to ensure that you finish your Ph.D."

Barry and I both enrolled in Columbia in September 1968. I registered as a full-time dissertation student, after having been on part-time status after Katie was born. That gave me access to free computer time and workspace at the Bureau of Applied Social Research. Two friends invited me to share an office there, and I began to integrate back into graduate student culture and the world of sociology. Barry started his new Ph.D. program and immediately met interesting colleagues, including another lawyer who had also returned to graduate school. He quickly got involved in student government in his department. After the spring riots, departments all over the university were beginning to understand that student input might be useful.

We enjoyed working in the same place, a few blocks from home. We could maximize our time together as a family and share the big changes Katie was undergoing. One morning shortly after we started the academic year, we walked into her room to find her standing tall in her crib with a grin of such absolute triumph it made us smile all day long. She had achieved the major human trait of pulling herself upright and we realized she would be walking soon.

Once I started hanging around other graduate students at the Bureau, I began to learn about dissertation research possibilities.

"Call Dr. Patricia Kendall," a colleague suggested to me. "She's looking for students to do secondary analysis on her 1962 survey of medical residents and interns. She's good to work with. I used her data and I've just finished."

The word 'finished' resonated. Dr. Kendall was a highly regarded member of the Columbia sociology community and probably would have had tenure there long ago if the Columbia Sociology Department gave tenure to women, which at that time it definitely did not. I had always viewed law and medicine as parallel and similar universes. I knew a lot about lawyers. It would be interesting to study doctors. I called Dr. Kendall. She had just left Columbia to teach at Queens College but agreed to let me use her data for my dissertation and work with me on a study of young doctors' career decisions about solo or group practice. Alan Barton would remain my official Columbia advisor. I began to move toward a feasible project and felt like I was finally on track, until suddenly I was derailed.

In late December, the day before Barry, Katie, and I planned to leave for Florida to spend Christmas with my parents, our babysitter Genevieve announced that she could no longer babysit for Katie, effective immediately. Our backup childcare provider was no longer available either. She had just moved back to Canada. I was about to comprehend the stark reality that having a career was not just about wanting one, working hard, and being willing to challenge the expectations for a good mother. It was almost totally dependent on good childcare, and good childcare was hard to find.

CHAPTER **35**

Epiphanies

MY DISSERTATION WORK went on hold in January1969 while I searched for a new babysitter. Although Barry usually stepped in to help with childcare, he couldn't do much because he was fully engaged with his first semester of final exams and papers. Our network of friends offered, at that moment, no leads. We had already ruled out nanny agencies. The women such agencies had sent us, on the few occasions we had used them, did not seem compatible with our lifestyle and values. Besides, their fees were high. There were no childcare facilities in the city for children under three that I could locate. In some societies, like Sweden and Norway, children are viewed as a national treasure and governments offer a wealth of child-serving resources for families. Not so in the U.S., with its strong individualistic and hands-off orientation to both families and children.

My only remaining option to connect with women seeking childcare work was to put a help-wanted advertisement in the Sunday *New York Times*. The first responses woke me up at Saturday midnight, right after the newspaper went on the newsstands. The second wave of calls aroused me at 6:30 a.m. Sunday morning and continued unabated all day. The voices were predominantly Caribbean or Puerto Rican.

"Just try me. I take care good care of your child. You see. Give me a chance."

I sensed and sympathized with the women's need and desperation.

How could I fairly sort out the best candidates to interview from among the onslaught of responses? My first question was usually about a woman's local references. Many had none.

"How can I get references if I can't get a job?" one woman asked.

In the end, I had half a dozen prospects whose English I could understand and said they had references and some childcare experience. After checking references I was down to three, for whom I set up interviews at home with Katie and me. Among the interviewees, Miss Bird seemed like the only viable candidate. She claimed substantial nanny work and the person she listed as her last employer spoke well of her. She was a talkative, cheery grandmotherly type, willing to come four days a week, could start immediately, and Katie liked her. We hoped she might stay with us for years.

On day one she explained she would be late the next day because she had a scheduled, though previously unmentioned, appointment for a pap smear. I, being supportive of preventative healthcare and the employee right to get it, agreed. On day two, when she finally showed up, she asked for a hammer to hang a large calendar in our small kitchen, "to make the place seem a little more homey for me." On day three she explained what kind of food she wanted us to provide for her lunch. She particularly liked lamb chops.

"I feel displaced from my own home," Barry complained.

On day four we fired her with a week's severance pay. I wondered if she made a business of applying for jobs and getting fired in the first week.

Where could I look next? How could I possibly do a dissertation without childcare? Or ever have a career?

As I searched through my address book trying to find someone I had not already contacted, I remembered a woman outside my usual network who was particularly resourceful and might have some ideas. Without much hope I gave her a call, and our luck turned unexpectedly. Her daughter had just been admitted to nursery school. She and her husband planned to cut back their much loved, full-time nanny Mrs. Restell to two days a week. We interviewed Mrs. Restell the next day. She was a neat, pleasant-looking woman in her late fifties with laugh lines in her face and reddish-gray hair tucked up on her head. She had a lifetime of experience with children and she and Katie bonded immediately. With Mrs. Restell, a dissertation seemed possible. I started back to work on my proposal.

My office mates at the Bureau were irreverent, funny, and usually up on the latest gossip around the department and university, an especially valuable commodity in our ongoing revolutionary environment. I felt the sense of connection and camaraderie that I needed to keep going in the essentially isolated work of data analysis and writing. One of my colleagues was just finishing her dissertation, using the same data set I would be using, so many of the files I needed were already in the office.

In March 1969, shortly after Katie celebrated her first birthday, I turned in a progress report to my advisor Alan Barton. Never one to give lavish praise, he said it seemed okay. That was enough. At last I was on track, past the point where someone would tell me to start over on a new topic. I met with Dr. Kendall at her nearby apartment every few weeks to get feedback on my work. My goal was to finish my dissertation in time to get it approved and submitted to the Graduate School by its fall deadline of December 5, 1969. That gave me about nine months to finish.

Katie thrived. Sometimes Mrs. Restell brought her up to Columbia at the end of the day where Barry or I met her under the Alma Mater statute. There she endlessly practiced climbing up and down the wide stone steps. As the weather warmed we moved to the sunny plaza in front of the new Business School building, with its small decorative blue-tiled pools, cooled by trickling fountains. At first Katie sat on the wide edges of one of the pools, giggling and dipping her toes in the shallow water. As she got taller she slipped in all the way and sloshed back and forth with other kids, flirting with the water sprays that spouted from each corner. It was a lighthearted, joyful spot for all of us on a campus plagued with anti-war demonstrations, unconditional demands, and strikes.

One day in August 1969 I sat in my Bureau office in a funk. My desk was cluttered with folded lengths of computer output filled with tables, files of partially finished analysis, and rough drafts of chapters on the history and current status of medical practice. Research methodology books lay in disarray on the bookshelf by my right hand. I felt scattered and hopeless. The December deadline for the submission of my dissertation was fast approaching. Even though Barry was taking care of Katie in late afternoons and on weekends so I would have extra time to work, I couldn't imagine meeting it.

I had moved from the cramped desk between two file cabinets, that I had occupied when I first arrived in the office, to the larger desk of my colleague who had successfully finished her degree and moved on to real life. I had hoped the desk might be lucky for me too, bring *me* a successful defense and a real life. At the moment that seemed unlikely

I was alone in the office. The door was closed. I leaned forward, chin cupped in my hands, my head swirling with 'can'ts,' 'won'ts,' and 'nevers.' The sun from the window behind me slanted briefly across a piece of unfurled computer printout on the desk. A sense of defeat rolled over me. I couldn't imagine ever finishing. Except that I had to. I couldn't let all my years of work go now. I didn't want Katie to grow up, as I had, with the model of an *almost* successful mother.

I put down my hands and lifted my head. "Okay," I said out loud to myself. "What have I got?"

Slowly I began to pile up the various pieces of paper strewn about my office in a rough order that followed the basic framework of a dissertation. Oblivious to the usual noises outside in the hall, I gathered manila folders and unanalyzed computer tables, pulled out fragments from drawers, and shuffled rough ideas in with developed ones. When I had cleared my desk and heaped all the material into one pile, I leafed through it, rearranged a few pages, and created a table of contents that I laid on top. Then I stared at the haphazard-looking stack on my desk with awe.

"I have here a rough draft of my dissertation," I told myself. "Now I'm going to start revisions."

The psychological impact was electrifying.

Suddenly instead of feeling that I was flailing around, bouncing erratically from one paper, one idea, to another, I saw a dissertation. It needed a lot of work, but it was there. The moment was a turning point.

In early October I found a typist, a major necessity for completion of a dissertation in that pre-computer era. By late October I guessed my chances of making the December deadline were 50/50. When I showed my work to my advisor Alan Barton he was even more pessimistic, but I decided to aim for the December deadline anyway. I understood the work wasn't brilliant, probably didn't have enough exciting findings to make into a book, but it should at least yield an article or two.

Barry was now in his second year of graduate school, busy with classes and his work as a teaching assistant. He was also writing a book with Professor Alan Westin about a 1967 case in which the U.S. Supreme Court had affirmed an Alabama court's conviction of Martin Luther King. Somehow he still always found time to read and comment on my dissertation drafts. We were now starting to feel the real financial pinch of our both being full-time graduate students. I needed to finish my degree, not just for Katie and my mental health, but because we needed me to get a job.

In late November I took my finished, neatly typed dissertation to Dr. Kendall for a last review before submission to the Graduate Office. Two days later I stopped back to get her comments.

"I don't think this will do," she said in a harried voice. "I'm not sure what the problem is....."

What did she mean? She'd been working with me chapter by chapter for months. How could she say this now? I stood in her bookshelf-lined living room unable to respond, just stared at her in disbelief.

"I can't make this decision," she finally said. "Take it to Alan Barton. He knows the requirements better than I do. Whatever he says I'll go along with."

I cheered up a little. As my official advisor, Alan had seen a recent version and had been reasonably positive.

"I think this can go forward," Alan said the next day after looking through it, "but I want to read it carefully before the defense and lay out necessary revisions."

It sounded like I might have a tough defense, but at least we were moving in the right direction. After I dropped my dissertation off in the Graduate Dean's office the day before the final deadline, I started preparations to go to Florida with Barry and Katie to celebrate Christmas with my parents. All I wanted to think about was tinsel, sand, and sunshine.

The days of January eked by with no word from the Graduate Office about a thesis defense date. Rumors were that the office was overwhelmed with defenses. Since the previous year's riots many faculty members had submitted their resignations, and we all wanted to get out before the professors we knew left Columbia. The notice of my defense date arrived the end of January. It was February 11, 1970 at 10:00 a.m. in 301m, Fayerweather Hall.

I had never been in 301m Fayerweather Hall and immediately went to investigate. It was right above what had always been my favorite place in the building, a high ceilinged, elegant, wood-paneled seminar room full of light from a line of tall windows on two sides, with a long, inlaid, antique table. I'd had several classes there and had fantasized about someday defending my dissertation there too. Not now. The downstairs seminar room was closed off and unusable. Its table and beautiful woodwork had been destroyed during the 1968 building occupations, reputedly burned as firewood. Room 301m, just above it, was reached by a utilitarian set of stairs rising off the side of a sterile classroom. It was functional, but dreary, predominately gray.

The defense went okay. My advisor Alan Barton was supportive and his concerns and suggestions for change seemed manageable. Dr. Kendall weighed into the discussion positively throughout, in spite of her initial doubts. The other two examiners raised no serious issues. I passed with revisions, the most common form of pass. I began to allow relief to surge through my body. I was actually going to be Anne Rankin Mahoney, Ph.D. After everyone shook my hand I fled down the steps to Barry.

"Passed," I said. "Let's get out of here. I'm ready to party."

And party we did. The next weekend. We invited everyone we knew.

The pressure was off. I was on my own time schedule for revisions and I could spend lots of time with Katie. Each week we had special Wednesdays together when we went exploring to a museum, playground, or library. She was just over two, with a tousled head of dark hair and big brownish green eyes that she turned beguilingly on everyone around her. We made friends every time we took the bus together. She had been an early walker; now she was an early talker, with lots of questions.

"Wha dat?" she'd demand, pointing her finger.

On weekends Barry, Katie, and I went adventuring together, often in Central Park, where we frequently visited the zoo and the carousel and sometimes got talked into buying a balloon. One day Katie's balloon got away and floated up into the blue sky before we could secure it. I watched mesmerized, remembering my first Thanksgiving in New York when I had seen another child's balloon break free, as I had wanted to break free. Katie's face puckered into a frown and her mouth opened in protest.

"Look Katie," I said in the moment before the cry came out, "Look at how beautiful your balloon is flying in the sky so free. It's going on an adventure."

Katie shut her mouth and stared at the balloon, unexpectedly quiet. "Fy," she said, and pointed.

The moment I had been unable to ever actually visualize arrived in mid-May 1970. The requisite number of copies of my revised and finally approved dissertation had been perfectly typed with all the margins and references exactly right. My parents were in town to help me celebrate. Barry and I had purchased a bottle of Piper-Heidsieck champagne, the same kind we'd had for our wedding. It was ready to pop as soon as I came back from depositing my completed Ph.D. dissertation in the Graduate Dean's Office at Columbia.

There seemed to be a lot of action on campus as I climbed the steps toward Low Library where the Graduate School offices were located. As I grew closer I realized we were in the midst of one of the demonstrations that still periodically closed parts of Columbia. The doors to Low Library were blocked by strikers and picket signs. I stopped and stared at the scene. Although I didn't agree with non-negotiable demands, my sympathy was still with the complaints of the strikers. I was not about to cross the picket line.

After watching for a moment, I turned around and trudged back down the steps, still clutching my precious package. We'd have the champagne anyway, I decided, to celebrate my *attempt* to deliver my finished dissertation. I'd try again in a few days.

Dissertation complete I began to wonder if I really wanted to work. The available jobs were all fulltime and a long commute. I loved my time with Katie and we were thinking about having a second child. Besides, the general expectation that I should stay home if I were *really* a good mother still nagged at me.

"You can stay home if you want," Barry assured me. "We can manage that."

Then he chuckled. "But I give you about two weeks before you change your mind."

I laughed too, suspecting he was right.

Not long after our conversation I found myself standing on a pile of books on top of the kitchen counter, wavering back and forth as I tried to reach the top of the high cupboards so I could wipe them clean with a damp cloth. I had been cleaning the shelves for some time, periodically grasping at them to keep my balance. Katie played below me on the worn red and blue speckled linoleum, squawking for attention.

"You no kean," she complained.

"Just be patient," I responded with annoyance, "Mommy won't be much longer."

I looked down at her angry little face, steadied myself, and suddenly registered the situation. This was what I was doing with my newly acquired Ph.D. and my precious time home with Katie, ignoring her to scrub a spot no one in the world would see or care about. I was imitating the friends of my mother back in my 1940's childhood in Linesville, equating cleanliness with mothering. Free to fly at last, after so many years of pushing boundaries in my effort to achieve both family and career, how had I allowed myself to get stuck here, precariously balancing on a pile of books in the name of being a good mother?

CHAPTER 36

Rich in Love

A FEW MONTHS later, in fall 1970, as the ginkgo tree leaves were beginning to turn the sidewalks in Riverside Park yellow, I took Katie, now two and a half years old, to visit the West Side Montessori School where Barry and I hoped to enroll her when she was old enough. As we turned from Broadway toward the school on West 99th Street I stopped suddenly, flooded with memories. I had lived on the 18th floor of this corner apartment building when I first moved to New York in June 1961. How unsure of myself I'd felt nine years ago, how emotionally poor I'd been then, so desperate for a close relationship at any cost to myself.

Now I felt rich in the love I shared with Barry and Katie, and I had completed the Ph.D. that had seemed a hopeless dream then. Barry was doing well on his doctoral work too, now starting his third year, studying for his comprehensive exams while teaching as a part-time instructor at City College of New York and Barnard College. After my epiphany cleaning cupboards on top of our kitchen counter, I'd gone searching for a job as a sociologist. In a short time, I had found a part-time position teaching sociology, family, and research methods in the M.A. nursing program for college graduates, located at New York Medical College in nearby Flower Fifth Avenue Hospital. Surely life was full now. Full enough.

Except it wasn't. The urge for more still impelled me forward. Our family was not yet complete. Barry and I wanted a second child, but we had recently suffered a miscarriage. The doctor told us not to worry. I tried not to and hoped that I might already be pregnant again, but that was probably wishful thinking. My career wasn't complete either. I still wanted to teach sociology in a college or university. Work in the nursing school was interesting, but far from the career I envisioned. I worried that it gave me little chance to build the research and writing record I would need to be considered for a full-time academic position in the future. This was one of the drawbacks of part-time jobs, often sought by women with young children because of the scarcity of good childcare.

Our situation changed substantially within a few months. Before the end of the year we were expecting our second child. My pregnancy progressed easily like the first one, with no threat of miscarriage. We planned to use the Lamaze method of childbirth again and had just started to practice our exercises, using Mrs. Bing's book.

On May 6, 1971, three years after he started graduate school, Barry passed his comprehensive exams in political science. He told me the next day that he was "ready for a break from school" and wanted to get a job for a year. He was in the midst of describing to me the kind of work he wanted when the phone rang. The caller was one of Barry's former colleagues.

"Would you be interested," he asked, "in a fulltime position with the New York State Division of Criminal Justice starting in September?"

After Barry hung up, the two of us sat stunned by the synchronicity of the call. We stared at the phone as if it were magical. The job was exactly what Barry had been visualizing and the September start date was perfect. It would give us all some time to adjust after the birth of our baby in early July.

I had come to realize, that as a non-nurse, I would always be viewed as an outsider at the nursing school where I taught. My classes were considered a nice addition to the curriculum, but essentially fluff. Still, most of the students seemed to appreciate the social cultural perspective I provided. I enjoyed working with them and decided to stay at the nursing school a second year.

The future seemed rosy until Mrs. Restell, who had been everything we could ever want in a nanny for over two years, announced that she and her husband had decided to retire. She would be leaving us the end of June. My world tumbled. Our baby was due on July 7th. In the fall, both Barry and I would be working at real jobs more than a half hour from home. No one I knew had any childcare suggestions. The advertisement I put in the *New York Times* yielded more replies than I'd ever had before, but no acceptable candidate. After Mrs. Restell, no one else came close. Should I quit my job? We couldn't afford for me to quit my job! Even with Barry starting work in September we were feeling the financial strain of our many years as students.

"Have you looked in the *jobs*-wanted section as well as listing a job in the *help* wanted section?" Barry asked.

I was sure there was no such section, but I rifled through the classified ads to please him. There, in a narrow band of six tiny 'job-wanted' ads, was one from Marilyn, who wanted to take care of children. She was married, an artist, and finishing her B.A. in night school. Katie and I interviewed her the next day. We both liked her, but she was hesitant about caring for a newborn baby. She didn't have any experience with babies, she said.

"Most new mothers don't have any experience with newborns either," I countered, "and they do just fine."

She nodded in acknowledgement and accepted the job when we offered it to her. Marilyn agreed to start in late August and stay for a year. She couldn't replace Mrs. Restell. No one could. But because Marilyn was so different from her, we could accept her as who she was – a bright, creative young woman, full of energy, inexperienced with babies, but willing to learn. I planned to take most of the summer off from the nursing school, when no students were present, but move back toward my three-quarter time status when classes resumed in September, just as Barry started his new job.

We decided on the names Michael or Lisa for our baby and set up a porta-crib in the front corner of the living room to serve as a temporary nursery. The spot, surrounded by a jungle of large plants we had agreed to take care of over the summer for our downstairs neighbors, looked like a tropical spa. Katie helped excitedly with preparations and regularly put her hand on my belly to feel 'our baby' kick. Our anticipation also brought concerns. Could we love a second child as much as we loved Katie? Everyone said we would, but it was hard to visualize. How would Katie react to the reality of having to share her mommy and daddy? I also worried about how well I, as an only child, could manage the chaos of two children.

What I assumed was my last appointment with the obstetrician began routinely. The previous week the doctor had told me the baby was big, but probably not as big as Katie had been at birth, and was in perfect position to be born. I climbed up on the examining table in high spirits, ready for him to tell me I would go into labor any minute.

It took me a few minutes to realize that somewhere early in his examination the doctor had stopped his usual casual conversation. He was listening through his stethoscope with unusual intensity as his hands moved over my abdomen gently exploring, returning again and again to the same places. I felt a sudden flash of fear.

At last he looked up. "Sorry for all the poking and prodding. The baby has flipped into breach position and turned itself around, but the heartbeat is still strong."

"You said it was in perfect position."

"Last week. Not now. But the baby sounds fine."

The doctor kept reassuring me that our baby sounded fine, as if there was a possibility that it might not be! What was going on?

Actually, now that he mentioned it, I remembered an unusual amount of activity in my abdomen two nights earlier. But how could a baby get upside down and turned around?

"I'll be gone over the July 4th holiday weekend," the doctor said, "but don't worry. There is no way the baby will be born in the next few days. Come back next week on July 7th."

Gone over the weekend! No way the baby could be born! Don't worry!

I threw aside the white towel and pushed myself into sitting position on the narrow table. Of course, I worried. It sounded like our baby was just surfing around inside. What if the umbilical cord got tangled around its neck as it surfed?! What if it got kinked so our baby couldn't get food and oxygen?

A perfect blue sky hung over sunny, breezy New York City that Fourth of July weekend. Barry and I especially enjoyed the City on holidays. Buses were uncrowded, pollution was low, and there was no wait for the playground swings. The three of us visited a new, brightly colored set of play equipment in Central Park, just off Fifth Avenue. Katie clambered, climbed, slid, and swung as long as she wanted, then played tag around the slides with Barry. I moved around the playground with them, seeking shade and a place to sit, worried, in spite of the doctor's assurances, that each sensation in my abdomen signaled the start of labor or more baby athletics.

Later that night my worry intensified when I was awakened by a small earthquake rolling across my abdomen. I lay still, almost afraid to breathe. It seemed like I should do something, but what? After a few moments of upheaval, I felt more comfortable and was relieved to feel the baby still kicking. Had our baby flipped back? The next night the same thing happened. How could I keep our baby safe? What was best? Should I let it move or lie as much on my stomach as possible to give it less room to flip? What if I did the wrong thing and it got tangled up?

"Please stay put Michael/Lisa," I whispered. "Please don't surf anymore."

CHAPTER **37**

Manhattan Family of Four

BARRY AND I went together for my July 7th appointment. He held my hand tightly as we sat beside each other in the waiting room. What if our baby wasn't okay? What if something bad had happened when it surfed around inside? The nurse's usual cheeriness as she called me into the examination room seemed inappropriate.

The doctor came in almost immediately, with my chart in hand. After a quick greeting he began to probe my abdomen silently, listening intently through his stethoscope. I lay terrified at what he might find, going over in my mind whether anything had seemed different since the commotion in my middle the past two nights. After what seemed like way too long to yield a good outcome, he looked up and smiled.

"The baby has turned back and sounds fine," he reported. "No signs of labor, but since this is your due date, I'd like to induce labor and deliver before the baby turns again. I'll set up an appointment at the hospital for 1:00.

A lightness of relief spread through my body. "Okay," I said. Delivery today sounded wonderful. I did not want to go through another terrifying night of baby surfing.

My second labor was just as slow, boring, and uncomfortable as the first, in spite of Barry's enthusiastic Lamaze coaching. The sun was long down before we moved to the delivery room, where the nurses set up the mirror and Barry again stood behind my head.

"It's Michael," shouted Barry as a lustily crying baby with a full head of red hair appeared.

"Eight pounds four ounces," the nurse announced as she wrapped him warmly and handed him to us. We gazed intently at our new family member, delighted with everything about him, surprised at how tiny he was compared to three-year-old Katie. He stopped crying and looked at us, as interested in us as we were in him

The next morning, I took Michael, his small body snuggly warm against mine, for a walk around my hospital room. At one point I gazed down at him and felt a wave of such overwhelming love that I had to stop walking. I placed my finger into one of his tiny clenching fists; my nagging question had been quickly answered. Yes, we could love Michael as much as we loved Katie.

Michael and I came home after just a day and two nights in the hospital. No infections this time. Katie was excitedly waiting as we walked in the door. She climbed up on our soft orange couch; we laid him in her arms and sat beside her. We were now a family of four. After he met his sister, Michael met his Mahoney grandparents. Then Barry and I attempted Michael's first home diaper change. We quickly learned that diapering a boy baby posed different hazards than diapering a girl. When we finally lay him in his jungle crib he gazed transfixed at the surrounding foliage. We joked that he might imprint his early leafy environment and grow up to seek a life in the tropics.

After the baby nurses and my parents had all come and gone, and before Barry started his new job in September, we decided to go on a short family vacation, just the four of us. We found a two-bedroom cottage with room for a crib on Indian Lake in the Adirondacks beside a small sandy beach. Katie could swim every day and we could take short walks with Michael to show him the trees and the lake. It was a time of just being together, consolidation of our family foursome.

Katie's views about Michael changed radically and rapidly over the next few weeks. One day she said she loved him and wanted to marry him. A few days later she tugged at my skirt and demanded insistently, "I want Michael go back in egg!" When our new nanny Marilyn arrived in August she empathized with Katie immediately. She too had a younger brother and understood Katie's ambivalence. She encouraged her to talk about her dreams and paint and draw her feelings about Michael.

Mike, as we soon began to call him, was an easy, cheerful baby, with red-blond hair, bright blue eyes, and an impish grin. As fall approached and his spot by the windows began to get chilly, we started giving him naps in the big crib in the room where Katie slept. One day Katie, who had long ago moved into her own real bed, announced that she wanted Michael to sleep in her room every night.

One fall evening, after Barry had settled into his new job, we sat down at our dining room table to consider our future. Barry wanted to work at the New York State Division of Criminal Justice for a little over a year, until the end of December 1972. Then he planned to return to Columbia to work on his dissertation. Hopefully it would be substantially done by June 1973. What did we want to do after that? I still hoped to find a job teaching sociology full-time in college or university. Barry, with his varied experience in law, teaching political science, and administrative and policy work at the Division of Criminal Justice, had a wider range of options. Barry suggested that since the pool of jobs for me would be relatively small and his would be larger, I should look for a job first. When I found something I liked, he would search in the same location. This was almost unheard of. Usually the man, as 'head of household' and with a higher earning potential because he was male, found a job first. Then his wife 'followed' and tried to pick up whatever work she could, regardless of whether it was in her field.

We had decided early in our marriage that we did not want to live in the suburbs with their long commutes, nor get into the moneymaking rat-race necessary to afford a bigger apartment and private schools for the kids in Manhattan. We'd have to move away from the city, we'd said, way back when the actual reality of such a decision was far in the future. Just where would we want to live? We pulled out the U.S. map, spread it out on our blue tablecloth, and stared at it. The whole country lay open to us. It was seductive, unsettling, terrifyingly unknown. Where we settled in that huge expanse of America would shape the direction of our lives and the lives of Katie and Mike. We were both interested in Colorado and put that and the whole southwest at the top of our list. We agreed that urban areas would be most likely to offer interesting work opportunities for both of us. For me, that eliminated the many colleges in small communities. We decided we would aim to move out of the city in summer 1973, in less than two years. Michael would be two, and Katie five and a half.

Meanwhile, we continued to build our lives in New York City. Katie was firmly ensconced in West Side Montessori School. Barry and I devoted most weekends to Mike and Katie. The Columbia campus was still one of our favorite playgrounds, and Mike, like Katie before him, learned to maneuver steps at Columbia, crawling at first, then walking and climbing. Mike was exploring everything, ranging much further outside the parental circle than Katie ever had. As he tried to climb the walls of our apartment, something Katie had never attempted, I began to doubt my long-held conviction that most of the differences between boys and girls existed because we treated them differently as young children. Our apartment rocked with Kate and Mike's giggles, squawks, and commotion. I discovered I loved living with two children, at least most of the time, but our apartment was shrinking by the day.

In spring 1972, Barry and I decided that one way to expand our living area in the hot summer months was to rent a weekend summer house. We remembered our special times together on Fire Island and wanted a similar experience for the whole family. The seashore didn't seem practical, but we could manage a house in the mountains. We bought a used car, that Katie immediately dubbed "Sam," and a few weeks later we found a five-bedroom house in the Hunter Mountain ski Area in New York. It had a large front deck with a high railing and locking gate, a perfect play area for Mike, who was just starting to walk. Although the two and a half hours commute every Friday night was long, it turned out to be a boon. The kids fell asleep almost immediately in the back seat and Barry and I had precious, undisturbed time for conversation.

On our first weekend at the house I noticed a small green patch beside the driveway and realized how desperate I was, after eleven years in the city, to get outside and dig. We got permission to use it for a garden and on the first Saturday in June, Katie, Barry, and I cleaned it out and turned soil all day to plant basil, lettuce, and squash. Even Mike got into the act, down on his knees pushing the dirt with his hands. The next weekend we filled the empty flower boxes on the windowsills with fragrant purple, pink, and red petunias. Every Friday night as we drove down the crunchy gravel driveway and breathed in the strong perfume of those petunias, we knew we were home. We jumped out of the car to check our garden's growth by the headlights even before we unlocked the house.

Sunny, tow-headed Mike started the summer toddling and in no time was running everywhere in his navy sneakers that were almost as wide as they were long. Sometimes we lost him in wildflowers and grasses just his height. He was also beginning to talk. Among one of his earlier phrases was, "Katie you not da boss a me." Clearly we had two very independent and vocal children. We were delighted. In the scenic, and lifeguard protected, pool created from a bend in the creek that flowed through town, Katie practiced the swimming she had learned at our YMCA "mother and tot" swim classes. Mike practiced his walking--straight into the water. The summer was magical for all of us. Family life was good, and I felt like I was being a good mother, even though I was working.

In July 1962 I left the nursing school and started a new part-time job as a staff member for the American Bar Administration's Juvenile Justice Standards Project at the New York University School of Law located in Greenwich Village. Working again in law and sociology felt like coming home. One of the issues that especially interested the

Standards Project was the treatment of "status offenders" (known as Persons In Need Of Supervision, or PINS, in New York state) who had committed no crime. They were brought into juvenile court, often by their parents, not because they had been accused of any crime, but because they were difficult to manage. Often these children ended up receiving harsher treatment from the juvenile court than the kids who committed a crime.

There was growing concern among juvenile justice reformers that the status offenders should be removed from the juvenile court. Over my time with the Standards Committee I did a study on PINS in a New York juvenile court that showed that concern was warranted. It documented that being classified as a PINS had potentially serious long-range effects on a child's life. The study, entitled "PINS and Parents" was published in *Beyond Control: Status Offenders in the Juvenile Court*, a book edited by Lee E. Teitelbaum and Aidan R. Gough.

In mid-July, soon after I started my new job, we were faced again with the problem of childcare. Our nanny Marilyn, who had agreed to work for us for a year, reminded us that her year was up, and she would be leaving in August to get back to full time work on her art. Once again, I faced the daunting task of trying to find good childcare and worried about what I would do if I couldn't. Our *New York Times* help wanted advertisement yielded two possible candidates. One was outstanding, a certified early childhood teacher from Northern Ireland. We were ecstatic. She was young, enthusiastic, obviously well trained, and she and the kids connected immediately. When I paid her on Friday, at the end of the first week, I told her she was so good I wanted to give her an immediate raise. She seemed strangely subdued, not as pleased with her raise as I would have expected. I asked her if the day had gone okay and if the kids had been behaving well. She lit up. "Oh yes," she said, "the kids are lovely." Still, I couldn't shake off a sense of uneasiness. A few hours later the phone rang. I recognized the Irish lilt of her voice, though it sounded stuffy like she had been crying.

"I'm terribly sorry," she said, "but I can't come to babysit anymore.

I don't want it, but I have to go back home. My mother got a job for me in the village school without telling me and just sent me an express letter with a return ticket in it for this Monday. The situation is very bad in Northern Ireland. My parents are old. They need me."

I cried a long time after her call. The problem of childcare seemed so ongoing, insistent, demoralizing, I didn't know if I could keep going....

Finally, I roused myself. We had <u>no</u> childcare for Monday, and Barry and I both had to go to work. I had to find someone right away. There was only one thing to do--look at the other job applicants from the *New York Times* that we had interviewed. There was one person, Naomi, who might work out. She was a far second place, but she had had previous childcare experience and her work reference was positive. After talking with her again, I still felt less sure about her than any nanny we had ever had. Would she be able to offer enough stimulation for the kids, especially Mike, who would be with her all day while Katie was in Montessori pre-school. Mike and Katie seemed to like her, and she was willing to clean, which would ease my life considerably. With some reluctance we hired her.

One day, after Naomi had been working several months, my downstairs neighbor, a stay-at-home mother with kids just a little older than ours, stopped me in the lobby and asked me if my nanny was happy. What did that mean? Happy? What was happy? I asked her what prompted her question, what she had seen or heard that concerned her?

"Nothing," she said. She "just wondered." The encounter left me distressed and unsettled. We were expecting to leave New York in a few months. Any change of childcare providers, even if I found someone really good, would be, in itself, disruptive to the kids. I talked with Katie and Mike about their time with Naomi and they seemed content with her. Barry and I agonized over what to do. We finally decided to keep Naomi, but to closely monitor how the kids were doing. All the guilt that I tried to keep buried about whether I was a good mother resurfaced.

Part Seven
Job Search

CHAPTER **38**

Word of Mouth

MY SPIRITS ROSE at the sight of a table covered with thick, loose-leaf binders full of job possibilities at the August 1972 annual sociological meetings. Barry and I planned to move out of New York City in August 1973, and this was where I hoped to find the college teaching job I had been working toward since I graduated from college in 1959. My optimism diminished as I began leafing through the listings. Few were relevant to my own search. The 'best' jobs, the full-time tenure track college positions I was looking for, were still filled mostly by word of mouth through the old boys' network of male professors. It was easy for women to find the off-beat or part- time jobs like the ones listed in the binders, the ones isolated from academia like I'd had at the nursing school and the Juvenile Justice Standards Project. Access to the academic jobs remained predominantly the purview of men.

In college in the late 1950s I believed I could be anything I wanted if I got the qualifications. Now I had a better understanding of the systemic and attitudinal forces working to undermine my chances of actually being able to do that. My women colleagues and I were all networking frantically at the conference trying to locate good positions as sociologists. We ran into each other occasionally in the book display or a professional session and quickly exchanged information. None of us were having much luck. On the last day of the conference, after four days of search, I had no real leads. There would not be another big job market like this again until next August, *after* Barry and

I had hoped to move out of New York. As I wandered aimlessly, trying to figure out what to do, I spotted one of my former Northwestern instructors down the hall.

"Larry," I called, clattering after him in my medium high heels. He too specialized in sociology of law. We had run into each other a few times since we had both left Northwestern and usually exchanged news about what we were doing. He knew about my work at Vera and Columbia Law School. I wondered where he was currently teaching. Larry stopped, turned around, and waved.

"I'm at the University of Denver Law School now," he said after we'd exchanged pleasantries. "They have a thriving joint degree program between Law and the Sociology Department. Gresham Sykes is there too."

Sykes had also been one of my professors at Northwestern. He co-taught the methodology seminar with Aaron Cicourel, the one in which I did so well.

"Any job possibilities there?"

"Sykes is leaving, and Sociology is looking for someone to replace him. You ought to apply. You've got the background. Just go up to room 540 and tell them I sent you."

"Shouldn't I call or something?"

"I don't know the phone number, just go knock on the door."

A few minutes later I hesitated in front of a door marked 540. Larry had said 'upstairs', but what if he really meant one of the other conference hotels? What if I'd gotten the number wrong? The idea of just knocking on a hotel door and announcing my interest in a job seemed a little scary. But this was my only job lead. It was in Colorado, our first choice of location. I knocked.

"Larry Ross sent me," I said when a man about my age opened the door. "He told me you were recruiting for a position in law and sociology."

After asking me how I knew Larry and ascertaining that I had a law and sociology background he asked me to come back in half an hour. When I returned I met with two young faculty members from the University of Denver, or DU as they called it, for what they stressed was a conversation, not an interview. The University included a liberal arts college, graduate programs, and several professional schools, including a law school. The eight sociology faculty members all taught undergraduates and graduate students in their MA program and new Ph.D. program. They needed someone to teach law and society, juvenile delinquency, and family. The job they described was a tenure track position and had everything I wanted. Because I was currently working on my study for the Juvenile Justice Standards Project about Persons In Need of Supervision, I had current research and a potential publication to talk about. Our conversation was informal and pleasant. I sensed they were interested in me.

A few days later a secretary from the department called and asked me to submit an application. This is it, I thought, exhilarated. I had no mentors to clue me in to the vagaries of the academic job search, no experience with the heightened friendliness and hospitality that department members exuded to job candidates during academic recruitment season.

Weeks passed and nothing happened, not even an acknowledgement of my application. After the bonhomie I'd experienced with the two DU representatives I didn't know what to think. Assuming they had eliminated me, I started sending out letters to every institution of higher education I could locate in Colorado and the Southwest.

One of my first rejections came from the chair of a sociology department in the southwest with whom I had exchanged two letters about a law and society position they were advertising. I had mentioned in one of them that I was married, and my husband would also be looking for a position in the area. Clearly a mistake. The rejection letter started out:

"We are sorry we cannot offer you a job because there is no position for your husband at the university."

What? I reread the letter. Yes, that's definitely what it said. I decided I couldn't let the letter pass without some kind of response. Focus on affirmative action in hiring and equal treatment of male and female employees was just beginning to break into the awareness of employers. Lawsuits were starting to challenge the acceptability of listing jobs by gender in newspapers, the firing of women because they were pregnant, unequal pay for women and men doing similar work, and hiring discrimination. I wrote back that I found it surprising and sexist that they wouldn't consider me for a job because there was no place in the university for my husband.

In just about the time it took for my letter to reach the departmental chair, I got a phone call, surely being taped, although they never informed me. The Chair sounded nervous and very formal, as if he were reading from a prepared statement. He apologized profusely for my 'misunderstanding' of the letter. Of course, he assured me, my consideration for the position was not connected in any way to my husband's employment possibilities. He would be happy to set up an interview with me for a position as soon as possible.

I didn't care to pursue that job further, but the speed of the department's reaction gave me a tiny sense of hope. Maybe we were making some progress in sensitizing employers to issues of gender discrimination.

I am appalled, as I think back, by how naïve I was as I started to prepare for my career. How could I have been so oblivious to the subtle and not-so-subtle ways in which we, as women, were kept within prescribed boundaries that markedly restricted the scope of our lives? Even today we are still trying to identify and demolish them.

CHAPTER 39

An Academic Woman's Tale

IN MID-NOVEMBER I got a call from the University of Denver inviting me to come for a job interview in five days. I hustled to get a plane ticket and landed in a near blizzard. One of the men I'd talked with at the Sociology conference met me and I began a three-day whirl of meetings, dinners, lunches, and drives through neighborhoods. There were only two women working in the department. I met one of them soon after my arrival, a young instructor just finishing up her Ph.D. from Princeton who facilitated my meeting with the department's graduate students. She was clearly very smart, and well- liked and respected by the graduate students. I looked forward to getting a chance to talk with her later in my visit, but surprisingly she did not reappear at any of the other recruitment events. I wondered why.

It was the other woman, Eleanor, who was on everyone's mind. Every person I talked with in the department and the university asked me if I had heard about or met her yet. Each then proceeded to tell me his or her version of 'Eleanor's situation.' The perspectives were all slightly different, like the varied stories of a single event in the 1950 Japanese movie *Rashomon*. Toward the end of my visit I finally met Eleanor. She was in her late fifties or early sixties, vibrant, energetic, and intelligent, with a strong concern for social justice. I liked her immediately. She took me to her house, and while she prepared dinner for me and two faculty members and their wives who would come later, she told me her story. It was the first I had heard directly from a woman who had tried to make it in a man's profession.

Eleanor had been in the sociology department longer than any other present member. One day she had obtained a list of sociology department members and their salaries from the University's Office of Grants and Contracts to include in a grant application she was putting together. She didn't pay much attention to the list at first. It was just another piece of paper she was piling up for the grant submission. Then as she glanced at it she suddenly realized that her salary was less than *half* of the lowest paid man!

"I was just stunned when I saw that list," she said. "I just couldn't believe what I was looking at. It was like getting punched in the stomach. I had always assumed none of us were getting raises. It had never dawned on me that I was the only one who wasn't."

I sat stunned too, trying to absorb what she was telling me.

"What did they say when you asked why?" I finally asked.

"I didn't need the money because my husband had a high income. The men needed the raises because they were trying to support families."

The department also refused to promote Eleanor to full professor. They said her publications, which were numerous, were not sufficiently research oriented.

"I was fed up," she concluded. She sued the department for gender discrimination and got a settlement but didn't tell me the details.

She talked with the School of Social Work about joining their faculty and they offered her a position as a full professor. She would join them in September at the beginning of the next academic year. It suddenly registered on me that I was probably, at least in part, her replacement.

"It's not that the department discriminates against women," the male faculty members in sociology all assured me when I asked about Eleanor. "It's that she isn't *really* a sociologist, doesn't fit into the kind of professional department we are trying to build. Social Work is more applied, it's a better place for her."

I'm embarrassed to say I bought their argument. I looked up and read some of Eleanor's publications. Much as I liked and respected her, the work did seem a little less weighty and more 'applied' than that of the other faculty members. But that explanation was far too glib. What exactly does 'applied' mean in sociology? Much of the research that sociologists do is essentially applied in that it seeks new understandings of how institutions, organizations, and families function so that they can be more effective and sensitive in what they do. My work at Vera had been applied research. The work of several other sociologists in the DU department was applied research.

After hearing so many different versions of Eleanor's story, I thought I understood what was going on. Actually, I didn't have a clue. I had yet to fully grasp what discrimination looked like. It was only years later, after I had heard the competence of every faculty woman I knew discounted for one reason or another, that I began to *fully* comprehend its dynamics. There was always an argument for why a woman didn't quite measure up. The dominant group, defined by gender, color, and class, in academia usually white men with a Eurocentric class background, set standards in 1973 that reflected their own limited perspective. They could always find a degree of difference between what they defined as good and the work of others who were outsiders or different. This was the same phenomenon that I had stumbled across in my study of American Black poets in 1959 in my first year of graduate school. Because their work did not conform to the criteria of good poetry established by white Eurocentric academics, Black poets had little chance of being published or viewed as the 'good literature' that English students should read. Women faculty members had a similar problem. Their perspectives, or methodology, or the topics they chose to study were often deemed less rigorous or important than those of men.

That this presumption of incompetence among minorities still occurs in academia today is evidenced by the books *Presumed Incompetent I: Intersections of Race and Class of Women in Academia* published in 2012 and *Presumed Incompetent II:*

Race,Class, Power, and Resistance of Women in Academia published in 2020 *by* Yolanda Flores Niemann, Gabriella Gutierrez Muhs, and Carmen G. Gonzalez.

Except for Eleanor's story, I thought DU offered everything I wanted. Classes were small. The department needed the courses in law, criminology, and family I wanted to teach. The position offered me the opportunity to work with both graduate and undergraduate students. Still I hesitated. Eleanor's story bothered me, even though a woman administrator in the university assured me that Eleanor's situation had been a *unique* one. (I hadn't yet learned that that was usually part of the defense of discriminatory behavior.) She also assured me that I could trust the Chair of the sociology department to be fair.

My visit to Denver highlighted the enormity of a decision to move out of New York City. Denver was still referred to as a 'cow town' in 1972, in the early stages of urban renewal. Its nondescript downtown was dominated by parking lots. Small ranch style houses seemed to dominate the areas where we could afford to live. Living in Denver would offer a different lifestyle than our family had ever had. When I got home, Barry was excited and eager to hear about everything. He couldn't understand my uncertainty about moving.

"I like DU. It's a dream job, exactly the kind of teaching I've been looking for, but Denver would be a big adjustment. And there's this wonderful woman sociologist who was discriminated against.... Something's not right about that. But if we never take available jobs, how will we ever get more women in men's professions?"

The chairperson of the sociology department told me not to expect to hear from them until late January, but again the time stretched beyond my expectation. Late January ran into early February.

CHAPTER **40**

Decisions

I TRIED TO turn my mind and attention to a new possibility. The feminist chair of faculty recruitment for the sociology department at the University of Colorado was trying to recruit women to the department. We were in communication about a possible visit to Boulder.

In late February, just as I was giving up hope of hearing anything positive from the University of Denver, the department chair called to offer me a tenure-track position as an Assistant Professor. I told him we couldn't decide until Barry had a chance to see Denver. We booked a flight immediately.

The professor at the University of Colorado, with whom I had been corresponding, suggested I set up an interview in Boulder while I was in the area. I agreed and spent the first day of our trip visiting the University of Colorado. Being on the Boulder campus brought back memories of my time there with Penny on our summer camping trip in 1960. On this campus I had launched a new phase of my life. Now I was here again, about to launch another, quite different, phase. Except that, in spite of the wonderful reception, interview, and get-acquainted party the recruitment chair had arranged, the University of Colorado didn't seem like the right place for me to start my college teaching career.

"The big classes aren't too bad," one professor explained, "because when class size reaches 90 you get a teaching assistant."

Ninety! I'd never taught a class over thirty, couldn't imagine doing the kind of teaching I liked to do with 90 students, even for CU's higher salary.

The next two days Barry and I spent looking around Denver, informally visiting with DU faculty members and looking around campus. DU with its small classes and more intimate environment, seemed more compatible with my style. The more I saw of the university, the more I liked it and the individuals who would be my colleagues. I was still bothered about the department's treatment of Eleanor, but I kept telling myself that it represented the end of an era. Nothing like that could happen again.

I came back from my second trip to Denver excited, all my hesitancy gone, ready to accept the DU offer; but now Barry was ambivalent. Although he had gone skiing in the mountains and returned to Boulder to see people playing tennis in the sunshine, a big Colorado selling point, he began to realize how deep his roots in New York were.

"I've never really gone away from home before."

He was right. He'd gone to college and law school relatively close to home and returned to New York to work after his six months in the army. His extended family all lived in close proximity on the East coast. His identity as a New Yorker was much stronger than my identity to any place I had ever been. He mulled the decision for a couple days.

"This is what we said we wanted to do," he finally said. "Let's do it."

I accepted the job. I had reached the goal I set for myself when I was a senior in college. Now I had seven years to prove myself, show that I was a good enough teacher, good enough scholar, to get tenure and stay at the University of Denver. The next set of challenges was just beginning.

In early April we reserved a three-bedroom, two-bath faculty house in a complex close to and maintained by the university. One bedroom would serve as Barry's office while he finished his dissertation and did some other writing. We could move in on

June 18th. One day Barry and I looked at each other with a mix of excitement and terror. We realized that moving day was exactly six weeks away.

The van was late. I stood in front of 245 W. 107th Street in mid-June 1973, head swiveling back and forth, willing it to come so we could start loading. Katie and Michael cavorted around me, playing tag on the sidewalk, using me as home. Each other, that's all the home the four of us would have for the next several days.

Ziggy, our butcher, had shaken his head the day before, when I stopped in his shop and told him this would be the last steak I'd buy from him, that we were moving to Colorado. "Colorado? Why? You're so brave." I didn't feel brave, just nervous that the van would never come. I couldn't think beyond that.

The van arrived an hour late. Three burly men jumped down from the cab. The driver approached us with a clipboard.

"You the Mahoneys?"

"Yes."

"Denver, Colorado?"

"Yes."

"Sign here."

We signed and handed him a check.

He nodded to the other two men, who opened the back of the truck with the rattling of chains and scraping of ramps. They pulled out a stack of white folded cardboard boxes and hastened upstairs to our apartment. There they set about shaping and filling the boxes with our lives--wedding gifts, children's toys including Kate and Mike's beloved plastic pink horse on wheels, my dissertation, Barry's in-process dissertation, old Vera files, all indiscriminately hoisted, hauled down, and buried in the dark bowels of the truck.

It began to sink in. Occasionally Barry and I connected, clasped hands, but mostly we worked, one up and one down, transferring our known lives from New York, where Barry had been born and raised, where Katie and Michael had been born in the same hospital as their dad, to Denver, Colorado, where none of us had any history, a place and future unknown.

I had walked into Northwestern University in 1959 determined to be a college teacher. Two years later I'd come to New York City with a suitcase and duffle bag seeking both love and meaningful work. Now we were uprooting our lives to move our family to my dream job, a tenure-track teaching position. The career-preparation phase of my life was over. I had an amazing, loving family, all with me. We were going on an adventure together to Colorado. I had been hired for the job I'd been working toward since I was a senior in college, the one my career counselor said I was well suited for, except that college teachers were usually men. I understood more now about why she had given me the test results with such hesitation and how naïve my 'that's okay, I like men' response to her cautious warning had been. In accepting this job as a college teacher, it was important for me to understand that I was still "a woman on a man's path." There were still red flags. Eleanor's experience in the department I was entering was one of them. Women were beginning to cross boundaries, but we were still a minority.

Barry and I stood with arms around each other and our two children, watching as the movers finally pulled the ramp up and shut and locked the mud-spattered yellow doors with a clang. The engine roared to life, sent a black stream of exhaust up its tall front pipe. The truck shifted into gear and roared away with everything we owned inside.

On our final trip upstairs to get the last items for the car, Barry and I stood together in the doorway, looking one last time at the place that had held so much of our lives together, so much happiness. Our breath still floated there, but all other signs of us had been lifted out. How could eight eventful years, so much living, be wiped away in a day?

Mike and Katie climbed into their nests in the back seat of Sam, our ancient blue Plymouth. Barry leaned over to kiss me. We all waved goodbye to our apartment and headed West. I shivered with anticipation and a little fear.

Epilogue

OUR OLD CAR Sam struggled with the gradual upward slope of our western journey. We had to stop a few times to add water to the radiator and let the engine cool. In spite of that, a few days after we left New York City we arrived in Denver and moved into DU's housing for new faculty members.

"And what department does your daddy teach in?" our neighbors asked our kids as we were getting settled.

Katie pulled herself to her full five-and-half-year-old height and replied with great pride, "My *mother* teaches in sociology."

I was lucky that the sociology department had hired another woman, Rita Braito, at the same time they hired me. Rita was a little older and much wiser than I. She was an important mentor to me. There were very few women faculty members at the university in 1973. Over the years the number of female members in all departments and at all professorial ranks grew. Eventually we were able to start a Women's Studies Program, in which I served three years as chairperson. My teaching and writing shifted over time from predominately law and criminology to gender issues and family, where my deepest professional interest remains today. In Fall 2016 DU installed its first woman Chancellor.

Our family thrived in Denver. Barry developed a career doing research, teaching and consulting on court and criminal justice system issues in the United States and abroad, working with several different reform-oriented organizations, all based at one time or another in Denver. He was founder of one such organization, The Justice Management Institute (JMI), serving twice as its president for a total of over nine years.

After graduating from East High School in Denver, both Katie and Mike went back to New York to climb the steps by the Columbia alma mater statue again, this time as undergraduates. They then moved on to explore the world in their own ways. Our three granddaughters have been crossing boundaries, geographical and otherwise, since their earliest years.

Barry and I went back to New York to visit our old haunts for our 50th wedding anniversary and had our picture taken in front of the brownstone where we were married. Sometimes we marvel at how well everything worked out, considering how little we knew about each other when we married. I think it worked because we knew the important things. Our ongoing mutual desire for equal engagement in both family and work, the kind of marriage I envisioned as I took the train to New York to live in 1961, made a big difference too.

References

(Includes some suggested reading for those who want to learn more about the Silent Generation and the era in which its members came to adulthood.)

Arendt, Hannah. English ed. *Love and Saint Augustine*. Chicago: University of Chicago Press, 1998. (The original dissertation was published in German in 1929.)

Arendt, Hannah. *Origins of Totalitarianism*. New York: Harcourt, Inc. A Harvest Book, 1976. (This was first published in English in 1951.)

Arendt, Hannah. *The Human Condition* (1st ed.) Chicago: University of Chicago Press. 1958.

Ares, Charles, Anne Rankin, and Herbert Sturz. "The Manhattan Bail Project: An Interim Report on the Use of Pre-trial Parole." *New York University Law Review* 38:67-92. January 1963.

Attorney General's Committee on Poverty and the Administration of Federal Criminal Justice ("Allen Committee"). Report submitted to the Honorable Robert F. Kennedy, Attorney General of the United States. February 25, 1963

"Awakening, Women and Power in the Academy." *The Chronicle of Higher Education*. April 6, 2018. (https://www.chronicle.com/interactives/the-awakening).

Baker, Kelly J. *Sexism Ed: Essays on Gender and Labor in Academia*. Chapel Hill, NC: Blue Crow Press. 2018.

Berger, Bennett M. (ed.) *Authors of Their Own Lives: Intellectual Autobiographies by Twenty American Sociologists*. Berkeley: University of California Press. 1990. (See part IV for the stories of four women.)

Bing, Elizabeth. *The Lamaze Method: Six Practical Lessons for an Easier Childbirth*. New York: Rutledge. 1967.

Breines, Wini. *Young, White, and Miserable: Growing Up Female in the Fifties*. Boston: Beacon Press. 1992.

Carlson, Elwood. *The Lucky Few: Between the Greatest Generation and the Baby Boom*. Tallahassee, Fl: Springer Science and Business Media B.V. 2008.

Collins, Gail. *When Everything Changed: The Amazing Journey of American Women from 1960 to the Present*. New York: Little, Brown and Company. 2009.

Coontz, Stephanie. *A Strange Stirring: The Feminine Mystique and American Women at the Dawn of the 1960s*. New York: Basic Books. 2012.

Cox Commission Report. *Crisis at Columbia: Report of the Fact-Finding Commission Appointed to Investigate the Disturbances at Columbia University in April and May 1968*. New York: Vintage Books.1968.

Friedan, Betty. *The Feminine Mystique*. New York: W. W. Norton. 1963.

Garvy, Helen. *Rebels with a Cause: A Collective Memoir of the Hopes, Rebellions and Repression of the 1950s*. Los Gatos, CA: Shire Press. 2007. *(*See chapters 8 and 11.)

Gluck, Shema Berger. *Rosie the Riveter Revisited: Women, the War, and Social Change*. New York: Penguin Meridian. 1987. (See chapter 1 "This Is the Way the World Was: The United States on the Eve of World War II.)

Goffman, Erving. *The Presentation of Self in Everyday Life*. Garden City, New York: Doubleday Publishers. 1959.

Hoffert, Sylvia D. *A History of Gender in America: Essays, Documents, and Articles*. New Jersey: Prentice Hall. 2003. (See chapter 11 "Femininity in the Twentieth Century, 1920-1975".)

Howe, Neil. "The Silent Generation: The Lucky Few (Part 3 of 7)" *Forbes*. August 13, 2014.

Hurston, Zora Neale. *Their Eyes Were Watching God*. New York: Harper Collins Pub. 1937

Hurston, Zora Neale. *Dust Tracks on the Road*. New York: Harper Collins Publisher. 1942.

Hurston, Zora Neale. *Every Tongue Got to Confess: Negro Folk Tales from Gulf States* New York: Harper Collins. (Collected in the 1920s). 2001.

Key, M.R. *Male/Female Language*. Metuchen, New Jersey: Scarecrow Press. 1975.

Manchester, William. *The Glory and the Dream: A Narrative History of America 1932-1972.* Pp. 576, 580. New York: Little, Brown, and Co. 1974. ("Never had American youth been so withdrawn, cautious, unimaginative, indifferent, unadventurous, and silent.")

McAndrew, Frank T. "Controlling the Conduct of College Women in the1960s: Why Did the Threat of High-Spirited Women Seem So Scary in 1962?" *Psychology Today.* Blog: Out of the Ooze. Posted February 25, 2017.

Meadow-Orlans, Kathryn P. (Editor), and Ruth A. Wallace (Editor). *Gender and the Academic Experience: Berkeley Women Sociologists.* Lincoln: University of Nebraska Press. 1994.

Merriam, Eve. *After Nora Slammed the Door: American Women in the 1960s—The Unfinished Revolution.* Cleveland & New York: The World Publishing Company. 1964.

Millay, Edna St. Vincent. *Collected Lyrics.* New York: Washington Square Press. 1959.

Miller, Casey and Kate Swift. *Words and Women.* New York: Anchor Press, Doubleday.1976.

Miller, Claire Cain. "Child Care Still Stirs Up Resistance." *New York Times.* Section B, page 1. August 16, 2019.

Miller, Warren. *The Cool World.* New York: Little Brown & Co. 1959.

Mintz, Steven and Susan Kellogg. *Domestic Revolutions: A Social History of American Family Life.* New York: Free Press.1988. (See chapters 7 to 10 that cover the depression through social changes starting in the 1960s.)

Moran, Barbara Baillet. *Voices of the Silent Generation: Strong Women Tell Their Stories*. NC: Greensboro, NC: Avisson Press, Inc. 2006. (See preface and part I "The Fifties and Its Silent Generation.")

Muhs, Gabriella Gutierrez, Yolanda Flores Niemann, Carmen G. Gonzales, & Angela P. Harris. *Presumed Incompetent: The Intersections of Race and Class for Women in Academia*. Boulder, CO: University Press of Colorado. 2012.

Niemann, Yolanda Flores, Gabriella Gutierrez y Muhs, and Carmen G. Gonzales. *Presumed Incompetent II: Race, Class, Power, and Resistance of Women in Academia*. Logan, UT: Utah State University Press: An Imprint of University Press of Colorado. 2020.

Parker, Patsy. "The Historical Role of Women in Higher Education." *Administrative Issues Journal: Connecting Education, Practice, and Research*. Vol. 5, No. 1:3-14. (Spring 2015).

Parsons, Talcott. *The Structure of Social Action*. Glencoe, Il: Free Press, 2nd Ed. 1976.

Rankin, Anne. "Pretrial Detention and Ultimate Freedom: A Statistical Study." *New York University Law Review* 39:641-655, June 1964.

Roberts, Sam. *A Kind of Genius: Herbert Sturz and Society's Toughest Problems*. New York: Public Affairs, Perseus Books Group. 2009.

Rosen, Ruth. *The World Split Open: How the Modern Women's Movement Changed America*. New York: Penguin Books. 2000 (See chapters.1-3. Revised with new epilogue in 2006.)

Rudd, Mark. *Underground: My Life With SDS and the Weathermen*. New York: Harper. 2009.

Stolz, Anthony. *The Silent Generation: A Memoir of the Depression Babies, The Parents of the* Baby Boomers. Stolz: First Books Library. 2002.

Tannen, Deborah. *You Just Don't Understand: Women and Men in Conversation.* New York: Ballentine Books. 1990.

Thorne, Barrie and Nancy Henley, eds. *Language and Sex: Difference and Dominance.* Rowley, MA: Newbury House. 1975.

Thorne, Barrie, C. Kramarae and N. Henley, eds. *Language, Gender, and Society.* Rowley, MA: Newbury House. 1983.

Time Magazine. "People: The Younger Generation." November 5, 1951. (http:content.time.com/time/magazine/article/0,9171,856950,00. html).

Weiss, Jessica. *To Have and to Hold: Marriage, the Baby Boom and Social Change.* Chicago: University of Chicago Press. 2000. (See chapters 1-2.)

Whitehead, Alfred North. *Science and the Modern World.* New York: The Macmillan Company. 1953. (First Published in Cambridge England in 1925. Whitehead was a British mathematician and philosopher best known for his work in mathematical logic and philosophy of science.)

Whitman, Svlvia. *V is for Victory: The American Homefront During World War II.* Minneapolis: Lerner Publications Company. 1948 (For the young reader. Includes interesting pictures and text about America during the war.)